## DATE DUE

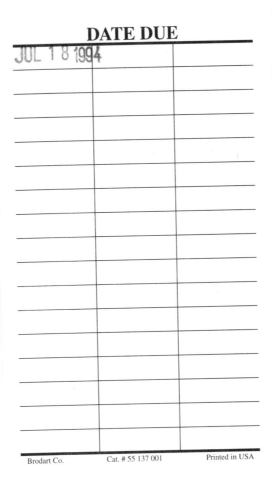

JUL 1 8 1994

| | | |
|---|---|---|
| | | |
| | | |
| | | |
| | | |
| | | |
| | | |
| | | |
| | | |
| | | |
| | | |
| | | |
| | | |
| | | |
| | | |

Brodart Co.  Cat. # 55 137 001  Printed in USA

# The Veiled Mirror
# and the Woman Poet

# The Veiled Mirror and the Woman Poet

H. D., Louise Bogan, Elizabeth Bishop,
and Louise Glück

## Elizabeth Dodd

University of Missouri Press
Columbia and London

5 4 3 2 1     96 95 94 93 92

Library of Congress Cataloging-in-Publication Data

Dodd, Elizabeth Caroline, 1962–
    The veiled mirror and the woman poet : H. D., Louise Bogan,
Elizabeth Bishop, and Louise Glück / Elizabeth Dodd.
        p.     cm.
    Includes bibliographical references and index.
    ISBN 0-8262-0857-6 (alk. paper)
    1. American poetry—Women authors—History and criticism.
    2. Women and literature—United States—History—20th century.
    3. H. D. (Hilda Doolittle), 1886–1961—Criticism and interpretation.
    4. Bogan, Louise, 1897–1970—Criticism and interpretation.
    5. Bishop, Elizabeth, 1911–1979—Criticism and interpretation.
    6. Glück, Louise, 1943–  —Criticism and interpretation.
    7. Classicism—United States. I. Title.
    PS151.D63    1992
    811'.5099287—dc20                                    92-29389
                                                              CIP


⊗™ This paper meets the requirements of the
American National Standard for Permanence of Paper
for Printed Library Materials, Z39.48, 1984.


Designer: Elizabeth Fett
Typesetter: Connell-Zeko Type & Graphics
Printer and Binder: Thomson-Shore, Inc.
Typeface: Goudy Old Style

*For my husband, Christopher Cokinos*

# Contents

# Acknowledgments

The kindness of many friends and colleagues has helped make this book possible. I especially want to thank Roger Mitchell for his guidance, his insightful comments, and his warm encouragement. I thank as well Scott Russell Sanders, James Justus, and Alvin Rosenfeld, who read an early version of the study. Janet Sylvester discussed with me some of the issues germane here, and I thank her for sharing her thoughts. My husband, Christopher Cokinos, read this manuscript repeatedly, each time thoroughly, and I am especially grateful for his keen eye and support.

I wish also to thank the Indiana University Graduate School and the Kansas State Department of English for grants that made research travel possible and both the Kansas State University Women's Studies Program and the Kansas State University Office of Research and Sponsored Programs for support during the completion of this manuscript. Kevin Ray, manuscript curator of the Washington University Olin Library, was very helpful and I want to thank him as well for his helpfulness while I studied the Elizabeth Bishop correspondence housed in the May Swenson Papers, Washington University Libraries, St. Louis, Missouri.

I also thank Roxanne Knudson, executor of the Literary Estate of May Swenson, for her permission to quote from May Swenson's unpublished letters to Elizabeth Bishop. Excerpts from the unpublished letters of Elizabeth Bishop are used with the permission of her estate, copyright 1992, and I thank Alice Methfessel, executor of the Literary Estate of Elizabeth Bishop, for her permission to quote from these letters as well as from an unpublished Bishop poem. I am grateful to Sandra McPherson for permission to paraphrase her correspondence with me and for making available to me an interesting postcard she received from Elizabeth Bishop.

I would also like to thank Ruth Moritz for her help in final preparation of the manuscript and Sara Fefer for her friendly and thoughtful help in bringing this book into print.

Finally, I have received permissions as follows to reprint the selections that appear in this work:

"The Dance" (excerpt), William Carlos Williams: *The Collected Poems of William Carlos Williams, 1939–1962, vol. 2.* Copyright © 1952 by William Carlos Williams. "Danse Russe" (excerpt) and "Spring and All" (excerpt), William Carlos Williams: *The Collected Poems of William Carlos Williams, 1909–1939, vol. 1.* Copyright © 1938 by New Directions Publishing Corporation. Reprinted by permission of New Directions Publishing Corporation.

"Oread," "Mid-day," "Orion Dead" (excerpts), "Calypso" (excerpts), "Iphigenia" (excerpts), "Eurydice" (excerpts), "The God" (excerpts), "Orchard" (excerpts), "Fragment Forty-one" (excerpts), "Amaranth" (excerpts), "Fragment Forty" (excerpts), "Eros" (excerpts), "Fragment Sixty-eight" (excerpts), "Envy" (excerpts), H. D.: *Collected Poems 1912–1944.* Copyright © 1982 by the Estate of Hilda Doolittle. Reprinted by permission of New Directions Publishing Corporation.

Excerpts from *The Complete Poems, 1927–1979* by Elizabeth Bishop. Copyright © 1979, 1983 by Alice Helen Methfessel. Reprinted by permission of Farrar, Straus and Giroux, Inc.

"It is Marvellous . . ." by Elizabeth Bishop. Copyright © 1988 by Alice Helen Methfessel. First appeared in *American Poetry Review* 17, 1. Reprinted by permission of Farrar, Straus and Giroux, Inc.

"The Flume" (excerpts), "The Long Walk" (excerpts), "Portrait of the Artist as a Young Woman" (excerpts) from *Journey around my Room,* edited by Ruth Limmer. Reprinted by permission of Ruth Limmer.

Lines from "You, Doctor Martin" by Anne Sexton in *The Complete Poems of Anne Sexton.* Copyright © 1981 by Linda Gray Sexton and Loring Conant, Jr., executors of the will of Anne Sexton. Reprinted by permission of Houghton Mifflin Company.

"The Departure" from *The Dead and the Living* by Sharon Olds. Copyright © 1983 by Sharon Olds. Reprinted by permission of Alfred A. Knopf, Inc.

Excerpt from "Lost One." Copyright © 1989 by Nina Bogin. Reprinted from *In the North* with the permission of Graywolf Press, Saint Paul, MN.

"To a Dead Lover," and "Leave-taking" (excerpts). Copyright © *Poetry Magazine,* 1922; copyright © Ruth Limmer, 1992. Reprinted by permission of Ruth Limmer.

First stanza of "The Shroud" by Edna St. Vincent Millay. From *Collected Poems,* Harper & Row. Copyright © 1917, 1945 Edna St. Vincent Millay. Reprinted by permission of Elizabeth Barnett, literary executor.

Excerpt from "Burning the Letters" by Sylvia Plath in *The Collected Poems of Sylvia Plath* edited by Ted Hughes. Copyright © 1981 by the Estate of Sylvia Plath. Reprinted by permission of Harper-Collins Publishers Inc.

Excerpts from "Nick and the Candlestick" (8 words); "The Moon and the Yew Tree" (21 words); and "Daddy" (8 words) by Sylvia Plath from *The Collected Poems of Sylvia Plath* edited by Ted Hughes. Copyright © 1981 by the Estate of Sylvia Plath. Reprinted by permission of HarperCollins Publishers Inc.

Excerpts from "Women," "My Voice Not Being Proud," "A Tale," "The Frightened Man," "The Romantic," "Sub Contra," "Late," "Knowledge," "Ad Castitatem," "Summer Wish," and "The Sleeping Fury," from *Blue Estuaries.* Copyright © 1923, 1929, 1930, 1931, 1933, 1934, 1935, 1936, 1937, 1938, 1941, 1949, 1951, 1952, 1954, 1957, 1958, 1962, 1963, 1964, 1965, 1966, 1967, 1968 by Louise Bogan. Published by The Ecco Press in 1977. Reprinted by permission.

"Jukebox" by Louise Glück. Copyright © 1975 by Antaeus/The Ecco Press. First printed by Antaeus in 1975 and reprinted by permission.

Excerpts from "The Lady in the Single," "The Egg," "Early December on Croton-on-Hudson," "My Neighbor in the Mirror," "My Life Before Dawn," and "Hesitate to Call" from *Firstborn.* Copyright © 1968 by Louise Glück. First published by The Ecco Press in 1983. Reprinted by permission.

Excerpts from "All Hallows," "The Letters," "The Shad-blow Tree," "Gretel in Darkness," and "The Murderess," from *The House on Marshland.* Copyright © 1971, 1972, 1973, 1974, 1975 by Louise Glück. First published in 1975 by The Ecco Press. Reprinted by permission.

Excerpts from "The Garden," "Lamentations," "Descending Fig-

# The Veiled Mirror
## and the Woman Poet

# 1

# The Veiled Mirror

Anyone who attempts to reduce poetry to large, sweeping categories moves into difficult territory. Narrative versus lyric; classical versus romantic; public versus private; pure versus impure; naive versus sentimental; abstract versus empathetic—all these categories are both useful and problematic, in that they identify certain generalities, both historical and aesthetic. But those generalities, by their very flexibility, may become stretched, shapeless garments, conforming very little to the specific bodies of work they intend to serve. Northrop Frye says of this difficulty's effect on the study of literature, "Our students are thus graduated with a vague notion that the age of sensibility was the time when poetry moved from a reptilian Classicism, all cold and dry reason, to a mammalian Romanticism, all warm and wet feeling."[1] I intend something in its own way problematic but with the clarifying effect of allowing familiar terminology greater precision for a certain kind of poetry. I wish to apply the admitted oxymoron *personal classicism* to a particular mode of poetry and investigate the ways—both professional and personal—it has been especially important to women poets.

Personal classicism is a poetic mode that has developed throughout the twentieth century—with roots in the nineteenth century. I find that some women poets combine personal impulses (those that appear in confessional poetry) with careful elements of control that allow them to shape and frame—and mute—what are at their core romantic, personal poems. Those elements chosen to mitigate the personal center tend specifically to mute or conceal the autobio-

1. *Fables of Identity: Studies in Poetic Mythology*, 130.

1

graphical details in the poetry and to imply a more "universal" approach. Many women writers have found themselves in the quandary Adrienne Rich describes: "I had been taught that poetry should be 'universal,' which meant, of course, nonfemale. . . . I had tried very much *not* to identify myself as a female poet."[2]

In personal classicism, certain aspects of romanticism—belief in the importance of the individual, use of a natural, spoken idiom, development of the lyric, emphasis on emotion as the basis for poetry—exist encased within a renewed interest in formal and tonal control. To adapt the language of M. H. Abrams's *The Mirror and the Lamp*, a book whose discussion of the movement from classical to romantic sensibilities helps clarify the combination of the two in contemporary personal classicism, it is as if these poets would lift the poetic mirror to their lives and selves, while making sure the glass is darkened, veiled, so it will not reflect with perfect clarity, and in the distorted images, each poet may both reveal and conceal the essence of herself.

Modern and contemporary poetry has been shaped to a very large degree by the concerns and discoveries with which romantic poets grappled. In fact, our debt is so great that Abrams finds that "our responses have been dulled by long familiarity with such a procedure not only in the Romantic poets, but in their many successors who played variations on the mode, from Matthew Arnold and Walt Whitman . . . to Wallace Stevens and W. H. Auden."[3]

Still overshadowing the recent arrival of language poetry, the new narrative, and new formalist verse among the pages of literary journals, the basic shape of the "greater romantic lyric" appears in countless contemporary poems, and we recognize the cultivation of romantic excitement especially among the confessional poets and their followers. Most modernist literature, in fact, roils in a continual obsession with the self, suffused with both attraction and distrust. Stream-of-consciousness narration, one of the great inventions in modern fiction, embraces the appearance of the personal in subject matter but much more importantly, of course, in style: the sense, created through technical or stylistic means, of a mind, a spirit, a personality at work. This is the very essence of the great stream-of-

2. "When We Dead Awaken: Writing As Re-Vision," in *On Lies, Secrets, and Silence: Selected Prose, 1966–1978,* 44. Italics are Rich's.

3. M. H. Abrams, "Structure and Style in the Greater Romantic Lyric," in *From Sensibility to Romanticism,* ed. Frederick W. Hilles and Harold Bloom, 528–29.

consciousness prose passages, from Nora's monologue at the close of *Ulysses* to the "Benjy" section in the opening pages of *The Sound and the Fury.*

In poetry, we often call such a sense of personality "tone," thereby placing importance on the speaker, the "self" who utters the poem. Modern poetry no less than fiction has been concerned with the self, pushing new romantic frontiers in the lyric. Modernism reveals its romantic legacy in continued reliance on certain major tenets of romanticism, such as the generative image and symbol and the status given to the artist's psychic experiences, as well as the declared avoidance of what each age perceived to be clichéd poetic diction and the intention to base poetry on the "common incidents of daily life."[4] Of course, what is "common and daily" has changed over the hundred years that separate the two movements.

Yet, despite so many years of exploration of and emphasis on the self—the self of the poet, it is understood—we also sense, in some writers, the continued urge to control the self, to hush the "natural" voice, and to mask the most personal emotions and thoughts. Pater, concurring with Schiller, may still hold sway: "The true artist may be best recognized by his act of omission." Even Jung, sounding like Eliot, assures that "the special significance of a true work of art resides in the fact that it has escaped from the limitations of the personal and has soared beyond the personal concerns of its creator."[5]

Some writers, who clearly subscribe to romantic notions of the important role a poet's personal experience and accompanying feeling should carry, have retreated at times to the concealing shelter of a kind of classicism. A significant number of these have been women poets, who have made aesthetic choices based on their daily struggles against sexism and stereotyping. The expectation that women poets will be "poetesses," who write autobiographical poems about passion that are formally and intellectually slack, is a specter that has haunted women sufficiently to bring them to overcompensate, to emphasize the formal and tonal control in their work, and to camouflage any portraits of themselves. The old classic notion that poetry should express the general nature of things—not the odd and origi-

---

4. Stanley Sultan, *Eliot, Joyce and Company,* 93; Ricardo J. Quinones, *Mapping Literary Modernism: Time and Development,* 126.

5. Walter Pater, *Appreciations with an Essay on Style,* 18; C. G. Jung, "On the Relation of Analytical Psychology to Poetry," in *The Spirit in Man, Art, and Literature,* trans. R. F. C. Hull, 71.

nal specific—still exerts power. And for most of this century, as in centuries before, the private lives and thoughts of women have not been recognized as representative of the "general." Even as the century draws to a close, woman is still subject to being cast as "other"; certainly as the century began, she was far too often trapped in that frustrating—and silencing—role.

### The Significance of Personal Classicism for Women
                    I remember
lying in bed at night
touching the soft, digressive breasts,
touching, at fifteen,
the interfering flesh
that I would sacrifice
until the limbs were free
of blossom and subterfuge: I felt
what I feel now, aligning these words—
it is the same need to perfect,
of which death is the mere byproduct.[6]

Many readers would identify these lines from Louise Glück's "Dedication to Hunger" as personal, confessional poetry, and in part, they are. The interior, taboo life of the self provides the poem's impetus: this section, titled "The Deviation," is about anorexia nervosa before it is about the art—the dedication—of poetry. Such a reliance on the taboo and the "deviant" informed the confessional movement of the early sixties, along with much of the poetry written in the following years under the influence of the confessionals. This interest in exploring the darkest, most private—and often shameful—recesses of the self almost seems to be the literary critic's dream. It is the logical extreme of romantic interest in the poet-as-speaker as a sincere, honest voice bearing witness to her or his own personal feelings and realizations, combined with modern psychology's developing exploration of sexual history as a way into self-realization.

But Glück's poem, for all its emphasis on the self, is about *controlling* the self: anorexia is, after all, a behavioral disorder based on a woman's need to exercise control over her own body, and by extension, her life. The method of control is denial, "sacrifice," and the

6. *Descending Figure*, 32.

result is the eventual disappearance of the physical self and the self's bodily desires and needs.

We might, by way of comparison, pose "The Deviation" beside a poem by a well-known male writer that also touches on a personal, private discovery of the self. The voice in William Carlos Williams's "Danse Russe" ends in celebration, not a desire to control or efface. Although written entirely in the conditional—"*If* when my wife is sleeping" (emphasis mine), followed by a series of other ifs—the poem nonetheless affirms the speaker's right to "celebrate" himself, to borrow Whitman's famous words, in his own house:

> waving my shirt round my head
> and singing softly to myself:
> "I am lonely, lonely.
> I was born to be lonely,
> I am best so!"[7]

Significantly, each line in the little song begins in the first person. It is very much a poem of our time, dominated by implied concerns of the self: What constitutes the self? What are the inherent needs of the self? What does it mean to be alienated or isolated from the collection of other selves?[8] This last question leads the speaker in "Danse Russe" to turn the simple separateness of his own existence into a private art as he dances naked in the north room of the house, waving his clothes, before the mirror.

Not merely as a matter of domestic decorum, it seems unlikely that the speaker in "Danse Russe" would have danced as he did before the twentieth century, except perhaps in the anomaly of a Whitman poem. The early romantics, for all their interest in the lonely self, continued to see human loneliness as a gateway through which people could commune with the natural order of being, with nature itself—and sometimes God—and did not focus on loneliness as a gateway further into the self, the kind of rambunctious narcissism that moves Williams's dancer. And certainly a speaker would not have even considered such a dance in the work of Pope or Swift. Even in the early twentieth century, if the lonely self had happened to be a female speaker in a woman writer's poem, she probably would not

---

7. *Selected Poems of William Carlos Williams*, 5.

8. For discussions of these concerns as they appear in poetry, see Karl Malkoff, *Escape from the Self: A Study in Contemporary American Poetry and Poetics;* Alan Williamson, *Introspection and Contemporary Poetry.*

have considered such a celebratory dance for very long, either. The speaker in Glück's poem turns the denial of her own needs and the diminishment of her own flesh into a private art. For a myriad of gender-related reasons, even if the speaker wanted to dance, not to "sacrifice . . . digressive flesh," she would most likely have found a more subtle method, under greater formal and tonal control, to express herself.

Personal classicism is that method. It is poetry founded on emotion, primarily sexual and familial love, often based on the writer's own experience. Any expression of universality is achieved, in good William Carlos Williams fashion, through the particular. To this end the language of personal classicist poetry generally has a natural, spoken quality, as if the speaker were talking to herself, or to one other person. The importance of a speaker who feels, remembers, and relates is paramount, and the imagery sometimes functions to reveal a landscape within the speaker's consciousness rather than to describe an objective, exterior setting. All of these elements contribute to the personal quality of the poetry.

Yet equally important is the achievement of control over the emotional subject matter. This is often produced through a tone of reticence, full of understatement and simple syntax. Specific tools of distancing may be important, such as use of personae or allusion—often to characters from classical mythology—who mute the sense of an autobiographical speaker, no matter how intimate the tone. Some, though by no means all, of the personal classicists work with traditional verse forms to impose an external shape upon their subject matter. Techniques such as these prevent the poetry from indulging its emotional subject matter and intimate speaking voice. More extreme forms of subjectivism—such as the sentimental women's poetry popular throughout the twenties and thirties or the confessional poetry that has developed since the middle of the century—have not, of course, emphasized this kind of control.

As I have suggested, personal classicism has been and continues to be a particularly important poetic mode for women writers of the twentieth century for many reasons, and the specific combination of these will differ somewhat for each individual writer. A reticent, controlled tone appears in much of the work of all four poets in this study; Bishop and Bogan further rely on formalist strategies to emphasize the rational qualities of their work. H. D. relies heavily on the use of personae to mask her own presence in her autobiographical poems; upon occasion others will also avail themselves of this strategy.

I do not intend to suggest that this is a movement of direct influences—indeed, these women do not cite one another as sources of inspiration; they usually name men as the models whom they most admire. Instead, these women seem to have independently come to similar conclusions about technique, shaped by similar (though not always identical) societal and personal forces. Personal classicism is not a single, simple response to a given set of historical or cultural forces. However, there are some prominent, largely general cultural catalysts.

Over the past two decades, feminist critics have shown how women historically have been excluded, in at least two different stages, from the Western literary canon. In the first, women were, by and large, simply denied access to learning, writing, and publishing, activities that were considered to be properly—and exclusively—male. The few notable exceptions, such as Anne Finch, Countess of Winchilsea, or Margaret Cavendish, Duchess of Newcastle, or Anne Bradstreet, were often considered "exceptional" in the worst possible way: abominations of womanhood or as Virginia Woolf says, "a bogey to frighten clever girls with."[9] Much of their writing deplored the condition of women, in general, and of women writers, in particular, with something of the anger and accusation that informs some contemporary feminist work.

Moreover, women depicted in male literature were either angels or monsters, creatures with whom no woman could identify, and as whom no woman would want to depict herself. Thus, as Sandra Gilbert and Susan Gubar have shown throughout *The Madwoman in the Attic*, women inherited an "anxiety of authorship," a fear that to write was unnatural, unfeminine, and would threaten to render them monsters and destroy their chances to become angels. This anxiety effectively stifled much creativity and most writing on the part of women until the nineteenth century.

In the nineteenth century, however, the exclusion of women from the serious literary canon entered the second stage and took on

9. In drawing the first of these two categories, I am abstracting from Sandra M. Gilbert and Susan Gubar's *The Madwoman in the Attic: The Woman Writer and the Nineteenth-Century Imagination*; for the second, their collection *No Man's Land: The Place of the Woman Writer in the Twentieth Century*, vol. 1 of *The War of the Words*. I, like many critics, am indebted to them for their insights. Virginia Woolf, *A Room of One's Own*, 65.

a different form. By the end of the century, women were writing a great deal and were very popular. As Jane P. Tompkins has pointed out, Harriet Beecher Stowe's *Uncle Tom's Cabin* "was, in almost any terms one can think of, the most important book of the century. It was the first American novel to sell over a million copies, and its impact is generally thought to have been incalculable." The sentimental novel, of which *Uncle Tom's Cabin* is the most famous example, was a form developed primarily by women writers, and its popularity and financial success were great enough to unnerve many serious male writers of the time. Sentimental poetry, published in magazines and book-length collections, sold in great numbers: Ella Wheeler Wilcox's *Poems of Passion* (1883) sold sixty thousand copies. As Gilbert and Gubar demonstrate, Hawthorne's famous diatribe against "a damned mob of scribbling women" was indicative of a perception prevalent among male authors that their own reading audience—and financial success—was being stolen by that "damned mob"; they feared, moreover, that pulp fiction would render readers uninterested in real—that is, male—art.[10]

Against a historical background fraught with such prejudices, serious women writers in the twentieth century have had to carve their own territory. They have been caught between the real need to distance themselves from the large number of popular women novelists and poets who confined themselves to stereotypical, sentimental depictions of hearth and home, and the need to distinguish themselves as women writers, writing from their own experience as women and not masquerading as male writers in the way of George Eliot or the Bells (Brontës) in the nineteenth century.[11] In spite of the fact that there now exists an examined history of women's writing—as many feminist critics have pointed out—that very history has in some ways harmed serious poets of the twentieth century, because some of it remains of primarily sociological interest, lacking the aesthetic

10. Jane P. Tompkins, "Sentimental Power: *Uncle Tom's Cabin* and the Politics of Literary History," in *The New Feminist Criticism: Essays on Women, Literature, and Theory,* ed. Elaine Showalter, 83; Cheryl Walker, *The Nightingale's Burden: Women Poets and American Culture Before 1900,* 122; Gilbert and Gubar, *No Man's Land,* 142.

11. For a look at the prominence of these popular sentimental women poets, see Walker, *The Nightingale's Burden.* Walker is sympathetic to these poets, pointing out that they frequently confined themselves to "hack work" and "sentimentality" because that was all the magazines of the day wanted to publish. She points out that Emily Dickinson published little and was, in fact, advised by an editor, Higginson, to consult published women poets, like Maria Lowell, to make her style less eccentric—less original.

values and complexities that distinguish serious art from strictly popular culture or political propaganda.

Of course, for some feminist critics, the immediate task is to change or dispense with existing aesthetic values so as to include such women writers. If our foremothers are excluded from the canonical fold, these critics reason, it must not be due to their lack of artistic achievement, even though such achievement admittedly must have been severely hampered by a social position of near-servitude and drudgery or merely ornamental leisure—neither of which allowed or placed value upon literary achievement by women. Various questions about what constitutes literature and whether artistic values may be inherently sexist deserve the investigation they receive from feminist critics. But a reductive argument can in fact be condescending toward both writers and readers, since it does not recognize the actual detriment that inequality can have on artistic values and production, and it assumes that readers will prefer to read material by women—any material—in order to form some kind of canon based merely on the gender of the author. Tokenism smacks of condescension, whatever form it takes.

Rather than rejecting traditional, mainstream aesthetics and embracing either sentimentality or anger as both structure and subject, the personal classicists have worked to adapt modernism—both its romantic and classical elements—to create a form based on female expression within the prevailing aesthetics of this century. They, too, want to achieve the universal through the particular—but they must find a way to prove that the female is just as much a part of the universal as the male, and they seek particulars and a method to present the self that will not exclude male readers while including women. They strive for a kind of stylistic balance and control in which to convey their own personal sensibilities.

In exploring and defining what I call personal classicism, I want to examine how romantic and classical elements come together to inform this poetic attitude and to trace its importance, due to influences from literary history, sociopolitical pressure, and individual sensibility, for a few women poets writing in this century. The struggle between poetic self-expression and self-silencing has had certain specific cultural implications for women and demands attention in a gender-informed study, yet it is quite probable that in the future, as these historical impediments drop away from the lives of women writers, the literary distinction between genders will also fade. It is still important, I think, to acknowledge that women and men may arrive at roughly the same type of literary effect for very different reasons: for example, both H. D. and her husband, Richard Aldington, chose to adapt and translate Sapphic fragments, but their choices were probably prompted by different influences and desired effects. H. D. came to see herself—her sexual as well as her artistic self— suggested in the figures of Greek women in ways that Aldington never could. As Jeanne Kammer has pointed out, "The *source* of aesthetic choice" may distinguish "the practice of women poets from men working in a similar fashion."[12]

### The Roots of Personal Classicism

In many ways, Emily Dickinson was one of the first practitioners of the mode as I conceive it. Her protestation to Higginson, "When I state myself, as the Representative of the Verse—it does not mean— me—but a supposed person" has been quoted by numerous feminist critics as evidence of the self-effacing stance Dickinson took toward her own work; it is also cited as a variant of the recurrent recourse to personae that her poems show, including "supposed persons" of the male gender.[13] Nonfeminist critics might see her remark as simply a variant on the mainstream notion, fostered in this century by Eliot and finding its culmination in the practices of New Criticism, that an artist is *and should be seen as* separate from his or her work. Dickinson was, after all, ahead of her time.

Perhaps both are right. Whatever "universal" qualities she naturally wanted to lend her poems (and Dickinson was original enough a poet to forge her own notions of universality and to fend off some of Higginson's advice) would have been reinforced by her constant awareness that her gender made her something of a special case. In 1954, Donald Thackrey wrote illuminatingly of Dickinson's ambivalent belief in the power of language, and he touched on her related interest in silence. Yet he did not discuss the probable connection between her status as a nineteenth-century woman and her understanding of silence's power, as have more recent critics such as Barbara Antonina Mossberg, Lynn Keller, and Cristanne Miller.[14]

12. "The Art of Silence and the Forms of Women's Poetry," in *Shakespeare's Sisters*, ed. Sandra M. Gilbert and Susan Gubar, 158. Italics are Kammer's.

13. *The Letters of Emily Dickinson*, ed. Thomas H. Johnson, 411–12.

14. Male critics in this century have commented on her as a "special case," too; Dickinson's perceptions were certainly accurate. Perhaps the most striking and offensive of such comments is that of R. P. Blackmur, who wrote, "She was a private poet who

Today we can see the connections much more clearly, in part because so many women have broken their own silence. It may be that the forces which have led to personal classicism needed to lessen enough for us to identify them correctly. In any event, Thackrey quotes a poem (421) in which Dickinson makes very clear one insidious connection between women and silence:

A Charm invests a face
Imperfectly beheld—
The Lady dare not lift her Veil
For fear it be dispelled—

But peers beyond her mesh—
And wishes—and denies—
Lest Interview—annul a want
That Image—satisfies.[15]

The woman in the poem *must* remain an "image" to command attention—to be recognized as having worth—and to preserve that image she must not show her true self. Significantly, she does not wear a true mask, an utterly fabricated facade; instead she simply "veils" herself, allowing for an "imperfect"—but not utterly false— perception of her. Similarly, a woman poet might choose to "veil" her "image" in the poem she lifts to mirror herself.

"A Charm Invests a Face" does not specifically deal with speech and silence but touches on a very literal problem for a woman: the pressure to *present* a pleasing, teasing, ornamental image rather than to simply be herself. It is a problem that women have not yet overcome, and it has had such pervasive power—even recognition—that Dickinson could trust her poem to do more than remark upon a woman in a veil.[16] Her poem is about all forms of missed commu-

---

wrote indefatigably, as some women cook or knit. Her gift for words and the cultural predicament of her time drove her to poetry instead of anti-macassars" (*The Madwoman in the Attic*, 543). Surely no one would characterize Yeats's indefatigable writing as analogous to the way some men whittle wood. Donald E. Thackrey, "The Communication of the Word," in *Emily Dickinson: A Collection of Critical Essays*, ed. Richard B. Sewall, 51–69.

15. All Dickinson poems are referred to here by number. They are numbered and punctuated as they appear in *The Complete Poems of Emily Dickinson*, ed. Thomas H. Johnson.

16. See Pamela M. Fishman, "Interaction: The Work Women Do," in *Language, Gender, and Society*, edited by Barrie Thorne, Cheris Kramarae, and Nancy Henley, esp. pp. 90–101. Fishman studied speech patterns between heterosexual couples, and her results showed that women have significantly greater difficulty than men in initiating

nication between women and men, including the power of men to prevent women not only from showing their true faces, but also from speaking their own minds. That interview alludes to more than mere eye-gazing between two lovers, after all; by further implication, the poem is about women writing poetry and it being read by men.

The poet's reasons for veiling herself will not be very different from those of the nonpoet's: the identity of each as a woman ensures that to be desirable—to be read or to be looked at—the woman must in some way alter the impression she makes so that it does not conform too closely to her true self. Mystery enhances charm—and more important, one's "real" or unadorned self might run a greater risk of rejection, being either physically or spiritually unattractive to those who are the woman poet's audience. The anger expressed in so many of Dickinson's poems—particularly those with images of volcanic power—toward confinement inherent in both religious and gender-specific roles would certainly not have met with approval or understanding from most mid-nineteenth-century readers, especially men. Half a century after Dickinson hid her strong-willed poems in little packets in her upper room, Yeats would write again of how a woman like Maud Gonne could destroy her beauty with willful opinions, and he would "pray" that his daughter should not suffer such a fate but think her own opinions "cursed" and by implication, therefore, not speak them.

In another well-known poem, Dickinson counsels herself and her readers to "Tell all the truth but tell it slant" (1129), to simultaneously reveal and conceal. Here she touches more directly on the task of the woman poet who must "dazzle gradually / Or every man be blind." The poem is about the need to use understatement, one of the primary literary devices I find among the personal classicists. It is

---

topics for conversation. In a limited sample, women made 62 percent of the attempts but raised only 38 percent of the topics which actually began conversations. Yet the men made only 38 percent of the attempts at conversation and succeeded in introducing 37 percent of the conversations. Women's "failures" were because the men failed to respond at all—they essentially ignored the women and thus condemned their topics to silence. The study concluded, "Conversation is more problematic for women, who work harder to make it happen." Another study published in the same volume (Candace West and Don H. Zimmerman, "Small Insults: A Study of Interruptions in Cross-Sex Conversations between Unacquainted Persons," 102–17) showed that in all possible combinations—men interrupting men, women interrupting men, women interrupting women, and men interrupting women—men are most likely to interrupt women speakers. In the sample, 96 percent of all the interruptions were done by males to females, again condemning the women to silence.

also about the power of being circuitous, since "Success in Circuit lies." For women who were essentially powerless in sociopolitical and legal realms, such verbal tools were surely familiar parts of their daily struggles to influence the men upon whom they were economically and socially dependent. Dickinson's readers will further recognize these as literary elements in the work; thus the poem is a kind of *ars poetica.*

Although Dickinson is clearly a precursor of the twentieth-century personal classicists, it is not my intention to treat her fully here.[17] Instead, I want to examine the relationship between modernism and personal classicism and to trace this heritage through contemporary work. It may be useful, therefore, to briefly reexamine just how romanticism and classicism have been perceived in the modernist movement, particularly by some of the important men who shaped that movement, since the standards male modernists articulated were those by which the early women personal classicists, such as H. D. and Louise Bogan, tended to measure their success. Men remained the most numerous and most powerful critics and editors, exerting real power over the women in the field. The blatant example of Pound's bullying methods with Harriet Monroe while he was her foreign correspondent for *Poetry* is indicative not only of Pound's personality, but also of a then typical working relationship in which men dominated.

### The Modernist Fusion of Romanticism and Classicism

For years readers have seen the contributions to modernism made by the romantics. Surely the use of the image as a way to connect the interior, emotive self with the exterior world is fundamental to the way modernism metamorphosed or "made new" the most treasured elements of the earlier poetry. Pound's "instantaneous" formula is really a kind of radical condensation of the aims of Abrams's "greater romantic lyric," a "descriptive-meditative poem," in which the external world—a natural setting, as in the countryside of England's Lake District, for example—provides the speaker with an opportunity to turn his thoughts inward, in a process of memory, thought, anticipation, and feeling. During this meditation, the speaker comes to some important realization, which constitutes the heart of the

17. Others have come very close to doing so, although they use a different terminology. See Barbara Antonina Clarke Mossberg, *Emily Dickinson: When a Writer Is a Daughter.*

poem. He "achieves an insight, faces up to a tragic loss, comes to a moral decision, or resolves an emotional problem," after which the poem usually takes another formal turn so as to end with a renewed view of the world around the speaker—although that view is colored by the internal, emotional change the speaker has undergone.[18] And the importance of the image necessarily implies the importance of the personality in which the perceived image registers.

In spite of the general recognition and acclaim for the image, there was no lack of difference of opinion among the early moderns about the best poetic trajectory to follow into the future. Even in the earliest years in London, before 1914, Ford Madox Ford espoused a kind of impressionism, wherein a writer could sacrifice realism—an attempt to show the world as it is—in deference to the way the world seemed to the writer.[19] Ford's doctrine insists upon a subjective quality that is very far from the attempts to achieve scientific objectivity that Pound and Hulme continued to pursue.

T. E. Hulme's *Speculations* is often credited with contributing to Pound's conception of verse that is "hard" and "dry." Hulme's demarcation between romantic and classical attitudes relies not only on aesthetics, but also on politics, philosophy, and religion. Michael Roberts notes that when Hulme calls "for a new classical art, he is not asking for imitations of an art of the past, but for one that will express the religious view of the world, and not the romantic or humanist view." What Hulme seeks in classicism is a belief in "objective ethical values," as distinct from the limitless belief in human potential that, in romanticism, places personality at the center of cultural attention.[20] Contrasting romanticism, what he calls "spilt religion," to classicism, Hulme writes, "Even in the most imaginative flights there is always a holding back, a reservation. The classical poet never forgets this finiteness, this limit of man. He remembers always that he is mixed up with earth. He may jump, but he always returns back; he never flies away into the circumambient gas."[21] This is a highly figurative description of the classical poet. Yet it points to a belief in limitation and hints at an interest in con-

18. Abrams, "Structure and Style," 528.
19. In this way Ford overcame his disregard for Yeats, as Michael H. Levenson shows in *A Genealogy of Modernism*. See esp. 119.
20. Michael Roberts, *T. E. Hulme*, 58.
21. "Romanticism and Classicism," in *Speculations: Essays on Humanism and the Philosophy of Art*, ed. Herbert Read, 118, 120.

trol beyond the artistic realms, which Pound and Eliot came to share, and which eventually, perhaps, led to their shared interest in authoritarian governments as instruments of cultural as well as political control.

Hulme defines the classical view of humankind as the belief that each person "is intrinsically limited, but disciplined by order and tradition to something fairly decent." More central to the early imagist movement, however, is Hulme's complaint of the romantic poets: "They cannot see that accurate description is a legitimate object of verse." He reemphasizes, "The great aim is accurate, precise and definite description." This is, of course, the major articulated aim of Pound, Eliot, and the imagists, from Eliot's call for an objective correlative, "a set of objects, a situation, a chain of events which shall be the formula of that *particular* emotion" to Pound's "Go in fear of abstractions."[22]

All these statements reveal a desire to point poetry's mirror outward, away from the writer's spirit or soul or emotions—which might be far too "damp" for modernist taste. Emotion is to be *implied* rather than stated directly; and when the emotion is located in a particular object, it must not distort the object itself, since realism, or "accurate, precise and definite description," is not to be sacrificed for greater self-expression. (Herein lies the difference between Ford and the Hulme/Pound/Eliot axis.)

In spite of these important differences, the early male modernists shared much in the way of their beliefs and goals for art in the twentieth century. And it was the collective similarity of purpose, the major intent of modernism, which set a context of classicism that emerging women writers would adapt into personal classicism. For, as the new poetics of imagism and modernism called for less and less obvious reliance on the interior self of the poet, the call to avoid "imaginative flights" carried an added weight for women poets involved with the movement. Popular women poets of the nineteenth century are all too vulnerable to the charge of being "flighty," since they cultivate the sentimental in poems that extol the spiritual virtues of love and family. Pound's admonition to "go in fear" might resonate more profoundly in a woman's ears than in a man's—H. D.'s, perhaps, or Amy Lowell's.

22. Ibid., 117, 127, 132; T. S. Eliot, "Hamlet," in *Selected Prose of T. S. Eliot*, ed. Frank Kermode, 48; Ezra Pound, "A Retrospect," in *Literary Essays of Ezra Pound*, ed. T. S. Eliot, 5.

T. S. Eliot also did much to articulate an ethic of understatement and self-shielding in his early essays; his was not the voice of abrupt dictum and manifesto—that was left to Pound—yet through his measured, scholarly arguments he introduced a critical attitude that would lead to New Criticism, and he called for a recognition and praise of intellectualism in art. Intellectualism favored classicism along the familiar classical/romantic dichotomy, being more interested in instruction than self-expression. This attitude resurfaces in Eliot's discussion of the artist in "Tradition and the Individual Talent": "What happens is a continual surrender of himself as he is at the moment to something which is more valuable. The progress of an artist is a continual self-sacrifice, a continual extinction of personality."[23]

Indeed, the author's personality is removed from direct participation in the poetic process since "the poet's mind is in fact a receptacle for seizing and storing up numberless feelings, phrases, images, which remain there until all the particles which can unite to form a new compound are present together."[24] Clearly, Eliot distrusted an expressive theory of art: the measure for the poem's success should not be the degree of sincerity or generosity of the poet/speaker. Instead, the poem depends upon a kind of metamorphosis in which whatever personal impetus lies behind the poem is rendered impersonal, and the poet's biography is unreadable in the finished verse.

Here is how Eliot contrasted classicism and romanticism, respectively, in his 1923 essay, "The Function of Criticism": "The difference seems to me rather the difference between the complete and the fragmentary, the adult and the immature, the orderly and the chaotic."[25] In other words, romanticism is intrinsically inferior to classicism, and a romantic poet had better be prepared to be labeled "immature" or "chaotic," and to always fail major achievement, due to his or her own mental and aesthetic limitations.

Of course in their own work many poets have ignored—or outright rejected—Eliot's beliefs, perhaps most notably the confessional poets and deep image poets of the fifties and sixties. Moreover, critics like James E. Miller, Jr., question the impersonality of Eliot's own poetry, calling it "a sophistic and sophisticated defense for someone

23. *The Selected Prose of T. S. Eliot*, 40.
24. Ibid., 41.
25. Ibid., 70.

wanting to write poetry 'talking about himself without giving himself away.'" Miller alludes here to Eliot's own statement in a 1951 lecture: "A poet may believe that he is expressing only his private experience; his lines may be for him only a means of talking about himself without giving himself away."[26] Certainly Eliot's extermination of the personal is questionable.

And in a sense, Eliot is describing the very course the personal classicist poets will follow. He wants his poetry to convey a personal tone while keeping himself safely shielded behind a mask, preventing an easy identification of speaker as poet, and of poetry as autobiography. Importantly, the fact that much of Eliot's subject matter places him in the role of the outsider—studies of impotence, abhorrence of sexuality, the homoerotic hints throughout *Prufrock and Other Observations*—includes him, to some degree, in the social position of the woman writer, whose personal life is marginalized, placed outside traditional literary territory. It is arguable that any writer from a marginalized background—whether cultural, racial, or sexual—potentially would have a vested interest in personal classicism, although gender is ubiquitous, applying to half the human race. From early in his career, Eliot successfully emphasized the work, not the creator, the process of composition independent from the writer's personality. His insistence on this approach to literature is echoed in the critical assumptions inherent in New Criticism. Consequently, he was not recognized as an early personal classicist whose work combined mask and autobiography; instead he contributed to the modernist period's classicist interest at the expense of its romantic roots.

Maturity, self-control, discipline—such terms taken out of literary context reveal an interest in containing or subverting the irrational ego. In context, they reveal attitudes toward presentation and form more than toward content itself. The tenets of imagism ostensibly speak of styles, not subjects, appropriate for twentieth-century writing. Ezra Pound, in his essay "Credo," described what he expected from the new poetry for the twentieth century:

> . . . harder and saner, . . . 'nearer the bone.' It will be as much like granite as it can be, its force will lie in its truth, its interpretive power . . . I mean it will not try to seem forcible by rhetorical din, and luxurious riot. We will have fewer painted adjectives impeding

26. James E. Miller, Jr., *T. S. Eliot's Personal Wasteland: Exorcism of the Demons*, 10.

the shock and stroke of it. At least for myself, I want it so, austere, direct, free from emotional slither.[27]

All three points of Aldington's and Pound's famous "Imagist Manifesto" emphasize excision. Herbert Schneidau likens the manifesto to Pound's call elsewhere for "straight talk, straight as the Greek!" and characterizes Pound's dictum this way: "classic directness in the accents of contemporary speech."[28] Thus, the modernist plan for poetry of the future is constantly harking back to the teachings of non-self-expression in a way that is hostile to romanticism.

Throughout much of Pound's early criticism we find this same concern with precision, concision, understatement or effacement of personal feeling. In "The Serious Artist" he writes, "The arts, literature, poesy, are a science, just as chemistry is a science. Their subject is man, mankind and the individual," further explaining, "The serious artist is scientific in that he presents the image of his desire, of his hate, of his indifference. . . . The more precise his record the more lasting and unassailable his work of art." Importantly, the writer is to present the object of passion, not to discuss—or explore—the passion itself. Elsewhere he advises, "Consider the way of the scientists rather than the way of an advertising agent for a new soap," and "In poetry there are simple procedures, and there are known discoveries, clearly marked." To Pound, "'Good Writing' is perfect control." To Eliot "it is not the 'greatness,' the intensity, of the emotions, the components, but the intensity of the artistic process, the pressure, so to speak, under which the fusion takes place, that counts."[29]

All of these statements display an envious (and finally fallacious) analogy between literature and science. They also rest on a fundamental belief in disciplined technique or, more precisely, the technique of discipline. What is important to recognize about the way such dicta must have sounded to aspiring women writers in the century's first decades is this: control of emotion, even eviction of personality, are primary stylistic goals in modern poetry. To fail to embrace these values is to fail to be taken seriously by the most prolific, vocal, and self-promoting (male) figures of the age.

Yet the study and expression of personality or emotion have traditionally been areas in which women (and early women writers) have

27. *Literary Essays,* 12.
28. Herbert N. Schneidau, *Ezra Pound: The Image and the Real,* 8.
29. Pound, *Literary Essays,* 42, 46, 6, 19, 49; Eliot, *Selected Prose,* 41.

excelled: from nurturing within the home to character development among the pages of Jane Austen, the very elements of humanity proscribed by modernism have been prescribed as women's domain. Moreover, the metaphor of the writer as scientist is yet another analogy in which the vehicle as well as the tenor is a profession that has traditionally excluded women. The woman poet wishing to succeed during the rise of modernism, therefore, finds herself in a quandary: how to achieve self-expression, writing out of her experience and perception as a woman, without incurring the disapprobation of the dominant cult of control. Personal classicism provides an answer to this problem: it mutes but does not seek to extinguish the female self and its life.

One might expect Marianne Moore to figure prominently in this study, as an example of a modernist woman who succeeded in achieving fame and recognition from her male peers and who certainly embraced the classical approach. Yet I do not find the hints of a truly personal tone, nor the interest in the individual spirit—although she certainly catalogues individual traits of objects and animals—that implies to me the commitment to feeling that distinguish the poets I identify as personal classicists.[30]

As I've begun to suggest, some of the important roots for personal classicism reside in the imagist movement; certainly important is the work of the poet recognized by her peers as the quintessential imagist, H. D. Imagism, with its emphasis on what is observed, on what is outside the self—frequently the natural world—allows a writer to effectively "surrender" (Eliot's term) the "I" in favor of the setting in which the "I" finds itself. Thus, the speaker emerges through implication: because the setting is seen, someone must be seeing it—the reader can infer something of the speaker by the way he or she describes the outside world.

Pound soon abandoned imagism when he decided it had become loose, sloppy "Amygism," no longer under his tight and discerning leadership. His impatience with Amy Lowell's promotion of the movement well after it had lost its initial power is somewhat justified; his

---

30. Although it can be argued that Moore's constant quoting from letters, conversations, newspapers, and the like is similar to the techniques of the personal classicists, I do not see in the *poems themselves* the kind of shielded emphasis on personal feeling that would warrant her inclusion here. She seems to me a mainstream modernist. For a thorough study of Moore's poetry, including information about her incorporation of private quotations, see Bonnie Costello, *Marianne Moore: Imaginary Possessions* (Cambridge: Harvard University Press, 1981).

disgust with the loosening of the "Amygist's" proclaimed rules, however, is not. Most of Pound's proclamations quoted above involve forbidding something as absolutely inappropriate to modern poetry; the "Imagist Manifesto" carries that same flavor of exclusiveness:

1. Direct treatment of the "thing" whether subjective or objective.
2. To use absolutely no word that does not contribute to the presentation.
3. As regarding rhythm: to compose in the sequence of the musical phrase, not in sequence of a metronome.[31]

Pound even published in the March 1913 *Poetry* a list of "don'ts" for aspiring writers.

Lowell, in comparison, was inclined to be more inclusive than exclusive, more inclined to affirm encouragement than to proclaim critical failure. In her 1915 Imagist anthology, she included six principles based roughly on the "Imagist Manifesto," but less prohibitive. Her second principle included sentences such as, "We do not insist upon 'free-verse' as the only method of writing poetry. We fight for it as a principle of liberty. We believe that the individuality of a poet may often be better expressed in free-verse than in conventional forms." The third principle was perhaps the most generous. "To allow absolute freedom in the choice of subject."[32] Lowell, as a woman and a lesbian, was keenly aware of the accepted bias against certain kinds of subject matter for poetry, and unlike Pound, she wanted to emphasize the importance of technique with the understanding that a writer might successfully apply those techniques to any subject she or he chose.

All this energetic search for a new poetry was a specific reaction to a mode that much needed reacting against: Georgian poetry. Even in an introduction to a Georgian anthology, an editor admits, "The faults of Georgian poetry . . . were technical slackness—the use of imprecise diction and facile rhythm; sentimentality of outlook; trivial, and even downright commonplace themes." Commenting on the preface to a 1921 volume *Selection from Modern Poets*, he says "Fifty minor poets writing durable lyrics about truth and beauty—that was the image of modern poetry which the Georgian movement projected. No wonder it became discredited in the eyes of discrimi-

31. Pound, *Literary Essays*, 3.
32. William Pratt, "Introduction," *The Imagist Poem*, 22.

nating and progressive readers."[33] He could have added "discriminating and progressive writers" to that group. None of the imagists—men or women—wanted to write what could be even remotely perceived as trivial, slack, and sentimental poems.

## The Call of the Archetypal

The classicist interest in the early twentieth century was not confined to formal interests, technique, or attitudes toward sincerity and self-expression. "Classical" includes classical mythology, which provided subject matter and framing devices, from the layered allusiveness of Joyce's *Ulysses* to H. D.'s and Aldington's work at "translating" poetry fragments. Of course, the interest in allusion to mythology is not in itself a new approach to literature, by any means. Instead, it reflects a continued self-consciousness of one's place—as a writer—in a tradition of retelling familiar myth that unites such disparate figures as Keats and Pope. It is this very awareness of continuity and one's place within the tradition that Eliot calls for in "Tradition and the Individual Talent," and one's place in the tradition can itself become subject matter for new art.

Yet there is also the sense of change in the modernists' reliance on myth: a newly conceived rediscovery of ancient Greece constituted an important part of what Hugh Kenner calls, in his lengthy study, "the Pound era." Kenner suggests that a *renewed* interest in the classics was general and widespread, and that the profuse amount of literary criticism on *The Odyssey* during the period from 1903 to 1910 was due in part to Schliemann's excavation of Troy.[34] Indeed, as *The Odyssey* became favored over *The Iliad* as the richer, more important text, its characters and themes appeared in modernist writings as divergent as Joyce's *Ulysses* and Williams's *Paterson*.

There is also among the high modernists, Pound and Eliot perhaps foremost, a kind of desperation in their turn to mythological allusion. Eliot's belief that modern people "know only / A heap of broken images, where the sun beats" and that the poet's task is to work with "These fragments I have shored against my ruins" as well as Pound's disgust for "a botched civilization" point to a modern world that suffers a cultural, ritual void.[35] High modernism turned to

33. James Reeves, *Georgian Poetry*, xvii, xvi–xvii.
34. *The Pound Era*, 42–44.
35. T. S. Eliot, "The Waste Land," *The Complete Poems and Plays, 1909–1950*, 38, 50; Ezra Pound, "Hugh Selwyn Mauberly," *Personae: The Collected Shorter Poems*, 191.

mythical allusion both to cast that void—as a paradoxical presence—
in high relief against the literary and cultural achievements of the
past, and, at times, to salvage relics from the past as cultural tonic
and sustenance, even while exploring new poetic frontiers that allowed for personal expression of horror, despair, and frustration at
the fragmentation of early twentieth-century life.

Many scholars and intellectuals have discussed the continuing
appeal of mythology as sustenance, as empowerment, in works of art.
Jung finds that myth bespeaks the archetypal and thus has a profound effect on the human psyche:

> When an archetypal situation occurs we suddenly feel an extraordi-
> nary sense of release, as though transported, or caught up by an over-
> whelming power. At such moments we are no longer individuals,
> but the race; the voice of all mankind resounds in us. . . . Whoever
> speaks in primordial images speaks with a thousand voices; he en-
> thralls and overpowers, while at the same time he lifts the idea he is
> seeking to express out of the occasional and the transitory into the
> realm of the ever-enduring.[36]

Writers, of course, want their works to evoke power, to transport their
readers. Modern use of mythological allusion promotes the sense of
connection with the distant past, and suggests that our contemporary
concerns and problems have something essentially in common with
the problems facing our ancestors. Perhaps in the twentieth century,
as we have marched steadily toward the brink of self-destruction
through two world wars, nuclear bombs and accidents at power plants,
and a growing ecological disaster that has, in Bill McKibbon's phrase,
put us at the "end of nature," the need for continuity has taken on
a desperate, poignant difference from our similar needs in earlier
centuries.

In any event, the mythical allusion in most modernist poetry
functions as a *complex*, not unlike Pound's vorticist image, fusing
past ("outward") with present ("inward"), though perhaps not quite
simultaneously if the allusion is at all obscure. In spite of the alarm-
ing fragmentariness of modern life, insisted upon in works as different as Virginia Woolf's *Jacob's Room* and T. S. Eliot's *The Waste Land*,
mythic allusion offers startling moments of luminous awareness,
where we see some kind of correspondence, if no overlying pattern.

36. *The Spirit in Man, Art, and Literature*, 82.

This correspondence need not be reassuring, however. As Charles Tomlinson points out, Eliot's early poetry shows a barely contained horror at the way allusive metamorphosis functions: "For the terrible thing . . . is that, although nothing connects with nothing, everything seems to be changing into everything else, that all these things are identical, that metamorphosis is not variety and fecundity, but the phantasmagoria of a divided self, of a mind that contains and unifies and yet, in need of spiritual metamorphosis itself, depletes and dries up." In contrast to Eliot's horror, however, Tomlinson sees Pound's use of mythical allusion in the *Cantos* as a much more hopeful and invigorating activity. Pound shows his energetic originality in his ability to "rescue" myth and "make us experience [it] on the pulses."[37] Thus the use of myth in the hands of a modernist like Pound—or, arguably, Eliot elsewhere—is one exactly of shoring up old structures so they will once again hold weight.

In the hands of a woman poet, the use of myth may be substantially different. Although one may argue, as some have, that there remain mythical hints that a matriarchal order preceded the emergence of the patriarchy, the vast body of existent mythology is shaped by—and helps to perpetuate the shape of—an order that has been largely hostile and oppressive toward women. The sense of "transport" and "overwhelming power" Jung speaks of will take on different meaning for a woman who sees an archetypal situation in her own subjugation. This power is often behind the personal classicist use of mythology as a mask through which to speak (well veiled) of one's own life, as in the work of H. D. And the implication, however subtle, that *such as it was for her, so it still is for me* carries a greater moral weight of indictment than if a woman should write simply of her own unhappiness. In a hypothetical example, to write of Jason's calculated abandonment of Medea and her children *and then to subtly imply that Medea speaks from modern times* is to give greater stature to the abandoned woman whose husband has never paid child support and for whom the courts have been sympathetic but ineffective: her life corresponds with the mythic and the tragic.

In addition, women writers may feel (correctly) that the women appearing in familiar myths often have been exploited by the existing narratives. For them, the archetypal appeal may not be to rescue ancient mythologies but instead to revise them through what Alicia

37. *Poetry and Metamorphosis*, 33, 48.

Ostriker calls "revisionist mythmaking": "They do not share the modernist nostalgia for a golden age of past [sexist] culture, and their mythmaking grows at least as much from a subterranean tradition of female self-projection and self-exploration as from the system building of the Romantics and moderns."[38]

To a certain degree, it appears only coincidental that the anthropological and historical interest in the world of Odysseus, Achilles, and the Greek gods familiar from the classics should flourish at the same time that writers displayed a greater interest in technical control, poetry as instruction, and limited emphasis on the poet's personality that could also be called classical. But in a sense, the relationship between form and content is so close as to render them, finally, inseparable. And as Kenner points out, Sappho's fragmented lyrics by their very nature are not expansive; they "compelled a new kind of detailed attention." In protest of J. M. Edmonds's translations of Sappho that "restore" through invention and guesswork entire missing passages, Aldington presented an epitome of reticence in "Papyrus"; his version contains, besides the title, only four words, and the overpowering presence of silence through ellipsis.[39] As is often the case, the subject matter—here, translations of an ancient yet compelling text—suggests the form. And as the original interest in translation moves into the realm of imitation, and then finally to style, the importance of a technique has become independently recognized.

This is not to suggest that the line may be drawn swiftly and without divergence from an anthropological discovery to a widely accepted style in poetic composition. Other factors, of course, come into play; Kenner even links the reticent nature of imagist lyrics to Henry James's interest in the enigma, in secrets, in "orgies of reticence."[40] The sensibilities of the writers who create in a given style have everything to do with the outcome of literary history. And social history—the effects of gender—have much to do with the development of sensibility.

In the 1990s one would like to be able to smile at Charles Tansley's refrain in Virginia Woolf's *To the Lighthouse*: "Women can't paint, women can't write." Yet we know that, until recently, women have had a small place in the literary establishment and have been constantly judged not simply as poets, but as diminutive "poetesses,"

---

38. *Stealing the Language: The Emergence of Women's Poetry in America*, 213.
39. Kenner, *The Pound Era*, 51, 54.
40. Ibid., 23.

or as "women poets," a kind set apart. We are not yet safely removed from the history of silence that has muted the achievement of recognized women writers.

The attention that women poets receive as "examples" of female art has fostered a feeling that technique, control, and reservation must be constantly exhibited in order to earn proper credentials and to protect women from the kind of dismissive criticism that was not uncommon through the first half of this century. Louise Bogan even accepted and internalized prejudices against women poets to the point that she believed women were inherently incapable of certain kinds of writing, and she privately dismissed her women contemporaries.

Moreover, the kind of silencing pressure that has affected poets is not by any means confined to the literary world. Western culture, and certainly American society, has emphasized the importance of retiring, even self-denying behavior for women in general—and that includes women poets. Thus, women have needed to strive on two fronts to win for themselves the ability to assert the self, rather than to deny it. Whatever course their personal lives take, personal classicism provides an aesthetic mode through which they may use quiet understatement, yet break through the silence.

### The Relationship Between Confessional and Personal Classicist Poems

Personal classicism began as an altered form of modernism, embracing—although for different reasons—much the same principles gleaned from romantic and classical roots, yet the mode has had a continued importance long after the preeminence of high modernism and New Criticism were assailed by the confessional poets. If the first personal classicists forged their aesthetic against both Georgian sentimentalism and the popular women "songbirds" of the nineteenth and early twentieth centuries, as well as against the possible skepticism or outright hostility their presence as women writers might have met from their male peers, the personal classicists who began writing and publishing in the late 1960s and after have received a very different burden.[41] They have come of poetic age dur-

---

41. Louise Bogan used the term "songbirds" condescendingly in explaining why she turned down an offer to edit an anthology of women's poetry: "the thought of corresponding with a lot of female songbirds made me acutely ill" (Letter to John Wheelock, July 1, 1935, in *What the Woman Lived: Selected Letters of Louise Bogan, 1920–1970*, ed. Ruth Limmer, 86).

ing the great popularity of Sexton and Plath and therefore must choose either to participate in the recognizably successful (or at least famous) activity of female confessionalism—or they must clear another path.

Indeed, in the thirty years since M. L. Rosenthal first introduced the term into the critical vocabulary with his review of Robert Lowell's *Life Studies*, the critical debate over confessional poetry has spent a good deal of energy debating the aptness of the name itself. Even Rosenthal expressed dissatisfaction with his terminology when he wrote in 1967, "It was a term both helpful and too limited, and very possibly the conception of a confessional school has by now done a certain amount of damage."[42] Other critics proposed alternative labels, such as A. Alvarez's "extremist poetry." Squabbles broke out over whether there was a specific, historic "school" consisting of only a handful of writers (Snodgrass, Lowell, Ginsberg, Plath, Sexton, Berryman) or whether it was a mode practiced by many other writers independently of these important few (including Delmore Schwartz, Theodore Roethke, even the later W. B. Yeats and the Pound of the *Pisan Cantos*) or whether, indeed, it was simply an extension of the personal lyric virtually unidentifiable from even Renaissance writers and thus undeserving of a new title.

Such disputes seem almost pointless now: clearly most students of literature recognize something about the poems of the first mentioned group that is different from most personal lyrics of earlier eras, and we see in the hundreds of little magazines scattered throughout America the impact those most famous confessional poems have had on contemporary writers. The difficulty is that most attempts at defining the mode have focused on either subject matter or technique—more often on subject matter—rather than any kind of fusion of the two, and this error makes it virtually impossible to come to any clear conclusions. Moreover, because no one has yet distinguished personal classicism from confessionalism, we find critics attempting to conflate the two into one impossible category—or to deny the utility of the category "confessional poetry" because it is not large enough to contain such differences in degree as clearly exist.

Steven K. Hoffman offers a perceptive definition for contemporary confessional poetry that would seem to include within its scope

---

42. *The New Poets: American and British Poetry since World War II*, 25. It is debatable whether the most "damage" was done to writers of criticism or of poetry.

many of the poems I wish to call personal classicist. He defines this "distinct historical movement firmly rooted in both the Romantic and modern traditions" this way:

> [It] synthesizes the inclination to personalism and consciousness building of the nineteenth century with the elaborate masking techniques and objectifications of the twentieth, a phenomenon which, under the veneer of self-absorption unprecedented even among the Romantics, makes notable inroads into myth and archetype, as well as social, political, and cultural historiography characteristic of high modernism.[43]

If this were, indeed, the final definition of confessional poetry's attributes, it would swallow too many poems into its great maw. I suspect that it is the willingness of critics to allow such vagaries to hold command that pushed Joan Aleshire to write an essay reclaiming the personal lyric from what she sees as a tendency to label "all poems with a high emotional content in which the speaker can be identified as the poet" as confessional.[44] She points out that the lyric has always been allied with emotion, and need not be totally supplanted by a misuse of the term *confessional*. The problem at hand is due to relying too heavily on only subject matter—"the personal"—as the criterion for judgement.

Lawrence Lerner mentions a matter of technique that I think is vital to understanding the method of confessional poetry. He identifies "a peculiar and disturbing intensity in the language, an attempt to render raw and disturbing experience through ugly and disturbing images that do not always seem to be under control."[45] The example he draws upon is Sexton's from a prose description of dreams of drowning: the speaker says she must "grapple with eels like ropes." Of course, Lerner's "ugly and disturbing images" could just as easily apply to the famous sunset in "The Love Song of J. Alfred Prufrock" where Eliot sees "the evening is spread out against the sky / Like a patient etherized upon a table."[46] I have already suggested that Eliot, in many ways, *is* something of a personal classicist, due to his eagerness to mask or extinguish marginalized attitudes and emotions. But it is important to point out that there is repeatedly in Sexton's poems,

43. "Impersonal Personalism: The Making of a Confessional Poetic," 688.
44. "Staying News: A Defense of the Lyric," 47.
45. "What Is Confessional Poetry?" 55.
46. *The Complete Poems and Plays, 1909–1950*, 3.

as in Plath's, and as in many of the avowedly feminist or lesbian poems that are being written today, a "peculiar and disturbing intensity of language" that is a matter not merely of diction but of syntax. There is a tendency in confessional poetry to adopt rhythms that build and intensify, and bespeak—viscerally—emotion that careens out of control.

One familiar example, of course, is Plath's "Daddy," which enforces the furious rhythm with its relentless use of rhyme. While the anger and sense of awakening power build rhythmically, the poem insists on indicting "you" as it intermittently rhymes "do," "shoe," "Achoo," "blue," "Ach, du. . . ." The words are often surprising. The poem plows through its gruesome images and comparisons—Daddy as Nazi, as Hitler, as devil—at breakneck speed, alternating long, jumbled sentences with shorter, staccato ones. Plath begins at top speed; the very first line's iambic tetrameter cannot be a calming meter. Where we should hear a caesura—we see one in the comma's placement—there is no relief because of the insistent, sing-song internal rhyme. After the perfect meter of that first line, we stagger over the irregular "Anymore," that begins line two, but we do not slow down. We, too, barely dare to breathe until the stanza closes.

In "Daddy," the angry, building rhythms are unmistakable. Of course, not all confessional poems display this tendency to the same degree. While many of Sexton's poems, particularly from her later collections, show a similar rhythmic intensity, some clearly do not. Yet even in her comparatively calmer poems, there often occur slight unexpected shifts in syntax that emphasize emotional intensity. The first line in her first collection, *To Bedlam and Part Way Back*, shows one such shift. "You, Doctor Martin, walk / from breakfast to madness."[47] Read aloud, the line is much more accusing and audibly angry than if the order were "Doctor Martin, you walk / from breakfast to madness." The tendency toward varying degrees of greater rhythmic unrest seems an important attribute for most confessional poetry.

Contemporary poets who work in the confessional mode continue to show this inclination. Sharon Olds—who often comes under attack for the looseness of her lines and the raw intimacy of her imagery—shows the same tendencies of the earlier women confessional poets who clearly influenced her. I've chosen "The Departure," from her second collection, *The Dead and the Living*, to represent her work here because of its similarity in subject matter to "Daddy." However, the

47. *The Complete Poems*, 3.

formal property I wish to demonstrate is evident in nearly all her work, including the poems most recently appearing in small magazines.

### The Departure
#### (to my father)

Did you weep like the Shah when you left? Did you forget
the way you had had me tied to a chair, as
he forgot the ones strapped to the grille
in his name? You knew us no more than he knew them,
his lowest subjects, his servants, and we were
silent before you like that, bowing
backwards, not speaking, not eating unless we were
told to eat, the glass jammed to our
teeth and tilted like a brass funnel in the
soundproof cells of Teheran. Did you forget
the blood, blinding lights, pounding on the door, as
he forgot the wire, the goad,
the stone table? Did you weep as you left
as Reza Pahlevi wept when he rose
over the gold plain of Iran, did you
suddenly want to hear our voices, did you
start to rethink the darkness of our hair,
did you wonder if perhaps we had deserved to live,
did you love us, then?[48]

Olds speaks in relentless questions: of the five sentences in this poem, only one is a statement. Moreover, Olds packs several questions into a single sentence, as in the last seven lines, where five clauses begin, "did you. . . ." Unlike some of Sexton's pieces that place their repetitions or refrains in the same position formally, Olds allows her questions to interrupt the forward movement of the line across the page. Of the eight appearances of "did you," three appear at the line's opening, two at the line's end, and the rest in various positions within the line. The phrase and the accusation, with their consuming interest in the past, keep popping up unexpectedly.

Like Plath in "Daddy," Olds makes outrageous comparisons: the father is a dictator, a strong man, a torturer, like the Shah of Iran. She suggests that injustice and cruelty on the small, private level of the family is comparable to the larger, public level of a nation, much

48. *The Dead and the Living,* 36.

as Plath compares her own condition to that of the Jews during the Holocaust. But it is not only the magnitude of the subject matter, nor the images with which that matter is conveyed, which make this poem indicative of the confessional legacy. It is also the visceral manipulation of sound and syntax.

Significantly, there is a tendency among women confessional poets to focus on anger more frequently than men do; among the male confessionals there is a greater interest in emotional agony that does not emphasize vengeful outrage to the same degree we find among women. However unflattering a portrait Lowell may paint of his parents in *Life Studies*, for example, he certainly never resorts to the extreme appropriation of world-class torturers to make his point. Moreover, the sense we get from that collection is more one of sadness over wasted lives, wasted opportunities, than resentment over mammoth indignities that were inflicted and opportunities that were denied. Clearly these last two concerns are primary interests of the women confessional poets, who are finally interested in "confessing" their own victimization.

Increasingly such wildness in metaphor and rhythm is a deliberate, political act; some women poets seem to identify poetic control with misguided complicity in patriarchal control, and therefore reject any traditional notions of aesthetic shaping. While personal classicists may share these political views, their aesthetic choices are very different. Personal classicist poets find the sources of their work in many of the same areas the confessional poets do: sexual and familial strife and disappointment; anger and indignation over the conditions of their personal and professional lives; grief or bitterness over loss. This kind of subject matter devolves from a belief that poetry speaks of life as it is lived, and poets with various stylistic approaches have shared this belief throughout centuries. It is important at this time in the appraisal of twentieth-century poetry to be able to distinguish confessional from personal classicist poets, noting in addition to their shared commitment to subject matter their crucial differences in formal and stylistic methods.

# 2

# H. D., *Classiciste*

## The Imagist Approach to Personal Classicism

"Well, I do not put my personal self into my poems. But my personal self has got between me and my real self, my real artist personality." H. D. wrote these curious lines to John Cournos apparently during her stay at Cornwall—the letter mentions her surplus of "sun, sea, wind, hills, birds, work both mental and physical"—with Cecil Gray, following the breakup of her marriage to Richard Aldington. She was at work on a biographical novel, either *Paint It To-day* or *Fields of Asphodel* and must have received some negative criticism from Cournos with which she agreed: "You are quite right about the novel and I shall certainly chuck it. . . . [T]he novel is not intended as a work of art. . . . It is a means to an end." In putting down honestly, or "straight," the personal "tangle" of her life, she hoped "to clear the ground" and then "turn to my real work again."[1] In other words, she distinguished her novel, primarily therapeutic, from real art. At that time, she considered her real work to be her poetry—she had not yet fully left her imagist phase—and it was the product not of her "personal self" but of her "real artist personality."

H. D. sounds very much like T. S. Eliot here, hinting at the artist's suppression of his or her own personality in order to shape that of the poet; this is good modernist doctrine. In 1917 Eliot wrote, "What happens is a continual surrender of himself [the artist] as he is at the moment *to something which is more valuable.* The progress of an artist is a continual self-sacrifice, a continual *extinction of per-*

1. Donna Krolik Hollenberg, "Art and Ardor in World War One: Selected Letters from H. D. to John Cournos," 147–48.

*sonality* [italics mine]."[2] "My real work"; "something which is more valuable"—both poets are discussing the way they see the artistic process at work in a writer's own life. H. D., however, takes the idea a step further, since she sees her "artistic personality" as her *real* self and sees that the personal life has not only ceased to merely feed but in fact has begun to obstruct her art. She has substituted the artificial for the personal as the primary self, not merely in her art but also—here in a personal letter to Cournos—in her life.

Her art, therefore, works to become a kind of screen that veils or "obscures" the personal; it is not simply an activity independent of the personal life. To use a favorite metaphor from her prose and poetry, her self is a palimpsest, with the "artistic personality" as the uppermost, visible layer. This letter's brief glimpse at H. D.'s attitude toward the connection between life and art gives a rare insight to her practice of personal classicism. Personal and impersonal are closely linked for H. D., and this close connection makes possible the occasional glinting of the personal from beneath the ostensibly outward or objective interests of the classical. She seems to be drawing her subjects from areas of interest much more far-reaching and inclusive than simply her personal life—from the world of ancient myth—but as I will show, those distant goddesses and ancient mortals who people Greek mythology and history mirror dramas from her own life; their emotions mirror her own.

Until recently, however, much of the critical attention H. D. has received has centered on her classicism—without the personal element—and the very subject matter of her work certainly demands significant attention as "classical" in a way the other poets in this study do not. With H. D. we do not merely speak of "classical" control and balance in the work—technique—as we shall with the poems of Elizabeth Bishop. Nor is it merely that her poems are interested in the external world, that they draw their significance from general truths and patterns rather than specific moments of personal realization and experience.

Instead, we must refer as well to the subjects she wrote about. She returned repeatedly to themes and characters from Greek mythology throughout her prose and her poetry. During her imagist phase she wrote dozens of poems with mythic, Mediterranean settings and speakers, from the much-anthologized "Oread," with its Greek moun-

2. "Tradition and the Individual Talent," in *The Selected Prose of T. S. Eliot,* 40 (italics mine).

tain nymph as speaker, to persona poems that have received greater
attention in recent years, such as "Thetis," "Circe," or "Calypso."
She based whole poems on Sappho's "fragments." A novel, *Palimpsest*, consists of three individual sections, the first titled "Hipparchia:
War Rome *circa* 75 B.C." Hipparchia is a Greek writer whom H. D.
identifies as the daughter of Cynic philosopher Crates and his wife
Hipparchia.[3] Another novel, *Hedylus*, takes both title and epigraph
from the *Greek Anthology*. H. D. translated several passages from
Euripides, as well as the play *Ion*. Her later, book-length poems draw
heavily upon Greek myth, especially *Trilogy* and *Helen in Egypt*. Even
in *Bid Me To Live*, a roman à clef set in World War I London, and
*Tribute to Freud*, a memoir of her psychoanalysis with Sigmund Freud
during the early thirties, we see her constant interest in the way classic myths and literature pertain to twentieth-century life; indeed,
most of her published work touches upon them in some way.

Other modernists also did this, of course; the intellectual community was full of excitement over a new renaissance of classical research. Throughout the male modernists' work, from Pound's *Cantos*
to Joyce's *Ulysses*, Greek myth appears time and again. But these other
writers did not pursue their use of Greek myth with either the same
perseverance as H. D. or in quite the same spirit. Pound was another
poet who immersed himself, as well as his poems, in the ambience of
literature and culture from another age, yet he did not restrict himself to only Greek classics. Instead, he moved from the Provençal trou-
badours to the Anglo-Saxons to Confucius to John Adams, among
his many subjects, and his ideogrammic patchworks of allusion
sought primarily to retrieve wisdom from the past, wisdom desper-
ately needed for this century. H. D., on the other hand, specialized
primarily in Greek mythology (although *Trilogy* combines Christian
myth as well); her retrieval of wisdom was also a revision of history, a
way to question and challenge patriarchal and militaristic tradition.

Alicia Ostriker has defined revisionist mythmaking as when "the
figure or tale [is] appropriated for altered ends, the old vessel filled with
new wine, initially satisfying the thirst of the individual poet but ultimately making cultural change possible." In "satisfying the thirst of the

---

3. As Thomas Burnett Swann points out in *The Classical World of H. D.*, "H. D.
does not explain how Crates, who lived in the time of Alexander (356–323), could have a
daughter who was still a young woman in 75 B.C.," 123. Here, as elsewhere throughout
H. D.'s creative work, she grounds character or situation in mythic allusion but adds
revision or improvisation, not merely vision.

individual poet" we should read, for H. D., real expression of her personal life as it conformed to a pattern already partly established by myth. Thus, revisionist mythmaking offered H. D. a method whereby she could both rely on the cultural, literary foundations provided by mythology, and also provide a new—her own, female—view of those very foundations. Ostriker also distinguishes between modernist mythmaking by the great male writers of the period and that practiced by H. D., since for the female revisionist, the work "contains no trace of nostalgia, no faith that the past is a repository of truth, goodness, or desirable social organization." Instead, the past can come under indictment; moreover, the past is not lost to us, at all, but rather continues to repeat its grim patterns; "the past is not then but now." The excitement a writer or reader feels when finding the world of the archetypal repeating itself in our contemporary lives may carry very different connotations for a woman. Rather than finding herself in the midst of a repetition of heroism or adventure, a woman is likely to find herself in the ancient position of victim. Gilbert and Gubar likewise hold that "excavation and innovation" inherent in the great male modernist texts are, in part, attempts to reimpose masculinist, patriarchal cultural standards.[4] These strategies are not only entirely lacking from H. D.'s work; they are, in fact, subverted.

In Barbara Guest's words, "With the instinct of sudden genius, [H. D.] recognized the form that suited her sensibility, and that form proceeded from Greek drama and Greek poetry." Guest suggests that H. D.'s "form"—imagism's understatement—derives precisely from her sensibility; I want to suggest further that her very subject matter is a product of both her sensibility and her study—and that form and subject combine in personal classicism, to allow H. D. a kind of controlled feminist emotion and a way to discuss events and feelings from her own life through a palimpsest, or through a mask. I agree with Louis Martz that the method of H. D.'s genius is consciously chosen, not merely serendipitous: "What is important is that the doctrines of Imagism provided H. D. with a discipline that enabled her to control the surges that arose from the depths of her violently responsive na-

---

4. Alicia Suskin Ostriker, "The Thieves of Language: Women Poets and Revisionist Mythmaking," in *The New Feminist Criticism*, ed. Elaine Showalter, 317, 330; Gilbert and Gubar, *No Man's Land: The Place of the Woman Writer in the Twentieth Century*, vol. 1 of *The War of the Words*, 156.

ture."[5] Through allusion to myth and through revisionist mythmaking, she treated again and again the condition of women both in antiquity and in the present, and some of these "women" are scarcely concealed portraits of herself. It is important to note here that this early development of personal classicism involves not merely a veil, but a complete mask. In later writers we will see less reliance on identifiable personae.

Yet before feminist critics turned their attention to H. D., many scholars did not recognize—or did not respect—this layering of the personal behind the allusive. They based either praise or blame on partial readings of her work, wherein she was "an inspired anachronism, a Greek reborn into modern times."[6] Douglas Bush leveled an early (1937) argument against her work: "At no time is she much concerned with dramatic fidelity to a mythological character or situation." He continued:

> H. D.'s devotion to Greece is obviously instinctive and sincere, yet the instinctive effort of a twentieth-century poet to write like a Greek indicates, no matter what the degree of success, a fundamentally romantic and precious conception both of Greece and of poetry. . . . But the Greece she dwells in has no real connection with the Greece of historic actuality. Most of her poetry has the air of an exquisitely chiseled reproduction of something, though it is a reproduction of something that never existed. . . . H. D. is a poet of escape. Her refuge is a dreamworld of ideal beauty which she calls Greece; her self-conscious, even agonized, pursuit of elusive beauty is quite un-Greek.[7]

Bush wrote this criticism before H. D.'s *Trilogy* appeared and before feminist criticism had drawn attention to the importance—and validity—of revisionist mythmaking. Of course she is not primarily concerned with "fidelity" to mythology as it has been passed down through traditional literary history. She adapts and changes plots and characters, sometimes inventing, sometimes restoring, in order to present her own vision.[8] *Trilogy* and later *Helen in Egypt* present H. D. not as a poet

5. Barbara Guest, *Herself Defined: The Poet H. D. and Her World*, 44; Louis L. Martz, "Introduction," in *H. D.: Collected Poems 1912–1944*, xiii.

6. Swann, *Classical World of H. D.*, 3.

7. *Mythology and the Romantic Tradition in English Poetry*, 502, 505.

8. See Swann's *Classical World of H. D.*, esp. 48, 44. With her restorative treatment of Circe, H. D. "appears to have revitalized a Homeric tradition diluted in its transmission through Roman and English poets. By the middle of the nineteenth century, Homer's strong hearted woman—who had good reason to turn Odysseus' swinish men

of escape, but rather one of vision, or as Susan Stanford Friedman suggests, of prophecy. The later work helps teach one how to read the earlier work as well, since the palimpsestic layering of different historical time periods and the free restructuring of myth are clearly her method in the longer poems—they are not mistakes in scholarship. These later works are, however, in spite of their larger scope of ambition, often less successful as poetry. The longer poems themselves explain, through their greater reliance on rhetoric, what the shorter poems enact.

I want first to focus on some of H. D.'s earlier, imagist poems to examine how imagism's close detail and specificity allow her to create both mask and personal voice. Much of the work that contributes most to the development of personal classicism appeared before 1930. *Red Roses for Bronze* (1931) is a transitional book, with many poems anticipating the more expansive, more rhetorical style of *Trilogy* and *Helen in Egypt*.[9]

When H. D. was introduced to American and British readers as one of the foremost imagists from the Pound circle in London, rather more was made of her style than of her subject matter. Her colleagues and friends were, after all, embarked on a similar stylistic venture, although some were more dogmatically theoretical than others, and since the use of mythology for contemporary literary material was already popular, the imagist critics tended to draw attention to the ways style could "make it [mythology] new."

Ezra Pound himself introduced her work to Harriet Monroe of *Poetry* magazine in 1912, and as foremost spokesperson for imagism, he emphasized her form and style. Significantly, he drew his analogy from the classics: "Objective—no slither; direct—no excessive use of metaphors that won't permit examination. It's straight talk, straight as the Greek!" Monroe continued in this vein in the contributor's note accompanying H. D.'s January 1913 appearance. Under the general title "Verses, Translations, and Reflections from 'The Anthology,'" Monroe published "Hermes of the Ways," "Priapus / Keeper-of-Orchards," and "Epigram / (After the Greek)." H. D.'s biographical note read, "'H. D., *Imagiste*' is an American lady resident abroad,

---

into hogs—had deteriorated into a figure as libidinous as Milton's Comus and considerably less colorful. She had become a stock enchantress." With Demeter, she has been "innovational." See likewise Susan Stanford Friedman's *Psyche Reborn: The Emergence of H. D.* for a discussion of how in H. D.'s work "probably for the first time in cultural history, 'Calypso Speaks' her own story" (236–43).

9. All quotations, unless otherwise specified, are from *H. D.: Collected Poems, 1912–1944*, ed. Louis Martz; Martz has in many cases restored sections of poems omitted at the time of original publication.

whose idenity [sic] is unknown to the editor. Her sketches from the Greek are not offered as exact translations, or as in any sense finalities, but as experiments in delicate and elusive cadences, which attain sometimes a haunting beauty."[10]

Both Pound and Monroe acknowledged H. D.'s scholarly debt to classical subject matter, but they recognized the importance of H. D.'s poems to be not their slavish adherence to Greek originals but their experimental delicacy. F. S. Flint, in a 1915 review published in the *Egoist's* special issue on imagism, had more to say about H. D.'s technique. He found that her poetry "must work on you as an evocation" and that it is "a kind of 'accurate mystery.'" Such words point to the mixture of romanticism and classicism in her work, identifying that mixture as deliberate—and praiseworthy—unlike the disapproval Bush offered. Flint continued: "She is lonely. If you dwell on the poetry of H. D. you will feel this loneliness more and more."[11]

Here Flint began to articulate the intent behind and the technique throughout personal classicism. He remarked upon the imagery's clear detail and went on to emphasize that landscapes in the poems are internal—they suggest moods and emotions through their specificity. He recognized the poem's romantic emphasis on the emotional state of the author; the "she" in his discussion does not point toward some "assumed person" or some specific mythic character—he implies that it is H. D., *Imagiste* herself, who is lonely. Most readers, however, make no such direct connection of the poem with the author's personal feelings, and H. D.'s approach encourages a more classical—less subjective—reading.

Interestingly enough, Flint mistitled one of the examples quoted, calling "Oread" "Pines." This error obscures the depth existing in such a compact poem, weighting only one aspect of the imagery—pines—and removing the personality whose emotional landscape is actually being depicted. Nonetheless, the poem remains a fine example of H. D.'s early experiments in image and voice.

Whirl up, sea—
whirl your pointed pines,
splash your great pines
on our rocks,

10. *Selected Letters of Ezra Pound, 1907–1941,* 11; *Poetry* 1.4 (January 1913), 135.
11. "The Poetry of H. D.," 72–73.

hurl your green over us,
cover us with your pools of fir.
(*Collected Poems*, 55)

Such a poem offers the opportunity for a writer not merely to translate emotion into landscape in the way "Oread" embeds the nymphs' loneliness and (perhaps sexual) longing into sea/forest imagery but also to translate personal life into legend. H. D. continued throughout her work to mix the romantic and the classic, subjective source and objective enactment: the personal event and the literary allusion. From her earliest imagist poems, H. D. discovered a way to express her own emotions and, indeed, important personal relationships and narratives, through imagist renditions of mythology.

A first, important element in H. D.'s development of personal classicism is her ability to speak convincingly as a voice both modern and ancient. The imagists came to demand that archaisms of language be dropped as merely ornamental; it took Pound some time to move beyond the student's infatuation with period language that marks much of *A Lume Spento*, but he finally articulated the matter this way: "No good poetry is ever written in a manner twenty years old, for to write in such a manner shows conclusively that the writer thinks from books, convention, and *cliche*, and not from life."[12] Some of H. D.'s most successful poems blend the modern with the ancient to achieve a kind of timelessness—the voice that speaks is equally mythic and contemporary. Likewise, some of her less-successful passages are marred not by their inexact mirroring of ancient originals, as Bush would have it, but by their inability to rise above the posturing and mannerisms suggested by an ancient text. Sections of her translation of Euripides's *Ion*, for example, grow tedious in their mannered apostrophe.

"Mid-day," from *Sea Garden*, is a clear example of how H. D. can present a speaker with a timeless, personally compelling voice within a structure of tonal control. Although the poem specifies no sex, this speaker shares much with the many female speakers throughout H. D.'s work, so to assume a woman here is not unjustified. Interestingly, the speaker lacks control of her own life, as do many of the women who speak in H. D.'s poems; she has the role of passive recipient rather than initiator, even of her own feelings. Tone achieves a kind of dignity, bravery, and an avoidance of melodrama while presenting the speaker's extreme feelings of anguish and powerlessness. As we will

12. *Literary Essays of Ezra Pound*, 11.

see, this tone characterizes the work of other poets who rely on a poetics of understatement, perhaps most notably Louise Bogan, with her constant admonishment against women writers who speak and write with "the protesting voice shrill."[13] Here is the poem:

### Mid-day

The light beats upon me.
I am startled—
a split leaf crackles on the paved floor—
I am anguished—defeated.

A slight wind shakes the seed-pods—
my thoughts are spent
as the black seeds.
My thoughts tear me,
I dread their fever.
I am scattered in its whirl.
I am scattered like
the hot shrivelled seeds.

The shrivelled seeds
are split on the path—
the grass bends with dust,
the grape slips
under its crackled leaf:
yet far beyond the spent seed-pods,
and the blackened stalks of mint,
the poplar is bright on the hill,
the poplar spreads out,
deep-rooted among trees.

O poplar, you are great
among the hill-stones,
while I perish on the path
among the crevices of the rocks.
               (*Collected Poems*, 10)

In the first twelve lines there are nine appearances of "I" or "me" or "mine"—yet the physical world, not the speaker, is able to act as subject, not object. Certainly the personal, emotional state of the speaker lies at the heart of the poem, since she describes her condition with six copulas in the passive voice: "I am startled," she says,

13. *Journey Around My Room: The Autobiography of Louise Bogan*, 150–51.

"I am defeated." The two most active verbs she applies to herself—
"dread" and "perish"—actually reveal her passiveness, her powerlessness. Yet this voice speaks with reticence. There is no biographical
narrative explaining her condition, none of the expansive development of a personality nor the detailed development of ornate patterns of rhythm and sound that would have marked, for example, a
Swinburne poem dealing with similar emotions. "Mid-day," with its
clean, swift presentation of images, natural objects taken as the ade-
quate symbol, as Pound would say, is surely a piece of imagist art.

Of course, using the natural world to present an interior, emotional
state is a standard practice in poetry, from the Homeric simile to a confessional poem like Plath's "The Moon and the Yew Tree," and the vital
relationship between the poet—seer and participant—and the world
has received commentary throughout literary history. "Mid-day" reveals two techniques of personal classicism: the reticence and simplicity with which emotions are rendered and the way the imagery
itself embodies them. In stanza two the speaker compares her thoughts
to the "shrivelled" and "scattered" seeds. While this comparison
employs an image selected from the natural world precisely for its
power of suggestion, the seeds retain an integrity independent of the
speaker, and so the level of emotional projection is diminished.

To continue the comparison introduced above, look at the first
lines of Plath's "The Moon and the Yew Tree": "This is the light of
the mind, cold and planetary. / The trees of the mind are black. The
light is blue."[14] The comparison is between two pitches since Plath
uses metaphor while H. D. uses simile; in "Mid-day" the speaker
exists as an emotional being in a world presented through imagery,
while in "The Moon and the Yew Tree" the world and its imagery
exist wholly within the speaker's emotional perceptions.

Another example of H. D.'s early development of personal classicism, "Orion Dead," presents a speaker whose sense of powerlessness
has a narrative explanation; the allusion is to the goddess Artemis's
accidental killing of her mortal lover, Orion. Artemis, too, speaks in
a world of imagery suggestive of her emotional state.

The cornel-trees
uplift from the furrows;
. . . . . . . . . . . . . . . . .

14. *Collected Poems,* 172.

The cornel-wood blazes
and strikes through the barley-sprays . . .
                    (*Collected Poems*, 56–57)

This scene is vibrant, full of plant life that is active and vigorously alive, in contrast to the dead lover. The scene corresponds to the goddess's desperate demand "So arise and face me." Her words suggest the initial, frustrated grief in the face of great loss which psychologists call the first stage of mourning: denial of the death itself.[15] Artemis threatens many violent actions, and so is not paralyzed to the extent of the speaker in "Mid-day" and at the poem's close she does "break a staff" and "break a tough branch."

But her action here does not assuage her grief and only results in further destruction of life. The poem announces her resulting despondency quietly, with the kind of metaphoric simplicity that draws her closer to the natural world, rather than redefining that world in terms of her own emotions. "I have lost pace with the wind," she says sadly, and the poem ends in a devastating understatement typical of personal classicism. It also ends with a situation common in H. D.'s poems: a woman (or, here, goddess) bereft in love. Time and again the female characters are abandoned—and misunderstood—by the men (or gods) they love; a primary example is Odysseus's insensitive departure in "Calypso": he speaks of all the "gifts" offered him by Calypso, while she laments:

He has gone,
he has forgotten;
he took my lute and my shell of crystal—
he never looked back—
                    (*Collected Poems*, 396)

Finally she pronounces: "for man is a brute and a fool." In "Orion Dead," Orion has only figuratively abandoned Artemis, but Artemis remains victimized in her bereavement; only by her brother Apollo's treacherous instigation has she accidentally killed Orion.

A second element of personal classicism developed through H. D.'s work is implicit in the very scenes she depicts, the characters she chooses for her poems and translations: in the personae and situations of her work, H. D. infuses her own contemporary concerns. Just as the voice (technique) of the poem contains both the archaic and the contempo-

15. See, for example, Robert Kavanaugh, *Facing Death* (Baltimore: Penguin Books, 1972).

rary, so the characters and situations (subject) contain the figure both of the myth and of a modern woman—frequently H. D. herself.

Personal classicism as a quietly feminist tool allows women artists to indict social, political, or personal situations without an air of high-strung, emotional vendetta. And their care in controlling emotion and anger in their work differs slightly from similar efforts among men. The writer who would create good art, yet who refuses to control rage, passion, sadness—emotion—is quite rightly considered to have a conflict of interest. Virginia Woolf has written splendidly on this topic; both the rhetorician and the creative artist must not be "harassed and distracted with hates and grievances" else "her books will be deformed and twisted. She will write in a rage where she should write calmly. She will write foolishly where she should write wisely. She will write of herself where she should write of her characters."[16] Dispassionate control must direct the artist, or else the art itself will be consumed with the passions, and nothing more than self-expression, however cathartic, will result.

The woman writer, all too often even in this century, has had a more difficult job in not only avoiding this conflict of interest but also the mere appearance of a conflict, to continue this metaphor. Woolf herself, for all her artistic wisdom, received from Max Beerbohm what Gilbert and Gubar call "a curious fan letter." It is, in fact, an outright attack on her creative work, contrasted with the praise Beerbohm gives her criticism because of its likeness to what her father would have written. He says of her fiction: "Your novels beat me—black and blue. I retire howling, aching, sore; full, moreover, of an acute sense of disgrace."[17] As Gilbert and Gubar point out, Beerbohm's own short story "The Crime" enlarges upon just what bothered him about her work: his protagonist attempts to burn a woman writer's novel, but the book proves too strong for his assault. In a description very like a rape scene, he pokes it and drags it over the coals of his hearth, but is unable to destroy it. Woolf, it would seem, is guilty of refusing to efface herself in her fiction—her criticism is all right because it does not sound like her, but rather like her father.

She also came under attack by Pound in a 1935 letter to T. S. Eliot concerning Henry Miller, who had "done presumably the only book a man cd. read for pleasure and if not out Ulyssesing Joyce at least being

16. *A Room of One's Own*, 62, 72–73.
17. Gilbert and Gubar, *No Man's Land* vol. 1, 125.

infinitely more part of permanent literature than such ¹/₂ masted slime as the weakminded, Woolf female, etc."[18] According to Pound, Woolf's work is culturally irrelevant when compared to Joyce's *Ulysses*, Pound's standard for permanent literature. Significantly, Woolf's modernism does not rely upon classical allusion for its controlling structure; instead, Woolf continually accomplishes her social or political criticism with humor—therein achieving through irony some objective distance.

It should come as no surprise that H. D., such a close associate of Pound—young sweetheart, student, friend—should choose to pursue part of the *Ulysses* model that Pound holds up. She does not attempt to "out Ulysses" Joyce, being more interested in women characters than in men, but she does rely on the sanctioned scrim of classical allusion. With these allusions, she portrays ancient Greek masks speaking thoughts and feelings of her own; the persona both reveals and conceals H. D.[19]

Her work in translation clearly shows this layering of convictions. While some of H. D.'s earliest published poems took the form of pseudo-translations, they were, as Harriet Monroe noted, "not offered as *exact* translations [italics mine]." *Bid Me To Live* contains a passage describing the character Julia's approach to translation that amounts to an explanation of H. D.'s own aims. Julia (H. D.) has gone to Cornwall with Vanio (Cecil Gray) and is at work "on a chorus-sequence that she had always, it seemed, been working on. It would take her forever to get what she wanted, to hew and chisel those lines, to maintain or suggest some cold artistry. She was self-effacing in her attempt; she was flamboyantly ambitious." From these few sentences it is clear that the restraint, the "hewed" or "cold" effect, is something she may need to bring to the poem; if it is not there to be "maintained," she must herself "suggest" it. The poet-translator is being "flamboyantly ambitious" in her project, having disregarded the male admonitions offered by her husband Rafe (Aldington), and Rico (D. H. Lawrence), both of whom emphasize periodically what she cannot do. Rico has told her she should not attempt to write in the persona of Orpheus, but rather to stick to her own part as the woman, in spite of the fact that in his own work "Rico [felt he] could write elaborately on the woman mood, describe women to their mar-

18. *Selected Letters*, 272.
19. I am indebted to Susan Stanford Friedman for her use of the phrase "reveals while conceals" repeatedly in her work on H. D. The poet herself uses the phrase in *Helen in Egypt*, 46.

row in his writing."[20] Rafe has examined rough, preliminary drafts of her work, pages not yet meant to be shown, and has hastily decided what has and what lacks worth. At Cornwall, Julia is free from such interfering voices and pursues her ambition; she remains, however, "self-effacing," and this choice of expression at first may seem curious.

But this sentence echoes the ones H. D. wrote to John Cournos, with which this chapter began: "I do not put my personal self into my poems." She attempts—in spite of her ambitious creation of a new version, a new vision—in her mythologically allusive work, as in her translation, to efface her personal self and instead let the artistic self take charge.

As many readers have pointed out, it is difficult to detect stylistic differences between "translations" and other, "original" poems. Douglas Bush, in frustration, chose to judge all her work by her translation, but the single criterion he chose to judge by was complete accuracy to the original. As he pointed out, H. D. does not translate works in their entirety, nor does she attempt to remove her own vision from her renditions. She begins *Ion* with a "Translator's Note": "For convenience, the translator [H. D.] has divided this play into nineteen sections. These are preceded by explanatory notes. But these notes are merely the translator's personal interpretation; the play may be read straight through with no reference, whatever, to them."[21]

Part of her poetic act was interpretation, adding to or organizing—shaping—the play as she went along. Again, a passage from *Bid Me To Live* is pertinent:

> She brooded over each word, as if to hatch it. Then she tried to forget each word, for "translations" enough existed and she was no scholar. She did not want to "know" Greek in that sense. She was like one blind, reading the texture of incised letters, rejoicing like one blind who knows an inner light, a reality that the outer eye cannot grasp. She was arrogant and she was intrinsically humble before this discovery. Her own.
>
> Anyone can translate the meaning of the word. She wanted the shape, the feel of it, the character of it, as if it had been freshly minted. She felt that the old manner of approach was as toward hoarded treasure, but treasure that had passed through too many hands, had

20. *Bid Me To Live*, 162, 62.
21. *Ion, a Play after Euripides*, 7.

been too carefully assessed by the grammarians. She wanted to coin new words.[22]

Julia, the translator—like H. D., the poet and translator—is interested in finding a juncture of form and subject that will be "new" and "her own." It is most profitable, therefore, to note the similarities between H. D.'s avowed translations and her original poems in the context of her personal classicism: in both kinds of work she was idiosyncratically selective, choosing details from mythology to both veil and reveal her own views and feelings. It is also interesting to note how similar Julia's attitude towards the "old manner" of translation is to Alicia Ostriker's discussion of women writers' "revisionist mythmaking" discussed earlier.

Frequently H. D. chose to translate the works of Euripides. She found in his plays intriguing, complex women characters, and plots that were in their own unfolding sympathetic to women. "Euripides is a white rose, lyric, feminine, a spirit," she wrote in 1919.[23] Finding him to be inclusive rather than exclusive toward a woman reader, she read him— and, in a way, rewrote him. From *Iphigenia in Aulis* she published choruses in the *Egoist*, 1915, and in *The Poets' Translations Series*, issued by the *Egoist*, 1916. All the speakers selected are women: the Chorus of Women of Chalkis or Iphigenia herself. The tale they tell is one that H. D. will return to in one way or another throughout later work: a militaristic and male code that literally sacrifices pacifist values—and here a woman herself—in favor of destruction in the name of honor.

The chorus in section nine of H. D.'s translation speaks of having seen and heard the many ships, and how "nothing will ever be the same— / . . . My mind is graven with ships."[24] It is inevitable that in the face of such militaristic determination, the mind grows "graven with ships"; nothing, indeed, could ever be the same. Significantly, H. D. conducted this work in the early years of World War I; she would return to these themes in *Trilogy* throughout the years of World War II.

Significantly, too, Euripides's play does not carry the buried misogyny of some other classical works. The prophet Kalchas may or may not speak the true desires of the gods; there exists the distinct possibility that he is a false prophet, and that his call for the sacrifice of Iphigenia is not the call of divine will but of human *philotimia*, the urge to be thought superior. Moreover, Achilles is not the great hero

22. *Bid Me To Live*, 163.
23. *Notes on Thought and Vision*, 32.
24. *H. D.: Collected Poems, 1912–1944*, 76.

of the *Iliad*. As William Arrowsmith points out, Euripides "make[s] Achilles such a priggish young man," who "sound[s] so callow." Instead, "there is only one person in this play who has an instinctive and passionate intuition of freedom; that person is, unmistakably, Iphigenia."[25] H. D. found his characters and themes sympathetic to her own convictions, and so it is not surprising that she should select passages from his work to translate. Euripides himself presented a certain variation on the tragic fall of the house of Atreus; his play layered, beneath the familiar tale from mythology, a message to his contemporaries about their own moral jeopardy in a war against the Peloponnesians. H. D. adopted this same mode for her own purposes; not only to suggest a political equivalency between wars from ancient Greece and from the twentieth century, but also to suggest that the mythic patterns of men betraying women still exist—even in her own life.

This notion that certain situations, certain relationships, certain emotional patterns repeat themselves throughout history in new incarnations—so that only the names are changed—pervades H. D.'s writing in many aspects. It gives her the palimpsest, the over-arching metaphor in the 1926 novel of that title. The palimpsest, the parchment in which one piece of writing has been scraped away to allow the recording of a new one, is a literary embodiment of layering. One "story," one text, is superimposed upon another, and if the erasure has been imperfect, some writing from the first may still be visible. In H. D.'s novel, the superimposition is not achieved by a modernist prose style in which certain sentences or paragraphs repeat in each story, as if the writing had bled through from the first layer into new contexts. Instead, H. D. creates similar characters and situations.

The main women characters are all intellectuals: Hipparchia of 75 B.C. is a poet, busy translating the work of Moero from Greek to Latin; Raymonde Ransome of London 1916–1926, is also a poet with the pen name Ray Bart; Helen Fairwood is a secretary-journalist, clearly well educated, helping a famous Egyptologist at work on a scholarly volume. In each story, the primary male character is in the military: Hipparchia is the mistress of a Roman military man, Marius; Raymonde Ransome's marriage to Freddie dissolved due to Freddie's infidelity while he was home on leave during World War I and

25. See "Editor's Foreword" to *Iphigenia at Aulis*, trans. W. S. Merwin and George E. Dimock, Jr., xi. Both Arrowsmith's foreword and Dimock's introduction provide helpful insight to the antimilitaristic undercurrent in Euripides' play in the context of the Peloponnesian War.

Raymonde was recovering from a miscarriage; Helen Fairwood's guide throughout Karnak is a postwar officer, Rafton.

All these stories revolve around the women's unhappiness with the men; each woman grapples to preserve a sense of her own identity against the domination or the reductive definitions the man offers. The first two stories explore, from slightly different perspectives as well as time periods, what is essentially the failure of H. D.'s marriage to Aldington. In the first, Hipparchia finds that she is not sexually attracted to Marius, in part because he is not her intellectual or cultural equal, in part because he has turned for sex to the more physical Olivia, based on Dorothy "Arabella" Yorke. She leaves him for Verrus, a character based on Cecil Gray, with whom she stays at the lovely Villa Capua (Cornwall). In the second, Raymonde Ransome is living and working alone in London, ten years after having "lost" Freddie (Aldington) to Mavis (Yorke) while recovering from a stillbirth. Raymonde explains to another young woman from whom Mavis has "stolen" a man: "I was so ill. I actually asked Mavis to look after Freddie, I was so ill. I asked her to look after Freddie," while Ermentrude asks in disbelief, "You mean she took your husband while that—happened?"[26]

All these stories are variations on a theme or a plot, and their underlying narrative similarity reveals the palimpsest: throughout history, against different backdrops, the same emotional situation—which H. D. selects from her own life—is reenacted. After Ermentrude has left Raymonde's apartment, Raymonde begins to write, transforming the reawakened pain to poetry. Through romantic-sounding apostrophe, she addresses Ermentrude, but then thinks:

> It was not really Ermy Raymonde was writing to. It was an abstraction. It was Beauty. Dead, bled, hyacinth bled from some once lovely bed. It wasn't really Ermy. It wasn't really Mavis. They were abstractions. They were symbols, the symbolic Syren, Circe and the symbolic Helen standing on the walls of a doomed symbolic city that held now that Malines, Rheims and Louvain were shattered. Antiquity behind antiquity of the comparatively just-past that was so much further than the very near past of decadent Athens. Decadent London. A city's finest artistic flowering comes usually in its decadence. Rome. Athens. Athens. Rome. Rome. Rheims. Raymonde had fled Mavis.[27]

26. *Palimpsest*, 113–14.
27. Ibid., 169–70.

H. D. flees Yorke repeatedly in her work and returns again and again to the years of World War I during which, in so many ways, the world fell apart for her. In 1915 she suffered a miscarriage, brought on, she believed, by the callous manner in which someone announced the sinking of the *Lusitania*—an event which showed how war now would focus on civilian targets as well as on traditional military targets; while such a perception at the time may have seemed excessive, the subsequent events in World War II as well as World War I confirm the horror heralded by the sinking of the *Lusitania*. After civilian ships, entire cities came under fire, from London and Dresden to Hiroshima and Nagasaki. Advised by a doctor that she should not become pregnant again during the war, H. D. avoided sex with her husband. He then began an affair with another woman living in the same building at Mecklenburgh Square: Dorothy "Arabella" Yorke.

As depicted in the autobiographical novel, *Bid Me To Live,* the residence at 44 Mecklenburgh was cramped and emotionally explosive. Not only did Aldington and Yorke carry on their affair in H. D.'s own residence, but D. H. and Frieda Lawrence moved in as well. Whatever happened between Lawrence and H. D.—perhaps he initiated some kind of relationship and then rejected her physically, as suggested in *Bid Me To Live*—his certainly became another relationship of "romantic thralldom," to use Rachel Blau DuPlessis's term.[28] H. D.'s form of escape was refuge with another man; she agreed to accompany music historian Cecil Gray to Cornwall, where each could pursue creative work. Gray was composing opera; H. D. was writing and translating poetry.

When she became pregnant with Gray's child, H. D. made the decision not to stay with him and planned to have the child and register it in Aldington's name. Her husband, however, vacillated in his attitude toward her, first promising to support both H. D. and the child, then threatening to file a lawsuit if she claimed the child as his. Not only did H. D. lose the support of her husband during the war, her favorite brother Gilbert was killed, and not long afterward her father died from a stroke brought on by the news of Gilbert's death. When H. D. was literally dying with double pneumonia, her new friend Winnifred Ellerman ("Bryher") found her in a nursing home and hired the medical attention that saved both H. D. and the child.

28. See "Family, Sexes, Psyche: An Essay on H. D. and the Muse of the Woman Writer," in *H. D.: Woman and Poet,* ed. Michael King.

With Bryher, H. D. began something of a new life, both of them raising the child, Perdita, and continuing as life partners throughout most of the next forty years. Yet it is the years and events at Mecklenburgh Square to which H. D. returns in so much of her work as the twentieth-century level of palimpsest. To different degrees, she adopts masks and distancing techniques in the fiction and the poetry; both forms reveal her belief in the return of significant scenes throughout history.

Even her memoir *Tribute to Freud* shows this view of art and history, and her perception that Freud himself shared her view attracted her to him: "It was not that he conjured up the past and invoked the future. It was a present that was in the past or a past that was in the future." She recounts a memory from early childhood, during which her brother has stolen Papa's magnifying glass and made fire by focusing the sun's rays.

> It is only now as I write this that I see how my father possessed sacred symbols, how he, like the Professor [Freud] had old, old sacred objects on his study table. But the shape and form of these objects, sanctified by time, were not so identified. They were just a glass paper-weight, just a brass paper-knife or the ordinary magnifying glass that my brother is still holding in his hand. What will my brother say? He cannot say, "I brought fire from heaven." He cannot answer father Zeus in elegant iambics and explain how he, Prometheus, by his wit and daring, by his love of the unknown, by his experimentation with occult, as yet unexplainable forces, has drawn down fire from the sky. It is an actual fact. But my brother has never heard of Prometheus, he doesn't know any Greek.[29]

Her brother, here, even though he is innocent of the comparison, "is" Prometheus. "It is an actual fact," she says. So the world's continual manifestation of archetypal relations does not, for H. D., apply only to herself: it is the way of the world at large. However, in her writing she often chooses to focus on herself and the people nearest to her, and thus she creates a method of transforming strictly autobiographic material into something that appears impersonal, allusive in content, properly modernist in its intellectualism. She appears to be holding the poetic mirror to reflect the outward world, but in reality it is herself whose image registers in the reflection.[30] It

---

29. *Tribute to Freud*, 9, 25.

30. In support of this point, DuPlessis concurs with Norman Holmes Pearson. In *H. D.: The Career of That Struggle*, DuPlessis says, "The 'Greek' then becomes a conventional but protected projection of private feelings into public meanings" (14). In an inter-

is, however, herself transformed, metamorphosed to an earlier appearance of the archetypic pattern, and so she is not likely to be recognized. Her work differs from that of the male modernists since her classical allusions embody twentieth-century feminist attitudes, reinterpreting old myths; the characters of her poems both express and control her emotions, both revealing and concealing.

Like her novels, her poems return frequently to women characters who have been betrayed and abandoned by the men they love. This is a plot or trope far too familiar to H. D. from her own life. As a very young woman she had been involved with Ezra Pound. From 1905–1907 he wrote her the love poems collected as "Hilda's Book," now published as an appendix to *End To Torment*, her prose memoirs of those early years. He guided her education. And they became engaged, to the initial displeasure of the Doolittle family. Yet after she had determined to marry him, had settled in London to be with him, she found her engagement to be no certain thing. In *End To Torment* she recalls: "How funny, I remember how he said to me in London, . . . 'Let's be engaged—don't tell . . .' well, whoever it was, not just then Dorothy." Elsewhere she refers to the earlier days of 1906 or 1907, and her sadness at being left behind when Pound went on his foray to Europe: "'Anyway,' an old school friend confided, as if to cheer me up, 'they say that he was engaged to Mary Moore, anyhow. Bessie Eliot could have had him for the asking. There was Louise Skidmore, before that.'. . . The engagement, such as it was, was shattered like a Venetian glass goblet, flung on the floor."[31] Pound was not, it seems, exclusively devoted to H. D.

There are conflicting accounts of just how Pound and H. D. broke their engagement: Rachel Blau DuPlessis holds that H. D. refused Pound, because she wanted to be writer not muse.[32] She follows roughly the situation in *HERmione*, where Her (H. D.) chooses not to marry George Lowndes (Pound). DuPlessis's argument is deeply flawed, however, by the supposition that modern writers actually view other people exclusively as muses, not as real people, and believe that they cannot write without recourse to a bodily muse. There is certainly a real danger for a woman writer that in marrying she may be

---

view, Pearson explains that H. D.'s "personality was absorbed into the Greek metaphor with which she occupied herself. . . . Her nature imagery, for example, was never really Greek but came from her childhood reminiscences" of the Atlantic coast (436–37).

31. *End to Torment: A Memoir of Ezra Pound*, 30, 15.

32. "Family, Sexes, Psyche," 72.

asked to give up identity as writer for that of supportive wife; in marrying another writer she may be asked to throw her talent and energy
toward advancement of her husband's career.

But the term "muse" in modern times is at best a metaphor for that
drive compelling one to write, to be a writer. At times one takes "inspiration" from loved ones, family members, including wives and husbands.
To presume that Pound insisted H. D. be his muse, "the model, a nude,
the voiceless inspiration"[33] and so rob her of her own creative work, is
absurd. Indeed, he championed her early work as no one else did. H. D.
herself wrote about the men in her life for years—they were a sort of
inspiration to her—without apparently detracting from their own output.

Moreover, there is evidence as well that Pound himself chose to
marry Dorothy Shakespeare instead of H. D. Barbara Guest states:
"When she [H. D.] asked Ezra if they were engaged, he had answered
'Gawd forbid.' "[34] Even if H. D. did take the initiative to break off a
formal engagement to Pound, she clearly perceived herself to have
been abandoned in some way; the wistfulness throughout *End To
Torment* proves her emotional attachment and sorrow.

Pound was not the only lover to betray or disappoint H. D. Early in
her marriage to Aldington, after World War I had been declared but
before Aldington had been called up, John Cournos suggested the
Aldingtons visit his friends Carl and Flo Fallas in Cornwall. Flo and
Aldington had an affair that lasted until both Aldington and Carl
Fallas were called up for military duty.[35] The affair which destroyed
the marriage, however, took place slightly later, at Mecklenburgh
Square. At first Aldington did not seem interested in leaving H. D. for
someone else: the phrase repeated throughout *Bid Me To Live* is "I love
you, I desire *l'autre.*" But his later threat to bring H. D. to court over
the paternity of Perdita and his decision to stay with Yorke, as discussed earlier, constituted the abandonment H. D. depicts in her work.

D. H. Lawrence, as well, both loved and rejected her. According
to *Bid Me To Live,* he encouraged her in a spiritually demanding relationship, yet recoiled from her physical touch. In *Bid Me To Live,*
Rico writes Julia a letter proclaiming, "we must go away where the
angels come down to earth"; she understands this as a romantic invitation of sorts, and it is followed by others. Yet, when left alone with him:

33. Ibid., 74.
34. *Herself Defined: The Poet H. D. and Her World,* 29.
35. I rely on Barbara Guest's account of these events, esp. 78–79. Guest suggests that
the poem "Amaranth" refers directly to Flo Fallas.

She got up; as if at a certain signal, she moved toward him; she edged the small chair toward his chair. She sat at his elbow, a child waiting for instruction. Now was the moment to answer his amazing proposal of last night, his "for all eternity." She put out her hand. Her hand touched his sleeve. He shivered, he seemed to move back, move away, like a hurt animal, there was something untamed, even the slight touch of her hand on his sleeve seemed to have annoyed him.[36]

As Guest notes, "Since neither H. D. nor Lawrence was capable of an ordinary relationship, what was established between them became intense, arbitrary, passionate—ending in disappointment and anger."[37] They parted company unhappily, when H. D. left Mecklenburgh Square with Cecil Gray.

These three relationships, especially, constitute a pattern which H. D. reexamines repeatedly throughout her work. The metaphor of the palimpsest provided her with a formal and theoretical construct to pursue the events of her life, not merely as autobiography, but instead as manifestations of the great primal, archetypal bases of western literature and culture. Gilbert and Gubar have discussed the palimpsest as an aesthetic strategy wherein "surface designs conceal or obscure deeper, less accessible (and less socially acceptable) levels of meaning . . . conforming to and subverting patriarchal literary standards."[38] These are but two levels of the palimpsest; others are embedded in the symbolic, repetitive use of biography and allusion as practically interchangeable materials.

"Eurydice," written during H. D.'s stay at Corfe Castle during World War I, has recently drawn more attention than many of her other persona poems; it is a prime example of how she embedded herself in characters from mythology. The speaker, Eurydice, addresses Orpheus from the underworld; she is filled with anger and resentment at her lover's bumbling of his famous failed rescue. The first numbered section reveals the intensity of her recriminations:

So you have swept me back,
I who could have walked with the live souls
above the earth,
I who could have slept among the live flowers
at last;

36. *Bid Me To Live*, 66, 81.
37. *Herself Defined*, 72.
38. *No Man's Land*, 73.

so for your arrogance
and your ruthlessness
I am swept back
where dead lichens drip
dead cinders upon moss of ash;

so for your arrogance
I am broken at last,
I who had lived unconscious,
who was almost forgot;

if you had let me wait
I had grown from listlessness
into peace,
if you had let me rest with the dead,
I had forgot you
and the past.

Elsewhere, she continues to confront him with his own supercil-
iousness, asking what he saw in her, "the light of your own face, / the
fire of your own presence?" She laments what she has lost: not, notably, him, but the very presence of the living earth, listed in imagery
of flowers and colors. And her blame is again directed solely at him
in the fifth numbered section, where she declares everything she has
lost is due to his "arrogance" and "ruthlessness."

Full of the indictment she levels against Orpheus, she declares
her own personhood, remote and safe from any—even well-meaning—
meddling.

At least I have the flowers of myself,
and my thoughts, no god
can take that;
                (*Collected Poems,* 51–55)

As recent critics have often noted, H. D.'s speaker presents a feminist twist to the familiar myth, telling the woman's story through her
own voice. The sympathy aroused is not for poor Orpheus, who lost
his lover twice, but rather for Eurydice, who twice lost life upon the
earth; moreover, Orpheus appears, through Eurydice's accusations,
to be a self-important, unthinking fool rather than a great artist.

Here is a point that has not been fully recognized in most discussions of this poem: Eurydice makes no mention of Orpheus's great gift
of song. In H. D.'s revisionist mythmaking, the plight of the female

speaker at the hands of the egocentric male eclipses the traditional emphasis on the power of the poet. Indeed, a more traditional understanding of the myth includes a sense of tragic inevitability; the sensitive poet's song is the product of a love so strong that it empowers his own splendid talent, but it also compels him to look back to his beloved. How can such a sensitive lover not look back? H. D. subverts this interpretation both when Eurydice accuses Orpheus of looking back to see his own reflection and in her omission altogether of poetry's role.

Clearly, this is a persona poem and not a confessional poem adorned with ornamental allusion like Plath's "Lady Lazarus," nor is it a modern feminine lament of disappointed love like those written by Edna St. Vincent Millay. Yet within the persona, H. D. has merged her own sense of outrage and betrayal with that of her mythic speaker. H. D. probably wrote the poem before the events at Mecklenburgh Square and thus before her disappointing relationship with Lawrence and the escalation of Aldington's affair with Yorke, although he had pursued an affair with Flo Fallas. Yet already she could empathize with her speaker's nearly powerless resentment toward a poet-lover's arrogance and actual abandonment. The twisted path of her engagement to Pound included his own departure for Europe; his return to the United States with renewed romantic interest, during which time she followed him to New York City but found that there he had little time for her; his invitation that she come to London, where again she found that she was not his exclusive betrothed. The pattern is suggestive, and one does well to recall that such repetitive patterns echoing mythology fascinated H. D., and she inferred from them a kind of cultural isomorphism, not unrelated to interest in reincarnation and the occult.

"The God" is another poem in which H. D. embeds the personal in a mythic context, but here she does not rely upon an actual persona. Instead, she creates a setting and uses language likely to imply a speaker from mythology; the first two stanzas alone seem to place the speaker in ancient Greece already familiar from many of her more specifically allusive poems.

> I asked of your face:
> is it dark,
> set beneath heavy locks,
> circled with stiff ivy-fruit,
> clear,
> cut with great hammer-stroke,
> brow, nose and mouth,

mysterious and far distant
from my sense.

I asked:
can he from his portals of ebony
carved with grapes,
turn toward the earth?
                    (*Collected Poems*, 45)

From this language there is nothing to imply that she is writing of
World War I with the lines that follow soon after: "the earth is evil . . .
we are lost." Just as it is difficult to tell translations from "original"
poems, it is hard to differentiate between a persona poem and a personal, contemporary lyric. It is difficult to tell whether the poem in-
tends a reader to adopt a classical or a romantic assumption; whether,
to return to the language of M. H. Abrams, the emphasis lies on "the
emotions of the characters who were imitated, or from the emotions a
poet assumed in order to portray such characters more effectively" or
rather it lies upon "the 'natural' and uncontrived emotions of the poet
[her]self."[39]

The repeated use of masks and allusion, and the language of those
poems, carries over into poems that lack such specific allusions. *Bid
Me To Live* reveals that the poem was written at Corfe Castle for
Aldington, and H. D. certainly came to see the rocky coastal landscape as reminiscent of Greece. Louis Martz says in the introduction
to the *Collected Poems*: "The male lover is treated as a Dionysus de-
scended to earth, flooding the speaker with the 'cyclamen-purple' of
passion. . . . And yet there is a touch of foreboding, a sense that the
poem is already an elegy."[40] The sensual, figurative imagery and the
personal fear of rejection—that hint of elegy Martz mentions—are
carefully shielded behind an ostensibly Greek, archaic speaker. Part
three is the elegiac, wistful section:

As I stood among the bare rocks
where salt lay,
peeled and flaked
in its white drift,

I thought I would be the last
you would want,

39. *The Mirror and the Lamp: Romantic Theory and the Critical Tradition*, 290.
40. *Bid Me To Live*, 164; Martz, "Introduction," xx.

I thought I would but scatter salt
on the ripe grapes.

I thought the vine-leaves
would curl under,
leaf and leaf-point
at my touch,

the yellow and green grapes
would have dropped,
my very glance must shatter
the purple fruit.

I had drawn away into the salt,
myself, a shell
emptied of life.
                    (*Collected Poems*, 46)

In an earlier poem, H. D. had already used ripe fruit imagery, especially "grapes, red-purple . . . dripping with wine" to invoke sensuality; when the poem was first published in *Poetry* (1913), it was titled "Priapus, / *Keeper-of-Orchards*."[41] "The God" recalls the earlier poem's imagery and its protective cloak of allusion. The later poem's final section, with the "cyclamen, / red by wine-red" and the sea "cyclamen-red, colour of the last grapes, / colour of the purple of the flowers," does not name Dionysus, nor make any other specific allusion, yet the twentieth-century poet writing to her husband successfully shields the personal dimension of her poem with language and imagery recalling other, more clearly allusive, poems.

Of course, not all H. D.'s persona poems act as masks; not all of her poems carefully collapse her own experience with similar events from mythology. "The Look-out" from *Heliodora* (1924) is a fine, richly imagined monologue by Lynceus, the lookout for the Argonauts, and it does not appear to hold embedded in its language any veiled specifics from H. D.'s own life. It is quite probable that H. D. was interested in this speaker since Lynceus is something of an outsider—one who appears not to work since he does not sweat at the oars like his fellow sailors. He must indicate the safe passage and bear responsibility for all the dangers that he alone, from his exclusive vantage point, can see. At times he longs to be freed from such knowledge and to merely work blindly with his muscles, like the oarsmen. Yet although H. D. had plenty of reasons

41. *Poetry*, 1.4 (January 1913), 121.

to feel like an outsider—she was a woman poet, an expatriate, a bi-sexual, to name the most obvious—and although her sympathy with the character may have contributed to the sensitivity with which she wrote of him, such sympathy is rather different from the palimpsest or mask, and distinguishes her work that shows simply modernist mythical allusion, from that which shows personal classicism.

In the *Collected Poems, 1912–1944*, Louis Martz includes in the section for uncollected, unpublished work, three poems I want to look at carefully, "Amaranth," "Eros," and "Envy." These three poems seem quintessential in their melding of biography and myth. Moreover, they correspond to three published poems in such a way that a close examination of all six will reveal much about H. D.'s method. Both sets of poems involve elements of what I call personal classicism, but the published versions contain fewer personal details and more invocation of classical mythology. Thus, those chosen for publication have been revised so as to mask the personal more effectively.

Martz explains that the three are "preserved in a carefully bound typescript containing only these poems and bearing on the flyleaf the inscription in H. D.'s handwriting: "Corfe Castle—Dorset—summer 1917—from poems of *The Islands* series—." Although never published in this form during her lifetime, the poems did appear with some significant revision in the 1924 edition of *Heliodora*. As Martz points out, H. D. did not keep the three as a triad within the book, although they clearly play off one another; instead they are "dispersed among other poems, and masked as expansions of fragments of Sappho."[42]

H. D.'s choices in revision and editing reveal several important points about the way she muted and masked personal experience through the techniques of personal classicism. First, and most obvious, is that the attributions to Sappho came later—if not as an afterthought, since she alludes briefly to Sappho within the earlier draft, then as a literary embellishment to reduce the autobiographical sense of the poems. "Amaranth" from the 1917 typescript appears in *Heliodora* as "Fragment Forty-one" with an epigraph from Sappho: ". . . thou flittest to Andromeda." With the new title and epigraph, the poem takes the appearance of a reworking, an expansion, of the Sapphic fragment about betrayal—and so the betrayed speaker is identified not as the author herself, but as a distinct and recognizable literary personage, Sappho.

42. "Introduction," xiv.

The first three numbered sections are quite similar in both versions; the first is something of a dramatic monologue, where the speaker explores the extent of her loss aloud, wondering if things might have been otherwise. She repeats "Am I blind?" and "Am I quite lost?" and then finally answers herself, "Nay," declaring that she returns "to the goddess the gift / she tendered me."[43]

The first real change in this section does not occur until the penultimate stanza. The unpublished version declares:

> Nor do I cry out:
> "why did I stoop?
> why did I turn aside
> one moment from the rocks
> marking the sea-path?
> Andromeda, shameless and radiant,
> have pity, turn, answer us."
>                     (*Collected Poems*, 311)

The version published in *Heliodora* substitutes "Aphrodite" for "Andromeda"; the epigraph itself names Andromeda and makes the allusion very clear, so that within the body of the poem, H. D. decided instead to name the goddess of love herself—not merely a mortal beloved. Thus, in the published version, the allusion is not embedded deep within the poem where it might appear only to adorn the moment but rather frames the entire poem through title and epigraph; the published version also hints that love itself—through Aphrodite—is perhaps to blame, not merely one specific beloved. "Fragment Forty-one" therefore emphasizes that disappointment and betrayal in love are a recurrent problem, and not merely the lyric lament of one speaker. I should point out that both poems are clearly examples of personal classicism in their use of masks; but the published version applies these principles more acutely, and reflects a careful choice to increase the classical control of the personal.

The second numbered section follows the same line of editing as the first: the first few lines in the unpublished "Amaranth" read

---

43. I quote here the text from "Fragment Forty-one" as it appears in *H. D.: Collected Poems, 1912–1944*, 181. Unless otherwise specified, I will represent basically unchanging sections with the punctuation and lineation from the published versions that appeared in *Heliodora*, with page citations from the *Collected Poems*.

Am I blind, alas, deaf too,
that my ears lost all this?
Nay, O my lover, Atthis,
shameless and still radiant,
I tell you this:

I was not asleep.
(*Collected Poems*, 311)

Aside from two small changes in punctuation, the only change made in the published "Fragment Forty-one" in this section is the removal of the name "Atthis." Just as the change from "Andromeda" to "Aphrodite" seems to reveal H. D.'s belief that the epigraph suffices in framing the poem, so too with the removal of "Atthis."

Both poems continue this section with a bitter yet reserved tone, the speaker addressing the lover and insisting she was not "asleep," "unaware," "blind," or "indifferent." The final stanza declares

I was not dull and dead when I fell
back on our couch at night.
I was not indifferent when I turned
and lay quiet.
I was not dead in my sleep.
(*Collected Poems*, 183)

I think it is useful to recall here that throughout *Bid Me To Live,* Julia seems to be willing herself not to feel anything, and so to avoid the pain of her dissolving marriage; it seems, as well, that Rafe has accused her of not "feeling anything" in bed, and so originally he bases his own infidelity upon her sexual unresponsiveness. This speaker denies that she feels nothing, and doing so she asserts her own integrity and sense of self.

In the third numbered section, the speaker addresses "Lady of all beauty"—Aphrodite, apparently—and asks the goddess not to believe that the speaker has deserted her. The two versions differ slightly in detail and syntax; in unpublished "Amaranth" the speaker asks

say I have offered but small sacrifice,
say I am unworthy your touch,
but say not, I turned to some cold, calm god,
silent, pitiful, in preference.
(*Collected Poems*, 312)

In "Fragment Forty-one" she instead asks

say I have offered small sacrifice,
say I am unworthy your touch,
but say not:
"she turned to some cold, calm god,
silent, pitiful, in preference."
(*Collected Poems*, 183)

These are small changes, subtly animating the goddess further so that she is an actual syntactic presence within the speaker's thoughts, speaking through direct address; in allowing the goddess to speak for herself in "Fragment Forty-one," H. D. strengthens the sense that the poem "is" Sappho's, where deities are not merely literary allusions but potent forces. It is a subtle strategy, but does effect a slightly greater distancing of poem from poet.

The section ends with the speaker's daring sacrifice, one calculated to more than atone for any slight she may have inadvertently given the goddess. Again, there are minor differences in lineation, punctuation, and detail—one version distinguishes between the woman who offers "her swathes of birth" and the "older woman" who offers "pencils of chalk / and mirror and unguent box" while the other treats all these gifts as those of the one "woman." Here is "Fragment Forty-one":

I dare more than the singer
offering her lute,
the girl her stained veils,
the woman her swathes of birth,
or pencil and chalk,
mirror and unguent box.

I offer more than the lad
singing at your steps,
praise of himself,
his mirror his friend's face,
more than any girl,
I offer you this:
(grant only strength
that I withdraw not my gift,)
I give you my praise and this:
the love of my lover
for his mistress.
(*Collected Poems*, 184)

What the speaker from "Fragment Forty-one" offers is quite a sacrifice; it is a gift of "life and spirit"—a draining experience. And with this offering the poem ends.

Yet the earlier, unpublished version, "Amaranth," continues for two more numbered sections, and their content moves in a different direction from the resigned—even perhaps magnanimous—gesture that ends section three. Section four gives a sensual description of the male lover, and a description of love that is both wistful and angry:

> Let him go forth radiant,
> let life rise in his young breast,
> life is radiant,
> life is made for beautiful love
> and strange ecstasy,
> strait, searing body and limbs,
> tearing limbs and body from life;
> life is his if he ask,
> life is his if he take it,
> then let him take beauty
> as his right.
> (*Collected Poems*, 313)

The section continues, the speaker moving to address the lover directly, bidding him to "Take beauty, wander apart." Bitterly, she tells him in his "happiness to take beauty for that is her wish, / Her wish, / the radiant and shameless."

In "Fragment Forty-one," H. D. removes these conspicuous passages about a male lover, which would be glaring departures from Sappho's lesbian lyric. She does end the poem with "the love of my lover for his mistress," but by withholding this phrase until the very end she does not draw protracted attention to the change throughout the poem's development. Elizabeth Bishop also uses this technique frequently in her work, withholding the most personal moments or the most powerful feelings until the last line or so of the poem. For H. D., the slight break from the framing device of allusion mutes, understates, the personal connection she feels to her persona.

The fifth and final section continues the speaker's direct address to the lover—and shifts fully to a tone of anger and recrimination, mixed with the frustration of still loving even in the face of unfaithfulness, very different from the resigned ending to section three. The speaker is furious, declaring she "hate[s]" and "despise[s]" the you, asking bitterly, "was my beauty so slight a gift, / so soon, so soon forgot?" She continues sadly:

> Turn, for I love you yet,
> though you are not worthy my love,
> though you are not equal to it.
>                    (*Collected Poems*, 314)

The poem concludes with five stanzas in italics, spoken by the goddess, in vindication of the wronged speaker.

> *She too is of the deathless*
> *she too will wander in my palaces*
> *where all beauty is peace.*
>
> *She too is of my host*
> *that gather in groups or singly wait*
> *by some altar apart;*
> *she too is my poet.*
> . . . . . . . . . . . .
> *Turn if you will from her path*
> *for one moment seek*
> *a lesser beauty*
> *and a lesser grace,*
> *but you will find*
> *no peace in the end*
> *save in her presence.*
>                    (*Collected Poems*, 315)

The goddess claims the speaker—the poet—as one of her own, not to be excluded because of her earlier "small tributes" and not to be discounted as lacking beauty. Thus, on one level, "Amaranth" is about beauty, as indicated in part by the title's emphasis on the flower of everlasting loveliness—never fading—which everyone in the poem seeks. It is again interesting to note that *Bid Me To Live* makes clear that Bella (Yorke) is beautiful, fashionable, and that Julia feels challenged by Rafe's pursuit of Bella for body alone. In the final lines of the poem, the goddess gives a last statement on beauty. She seems to address the faithless lover, admonishing him that his mistress—a lesser beauty—will not offer him peace; only the poem's main speaker possesses beauty with that power. In speaking so directly of hate and anger, and in finally allowing an actual goddess to come to her support—and to speak something of a curse, even if couched as a prophesy—H. D. has created a poem full of vengeance. Clearly, she reduces the power of that vengeance in her editing for publication as "Fragment Forty-one."

Both poems use elements of personal classicism to frame the lament; each one reveals and conceals the personal center around which the poem is built. In the earlier version, "Andromeda" and "Atthis" appear as allusions embedded within the poem, serving to shift the poem's appearance away somewhat from that of personal lyric. In the later, published version, H. D. has placed greater emphasis on the use of allusion, framing the entire poem as a persona piece. In omitting the final two sections from the later version, she mutes the anger and removes the obvious presence of a male lover, although she maintains the quiet suggestion in "Fragment Forty-one's" final lines. She prefers the suggested over the explicit when dealing with the personal; she prefers the explicit over the suggested when dealing with the allusive.

Of course, it may be argued that in omitting the two final sections in her published poem, H. D. was just being a good editor, not necessarily a personal classicist, carefully removing lines that might wallow in self-pity or seem self-serving—as in the final vindication spoken in the voice of the goddess. And, indeed, those last five stanzas are weak; Woolf would probably say that here H. D. wrote of herself when she should have written of her characters—except that, in this lyric poem, H. D. *is* her characters. But I do not mean to suggest that H. D. wrote a fine autobiographical poem and then systematically edited it to remove all traces of herself. She began writing a personal classicist lyric and then edited it according to stricter personal classicist technique. She also improved it.

The second unpublished poem in the triad, "Eros," plays off the goddess's lines in "Amaranth": "Turn if you will" and the speaker's "Turn back." The first numbered section in "Eros" reads

Where is he taking us
now that he has turned back?

Where will this take us,
this fever,
spreading into light?
    (*Collected Poems*, 315–16)

Yet in *Heliodora*, this poem is titled "Fragment Forty," with epigraph reading: "Love . . . bitter-sweet," ascribed to Sappho. The

entire first section from the earlier "Eros" is omitted, with its connections to "Amaranth"; so, too, is the entire second numbered section, addressing the lover directly. Here is the section as it appears in
the unpublished "Eros":

> My mouth is wet with your life,
> my eyes blinded with your face,
> a heart itself which feels
> the intimate music.
>
> My mind is caught,
> dimmed with it,
> (where is love taking us?)
> my lips are wet with your life.
>
> In my body were pearls cast,
> shot with Ionian tints, purple,
> vivid through the white.
> (*Collected Poems*, 316)

Instead, "Fragment Forty" begins with the third numbered section of "Eros," a section which opens with allusion to Eros-Cupid's
"bow" and moves quickly to language from Sappho's fragment. Thus,
"Fragment Forty" omits the more personal—and more sensual—
passages in order to establish the allusive elements securely at the
start. Here is the first section of "Fragment Forty":

> Keep love and he wings,
> with his bow,
> up, mocking us,
> keep love and he taunts us
> and escapes.
>
> Keep love and he sways apart
> in another world,
> outdistancing us.
>
> Keep love and he mocks,
> ah, bitter and sweet,
> your sweetness is more cruel
> than your hurt.
>
> Honey and salt,
> fire burst from the rocks
> to meet fire
> spilt from Hesperus.

Fire darted aloft and met fire:
in that moment
love entered us.
    (*Collected Poems*, 173)

Throughout "Fragment Forty," the voice moves from more public meditation, as in the first section, to more intimate-sounding passages where the speaker seems to be speaking her thoughts aloud only
to herself. But nowhere does the speaker address her lover with the
intensity and passion of the second section in "Eros." Instead, only
after two sections about the god Eros—not about erotic experience—
does the speaker really introduce her own situation. At the end of
section two, wondering again whether Eros may be "kept," she answers herself, "nay, thank him and the bright goddess / that he left
us." From there—the hint that she and her lover have been abandoned by love itself—she moves in the third numbered section to discuss the bitter-sweet nature of love.

Ah, love is bitter and sweet,
but which is more sweet,
the sweetness
or the bitterness?
none has spoken it.

Love is bitter,
but can salt taint sea-flowers,
grief, happiness?

Is it bitter to give back
love to your lover
if he crave it?

Is it bitter to give back
love to your lover
if he wish it
for a new favourite?
who can say,
or is it sweet?
    (*Collected Poems*, 174)

The words sound inwardly addressed, as if meditating the precise
quandaries in which H. D. found herself in both her marriage to an
unfaithful Aldington and her engagement to an inconstant Pound.
Once again, the poem departs from strict allusion to Sappho. Al-

though the fragment chosen as epigraph for "Fragment Forty," unlike that for "Fragment Forty-one," contains no names of unfaithful
lovers, and indeed, only mentions the "bitter-sweet" quality of love,
H. D. continues this poem as an investigation of the same kind of
situation in "Fragment Forty-one." And, once again, she embeds a
male pronoun within the poem, suggesting a variation from Sappho's lesbian love poetry; the implication is that one bitter-sweet
betrayal is like another—the pattern repeats itself.

The next two sections allow the speaker to articulate her feelings
as well as her questions: both versions contain this stanza:

> I had thought myself frail;
> a lamp,
> shell, ivory or crust of pearl,
> about to fall shattered,
> with flame spent.
> (*Collected Poems*, 175)

In the imagist tradition, H. D. creates the feeling through an image.
She suggests the frailty of the self in the construction of the lamp—
shell, ivory, pearl—as well as in the nature of the lamp itself, something beautiful in its projection of light, and yet so delicate. The
description suggests several attributes traditionally assigned to feminine beauty, thus implying that the speaker is, indeed, a woman.

The final section continues to work with the imagery of light and
lamp, and also echoes—in both versions—the ambivalent adjective
from "Fragment Forty-one"/"Amaranth": love is said to stand "with
such radiant wings." That radiance remains ambivalent here, as well,
since in the final lines the speaker again returns to the violently bitter-
sweet nature of love: "yet to sing love, / love must first shatter us."

Just as with the changes made to turn "Amaranth" into "Fragment Forty-one," the changes between earlier and published versions of this poem reveal an increased reliance on personal classicist
techniques. The shift from echoing allusion deep within the poem
to framing the poem around a Sapphic epigraph; the removal of the
most personal, sensual section; the decision not to emphasize a connection between this poem and "Amaranth"/"Fragment Forty-one":
all these changes heighten the mask H. D. lifts over such personal
and even autobiographical roots.

The final poem in this early triad, "Envy," is revised to become
"Fragment Sixty-eight" in *Heliodora*, with the epigraph: ". . . even

in the house of Hades. —Sappho." Both versions of this poem hint at a soldier-lover, just as so many versions of Aldington throughout H. D.'s writing associate the lover with militarism—Rafe in *Bid Me To Live*, Marius, Freddie, and Captain Rafton in different sections of *Palimpsest*, even the hint of World War I in "The God." The poem's first line explains, "I envy you your chance of death," and goes on to elaborate on that envy in almost masochistically violent language. Here is the second stanza of section one, with the punctuation from "Fragment Sixty-eight":

> Though he [death] clasp me in an embrace
> that is set against my will
> and rack me with his measure,
> effortless yet full of strength,
> and slay me
> in that most horrible contest,
> still, how I envy you your chance.
> (*Collected Poems*, 187–88)

While declaring envy of the soldier-lover's "chance of death," the language evokes death as a sadistic lover, and implies therefore that love itself is akin to death. Similarly, "beauty" is violent, as the following stanzas show. The speaker declares, "What is beauty to me? / has she not slain me enough" and goes on to wonder

> What is left after this?
> what can death loose in me
> after your embrace?
> your touch,
> your limbs are more terrible
> to do me hurt.

> What can death mar in me
> that you have not?
> (*Collected Poems*, 188)

These lines continue the anger expressed in the early version of "Amaranth." They also expand upon the notion of beauty; in "Amaranth" beauty is the threat, since the lover turns to *l'autre*, shameless and radiant. But it is also the goal, since the goddess finally proclaims that the speaker possesses true beauty. In "Eros" the speaker's own beauty is frailty, delicacy. And in all these poems, the lover's male beauty is dangerous.

The poet's continued examination of beauty reminds one that H. D. was—although strikingly beautiful—self-conscious about her height and very insecure. *The Gift* recounts how early in life young Hilda imagined she was the beautiful Little Eva with long blond hair from a production of *Uncle Tom's Cabin:* "Although anyone could see that you had short hair with, at best, mousy duck-tails at the nape of the neck, yet you could toss your head and the gold curls."[44] H. D.'s ambivalence shows both resentment of the importance granted stereotypical beauty and the desire to be judged beautiful. As we shall see in Louise Glück's poetry, this struggle remains deadly among contemporary women who suffer from anorexia nervosa.

As Louis Martz recounts, the following section recalls a specific event from 1915 after the stillbirth of H. D.'s and Aldington's child, when Aldington came to visit his wife in the nursing home, bringing a "huge bunch of violets."[45] In the poem, the memory of those violets becomes torture, since, implicitly, the sentiment that brought them is now dead.

> What can death send me
> that you have not?
> You gathered violets,
> you spoke:
> "your hair is not less black
> nor less fragrant,
> nor in your eyes is less light,
> your hair is not less sweet
> with purple in the lift of locks;"
> why were those slight words
> and the violets you gathered
> of such worth?
>
> How I envy you death;
> what could death bring,
> more black, more set with sparks
> to slay, to affright,
> than the memory of those first violets,
> the chance lift of your voice,
> the chance blinding frenzy
> as you bent?
>                    (*Collected Poems*, 320)

---

44. *The Gift*, 19.
45. "Introduction," xvii.

The third section from "Envy" is omitted from "Fragment Sixty-eight." Like the sections omitted from the other two poems, this one focuses closely on the sensuality of the "you," the lover. Moreover, the language in the last section is changed slightly in "Fragment Sixty-eight" to coincide with the preceding cut. Here is the section omitted from "Fragment Sixty-eight":

> Could I have known
> you were more male than the sun-god,
> more hot, more intense,
> could I have known?
> for your glance all-enfolding,
> sympathetic, was selfless
> as a girl's glance.
>
> Could I have known?
> I whose heart,
> being rent, cared nothing,
> was unspeakably indifferent.
> (Collected Poems, 321)

Commenting upon the true "maleness" of the lover, so much more "hot" and "intense" than she expected, the speaker contrasts such overpowering self-presence with the lover's glance: "selfless as a girl's." Clearly, she approves of his apparent lack of egotism—his androgyny, really—implied by this gesture; the next section originally continues in this vein, since

> . . . the upward sweep of your arm,
> as you lifted the veil,
> was the gesture of a tall girl
> and your smile was as selfless.
> (Collected Poems, 321)

His "maleness," when it is finally revealed, ties in with the sadistic-erotic language describing death and is contrasted to the lover's sensitive, girl-like appearance.

In the final section, the speaker repeats much that has already been established in the earlier stanzas, lamenting that "the goddess has slain me / for your chance smile . . . she trapped me." Finally returning to the poem's opening, the closing lines in both again maintain that the speaker is envious of the lover's "chance of death."

What is most interesting about this section is the change in "Fragment Sixty-eight," removing the comparison of the male lover to "a tall girl." H. D. drops the stark contrast of masculinity with girlishness, thereby further justifying the epigraph from Sappho and distancing author from speaker.

In comparing the earlier versions with the revisions prepared for publication, we see that H. D.'s editing choices all were calculated to increase the power of classical allusion and to diffuse some of the personal nature in the poems. Thus, we see how the original inspiration for each one derived from personal experience; since H. D. continually saw the world as the reworking and repeating of archetypal patterns familiar from mythology, she tended to compound personal experience with mythic experience. I think, however, that her editing choices are not always the best, and "Fragment Sixty-eight" remains the weakest of these three poems. The decision to remove the male/female contrast also removed psychological complexity from the poem, leaving it merely one theme to repeat and one vocabulary with which to explore. The final stanza does little more than neatly return to the epigraph; so little distance has been traveled in the revised poem that such closure is unnecessary and seems merely arch. Furthermore, I think the Sappho epigraph in this case really was an afterthought, a way to make the poem dealing with personal pain and anger fit into the persona scheme prevalent in much of *Heliodora*; it seems a way to justify the erotic language about death when no justification is needed.

One could say that for H. D., the specific was the universal; in poetry, she sought to emphasize the universal quality while muting the autobiographical. Her greatest contribution to personal classicism, and one of the aspects of her writing which receives extensive attention in contemporary feminist criticism, is the development of the persona poem as a mask for personal—female—experience; she sought both to turn life into legend and to bring life to mythology. What sets her apart from her male modernist contemporaries, aside from her exclusive focus on Greek mythology, is the fact that she animates not male but female mythological characters. In a literary atmosphere where lyric poetry treating a woman's personal experience did not meet with critical respect, and where the formative movement—modernism—largely omitted female perspectives, H. D. found a poetic mode with which to solve both these problems.

# 3

# The Knife of the Perfectionist Attitude

## Louise Bogan's Poetic Control

My voice, not being proud
Like a strong woman's, that cries
Imperiously aloud
That death disarm her, lull her—
Screams for no mourning color
Laid menacingly, like fire,
Over my long desire.
It will end, and leave no print.
As you lie, I shall lie:
Separate, eased, and cured.
Whatever is wasted or wanted
In this country of glass and flint
Some garden will use, once planted.
As you lie alone, I shall lie,
O, in singleness assured,
Deafened by mire and lime.
I remember, while there is time.
                    (*The Blue Estuaries*, 13)

This poem first appeared in Louise Bogan's first book of poems, *Body of This Death*, published when Bogan was twenty-six years old. It almost certainly refers to her dead husband, Curt Alexander, whom she had married at nineteen to escape her difficult home life, and so it is a very personal poem, treating mutability of the body (*this* body) and of the body's sexual desire. Yet it is also something of an *ars poetica*

71

for the young poet. Bogan's work repeatedly combines the subjects of love, change, death, betrayal, and renunciation with the subject of poetry itself, and this early poem combines the speaker's personal remarks directed toward her dead lover with an active engagement with the work of one of Bogan's contemporaries, Edna St. Vincent Millay. "My Voice Not Being Proud," as Elizabeth Perlmutter has argued, "offers an affront to the sensibility discoverable, for example, in Millay's 'The Shroud,' with its melodramatic plea for death as the release from the pain of betrayal."[1] Thus, in its first three lines, Bogan's poem takes sensibility and poetic language among its subjects, in recognizable allusion, perhaps, to Millay's 1917 volume *Renascence*.

"The Shroud" has a theme common to both Bogan and Millay: renunciation of sexual desire, due to disappointment or betrayal. Yet the voice in Millay's poem is certainly not reticent; although I would not necessarily characterize it as "proud," it does "cry imperiously aloud" in a tone almost never found in Bogan's work. The poem begins,

> Death, I say, my heart is bowed
>     Unto thine,—O mother!
> This red gown will make a shroud
>     Good as any other![2]

These lines return to close the poem after two more stanzas of lament. If Perlmutter is right in supposing that Bogan means to refer directly to Millay—and I suppose she is, since Bogan was scrupulous about excising obvious influences or inadvertent borrowings and was furious when others seemed to borrow from her[3]—then "My Voice Not Being Proud" must clearly state Bogan's attitude toward poetic tone: calm, even stoical understatement will serve her in this poem and in nearly every other she will write throughout her life.

But Bogan did not believe that one could sever emotion from poetry. Repeatedly, throughout her life as a critic, she emphasized her firm belief that the source of the lyric was personal emotion. In

---

1. "A Doll's Heart: The Girl in the Poetry of Edna St. Vincent Millay and Louise Bogan," 172.

2. *Collected Poems*, 43.

3. A 1936 letter to John Hall Wheelock, her editor at Charles Scribner's Sons, makes clear her sense of violation when she "recognized my flavor, and my phrase in L. Wiggam's [*Landscape with Figures*]" and "when the [Frances] Frost plagiarism occurred." See Bogan, *What the Woman Lived: Selected Letters of Louise Bogan 1920–1970*, ed. Ruth Limmer, 132.

her earliest published essay (1923), titled "The Springs of Poetry,"
she implies in the first sentence that emotions are those springs:
"When he sets out to resolve, as rationally as he may, the tight irrational knot of his emotion, the poet hesitates for a moment." But she
is quick to explain that art cannot simply render up a natural spring;
it "must break away in some oblique fashion from the body of sorrow
or joy,—be the mask, not the incredible face,—yet the synthetic poem
can never be more than a veil dropped before a void." Thus, a mask/
poem without true, felt emotion behind it is only "synthetic" or "void"
at its core; Bogan clearly prefers poetry based on felt emotion—born
of personal experience. Almost forty years later, she wrote, "For a
writer's power is based not upon his intellect so much as upon his
intuition and his emotions. All art, in spite of the struggles of some
critics to prove otherwise, is based on emotion and projects emotion."[4]

But it is through the *treatment* of emotion that one achieves art.
Bogan's choices in poetic technique are largely modernist, as in her
calls for distance and objectivity and in her implied disdain for sentimentality. Although she began writing her first poems a few years
after Pound had ceased touting vorticism, and even though she remained very much an American poet, having little contact with the
London crowd, her interest in rescuing poetry from Georgian sentimentality was very similar to that of the expatriates in Europe. She,
too, had read Arthur Symons's *The Symbolist Movement in Literature*,
and her poetry reveals a trust in evoking emotion through imagery
without authorial explanation, although she never went through a
strictly imagist phase. Like many of the imagists, she learned from
French symbolism a way to suggest emotion rather than to express it
within the confines of the ego. And as with many modernists, her
education left her familiar with the classics, as she read Latin prose
and poetry before attending Boston University from 1915 through
1916.

Although personal classicism owes much to the mainstream tenets of modernism, the women who write in the personal classicist
mode are not mainstream writers. Their gender alone would set
them apart from the male majority, and they must be doubly aware of
any modernist critique of romanticism since, as women, they are
subject to stereotyping as creatures of irrational emotion—attitudes

---

4. "The Springs of Poetry," 9; Bogan, *Journey Around My Room*, 120.

such as Ransom's "A woman lives for love" and similar opinions compound the work of a woman poet.[5]

Bogan's work and career reveal this influence and the mutations and adaptations that some women make of their modernist heritage in order to accommodate their position as writers who are women. Her best work shows that a personal classicist aesthetic can lead to strong poetry, to real achievement, to poems that exhibit the strengths that students of modernism have praised throughout decades of criticism. In this work, Bogan realizes a modernism specifically modified to meet her needs and ambitions as a woman writer in the early to mid-twentieth century. For Bogan this mode of personal classicism preserves both lyric romanticism's emphasis upon emotion as the source for poetry and the desire for aloof mastery inherent in the classical aesthetic.

However, the overall shape of her career also demonstrates that the same gender-related impulses that lead women to personal classicist achievement can also lead toward excessive suppression of their own potential. In the urge to be modern—and therefore unlike most of the popular American women poets of the nineteenth century—Bogan was quick to cut, to abandon work, to excise whole poems. Whereas H. D. used personal classicist techniques to make reticently personal poems still more veiled and reticent—leading to their eventual publication—Bogan's personal classicist method resulted in her writing veiled personal poems and then omitting the least veiled of these from her published collections. Bogan's reticence sometimes became a kind of artistic repression and in her case, a final diminishment of her total work.[6]

In fact, Bogan sounded rather like Eliot when she wrote, in 1961, "The poet represses the outright narrative of his life. He absorbs it, along with life itself. The repressed becomes the poem." Rather like Eliot—but there are differences. In the 1923 essay, she also discusses "doubt and terror," which the poet feels when preparing to sort out, through a poem, "the tight irrational knot of his emotions."[7] Eliot does not discuss composition as "terror," and even though in *Four Quartets*

5. "The Poet as Woman," 784.

6. This final diminishment is also central to the argument of Gloria Bowles's *Louise Bogan's Aesthetic of Limitation.*

7. *Journey Around My Room*, 72, 70.

>       Words strain,
> Crack and sometimes break, under the burden,
> Under the tension, slip, slide, perish . . . [8]

he does not suggest that the tension is terror. Bogan's word choice certainly reveals her inclination to suppress, control, and subvert the personal or autobiographical life as it appears in poetry, an inclination she certainly shared with H. D.

In many ways, her situation was analogous to that of H. D.: she was a woman poet largely in agreement with the goals and techniques of modernism. Like H. D., she had left formal university training after only one year, and she was from then on self-taught with the help of male friends/tutors: Edmund Wilson was one of her adopted guides through much of the reading she did on her own, as was Morton D. Zabel. Also like H. D., she tended to see repeating patterns in her personal life, and she occasionally chose mythic personae as the speakers in her poems, although never to the degree of layered compression that H. D. explored. Both she and H. D. were single mothers for much of their lives, and although Bogan's daughter was not born out of wedlock, Bogan found that a single woman trying to support herself and her child could be met with suspicion. In a letter to Rolfe Humphries from her parents' home in Otter River, Maine, she explained that she used her husband's name when "living in towns where they think it's strange to be a spinster with a child."[9] After her divorce from Raymond Holden, she also kept his name for legal purposes, and it appeared on her mail slot. She adapted a form of modernism—personal classicism—to meet her own status as a woman writer breaking with traditional sex-role behavior in the first decades of the twentieth century.

*Body of This Death* confronts that status in poem after poem. It is in many ways an emotional, personal collection, discussing sexual passion, disappointment, and the speaker's bitter attempt to renounce desire. For the reader familiar with Elizabeth Frank's biography of the poet, the details will appear poignantly personal, apparently growing from her early marriage to Curt Alexander. After completing a year of study at Boston University, Bogan won a scholarship to Radcliffe. But that would have meant, apparently, staying within her

---

8. *Complete Poems and Plays,* 121.
9. *Selected Letters,* 7.

tumultuous and violent family, and Bogan chose instead to attain freedom through marriage, at the age of nineteen. Bogan's mother strongly opposed this marriage; she even claimed to have had a heart attack in an attempt to put an end to Louise's plans. The union seems to have had little foundation other than sexual attraction, and the time she spent in Panama, where Alexander's position in the army took him, was made wretched by her pregnancy. Bogan suffered in the extreme Panamanian heat, and she was often feverish as well. Perhaps most important, she had a growing conviction that she and her husband had little in common. By the summer of 1919 she had left him, planning to pursue the life of a writer in New York City. Ironically, his death of pneumonia in 1920 left her a widow.

"Betrothed," the seventh poem in the collection, tells this story more directly than do most of the poems. I will return to discuss it, but first I want to examine the poems Bogan chose to open the book. They are less recognizably personal than "Betrothed," and they exhibit some of the veiling strategies we have already seen in H. D.'s work: reticence, distancing, and adopting personae.

In the latter category, two poems clearly have *male* speakers or subjects, and Bogan valued both enough to include them in her final collection, *The Blue Estuaries* (1968). The first, "A Tale," with which Bogan chose to begin all subsequent collections of her work, differs from most of the poems to follow because it focuses on a male figure, whereas the rest of the book predominantly observes women facing the pain and chaos of their emotional lives. This male does not present a fundamentally different view: the land he seeks ("Where no sea leaps upon itself") is not unlike that found in "Medusa" ("The water will always fall, and will not fall") and what he feels is what most characters or speakers in Bogan's poems come to feel:

> But he will find that nothing dares
> To be enduring, save where, south
> Of hidden deserts, torn fire glares
> On beauty with a rusted mouth,—
> (*The Blue Estuaries*, 3)

He distrusts change and the passage of time and seeks a physical landscape that will embody a sustaining principle, not the mutability he fears.

This male character, appearing amid so many women, does not provide an alternative, and at least momentarily endorsed, view, nor does he strengthen the women's thoughts by voicing an opposing and clearly abhorrent attitude. Instead, Bogan uses her speaker's masculinity simply as a distancing technique to present highly emotional and potentially melodramatic themes without relying on a reader's sympathy for the figure's gender or inviting a reader to identify the suicidal despair as Bogan's. It may also have been an attempt to avoid initial labeling as a "woman poet" (a woman who writes only about women), although if such were her intent, the attempt did not succeed, since as Stanley Kunitz pointed out, even the dust jacket of *Poems and New Poems* (1941) relegated her to those ranks.[10]

Elizabeth Frank notes of "A Tale" that its "contemplative . . . 'I think' in the third stanza not only draws attention to the story *as* a story, but suggests again how separate from the matter, and even skeptical of it, the poet is." Separate, yes, but skeptical—never. All the images that either precede or follow this introjection are rendered with far too much clarity to be doubted. By moving the fulcrum of poetic form further from the speaker, Bogan achieves balance and calm, but this distancing does not cast doubt upon the validity of the poem's statement. Jacqueline Ridgeway sees the import of the moment more accurately, I think, in noting that the stanza "bring[s] the poet to the forefront as more than narrator and is one in which the goal, however symbolically, is defined not by the youth but by the poet."[11]

In this poem, Bogan combines an ability to place herself at some distance from the speaker with the capacity to enter at a key point to direct the reader's sympathies. Since she demonstrates her satisfaction with the poem by placing it in the opening position in three subsequent collections of her work, we may assume that she had fulfilled in her own mind the criterion of beginning with emotion but then "breaking away in some oblique fashion."

"The Frightened Man," unlike "A Tale," does present an indictment against men (or at least one man); the speaker's words are an unsuccessful attempt to explain his evident desertion of a woman. Placed between two somber poems with female speakers discussing their own pain in love and abandonment ("A Letter" and "Betrothed"), the poem suggests what has led the man to his own behav-

10. "Land of Dust and Flame," in *Critical Essays on Louise Bogan*, ed. Martha Collins, 63.

11. Elizabeth Frank, *Louise Bogan: A Portrait*, 57; Jacqueline Ridgeway, *Louise Bogan*, 8.

ior: a kind of debilitating fear due to a stereotyping idolatry of women. Interestingly enough, the speaker's fear is very like that of Prufrock in Eliot's famous poem of fear, uncertainty, and impotence; Bogan's method of presentation, however, has little in common with Eliot's. In tersely rhyming, two-stress lines, Bogan allows this speaker to rely on language so unremarkable it is very little more than the stock phrase; he makes no eloquent apologia like the woman's meditation in "A Letter"—a poem that she removed from later collections of her work.[12]

> In fear of the rich mouth
> I kissed the thin,—
> Even that was a trap
> To snare me in.
>
> Even she, so long
> The frail, the scentless,
> Is become strong
> And proves relentless.
>
> O, forget her praise,
> And how I sought her
> Through a hazardous maze
> By shafted water.
>                (*The Blue Estuaries*, 6)

Predictably, "frail" contrasts with "strong" and "relentless." The last stanza is the most powerful of the three; the other two rely on familiar language and perception. But even this last sentence's imagery relies too much on abstraction, not keen observation.

The frightened man himself may be something of a victim of stereotypical attitudes toward women ("frail" versus "strong" equals "desirable" versus "undesirable"), but he also perpetuates these attitudes, and Bogan implies, through the poem's placement between "A Letter" and "Betrothed," that he has emotionally victimized the woman whom he attempts to forget. The poem's strict form and lack of range in diction may be Bogan's attempt to simultaneously express and control anger; her own attitude toward the speaker is clearly more inimical than sympathetic. In placing this poem among her

---

12. Bowles explains Bogan "always chose the condensed lyric over the more revealing, long-lined poems like 'A Letter' even if . . . they were extraordinarily moving." See *Aesthetic of Limitation*, 80.

others, she has gained a kind of detachment through the presentation of another point of view: that of the irresponsible male. Here there is no danger of a shrilly complaining woman's voice, because there is no woman speaking in the piece at all; the woman's viewpoint is vindicated through implication. As discussed above, however, Bogan risked other aesthetic dangers with this approach.

From these readings one might expect to find throughout Bogan's work a varied and complex series of personae, masks from behind which Bogan speaks with emotional intensity. Such an approach might certainly be said to be a lesson from the modernists, or even more directly from H. D., but it is not the case for most of the poems in *Body of this Death* nor for her later books. More often she achieves a measure of distance through use of the third person, as in "The Romantic" ("In *her* obedient breast, all that ran free / You thought to bind, like echoes in a shell") or the definite article, as in "Sub Contra" ("Lest *the* brain forget *the* thunder / *The* roused heart once made it hear [italics mine]." Similarly, the second person, as in "Late," from *Dark Summer* (1929), occasionally proves useful in permitting Bogan to present emotionally charged imagery and rhetoric ("Stony wings and bleak glory") without seeming to indulge a first-person speaker. Sometimes, however, the poems do read in the first person, with a woman speaking quietly of her disappointment and pain in romance. I find some of these to be among her most successful poems; in them she builds tension between powerful sadness and the understated, controlled tone in which she speaks, implying wisdom.

"Betrothed" is a fine example of reticence in tone achieved in the first person, perhaps one of the most powerful poems in *Body of this Death*, and one that Bogan chose to include in all three editions of her collected work: *Poems and New Poems* (1941), *Collected Poems: 1923–1953* (1954), and *The Blue Estuaries* (1968). As Frank's biography details, "Betrothed" was published in *Others* shortly after the birth of the baby, Mathilde, and not long before Bogan decided to leave her husband and return to Boston, taking the baby along with her.

> You have put your two hands upon me, and your mouth,
> You have said my name as a prayer.
> Here where trees are planted by the water
> I have watched your eyes, cleansed from regret,
> And your lips, closed over all that love cannot say.

My mother remembers the agony of her womb
And long years that seemed to promise more than this.
She says, "You do not love me,
You do not want me,
You will go away."

In the country whereto I go
I shall not see the face of my friend
Nor her hair the color of sunburnt grasses;
Together we shall not find
The land on whose hills bends the new moon
In air traversed of birds.

What have I thought of love?
I have said, "It is beauty and sorrow."
I have thought it would bring me lost delights, and splendor
As a wind out of old time . . .

But there is only the evening here,
And the sound of willows
Now and again dipping their long oval leaves in the water.

(*The Blue Estuaries*, 7)

This is one of few free verse poems Bogan wrote throughout her career, since she came increasingly to believe real form in poetry could not be achieved in the absence of rhyme and meter. Her truly free verse ventures are rare; more often if she does not observe rhyme she writes in blank verse, as in her long narrative poem from *Dark Summer*, "The Flume." Yet "Betrothed" is a poem of stoicism and reticence, thus similar to the rest of Bogan's work.

The stress in the opening lines is roughly trochaic, laying weight accusingly on the "you" that begins the first two, yet the line is not defined here by number of feet, but rather by syntax. And the poem continues to simulate the quality of real speech: the second line reads "as a prayer" not "like prayer." The latter would easily create a perfectly trochaic line, but it would lose the natural rhythm of speech. The third stanza adopts rather arch diction, "whereto" and "traversed of," as if calling attention to the solemn nature of this meditation, but Bogan returns to simplicity in the fourth. This deliberate spoken quality (and we must consider it *very* deliberate, given Bogan's stringent attention to craft) implies sincerity.

Yet there is nothing here that Bogan, or a contemporary reader, would be likely to consider true confession. While personal, the poem remains unruffled in tone, and it indulges in few of the kinds of specific details that would make the speaker emerge as a distinct and identifiable person—she retains something of the quality of "Everywoman" about her. Bogan's careful mediation between abstraction and imagery keeps the poem in the realm of understatement, not confession. When "regret" and "love" appear in the first stanza, they are part of the body, that important and tangible presence throughout the entire book, as "eyes cleansed from regret" and "lips closed over all that love cannot say." This latter image itself implies reticence. When the speaker describes her thoughts of love in familiar abstractions, "beauty," "sorrow," "lost delights," "splendor," the final stanza quickly cuts her off with an image presented in the natural rhythms of speech. Tone becomes an increasingly important tool for writers using personal classicism in free verse. Bogan's collected works reveal a range of tones, from the light humor of "Variation on a Sentence" to the exploring hopefulness of the second voice in "Summer Wish" to the wistfulness in "Fifteenth Farewell." "Betrothed" shows an early development of syntax and idiom to suggest emotion without insisting on it and to allow figurative language and imagery to appear naturally expressive rather than ornamental.

Some other early poems written during the same time period (prior to 1923) were not included in the first collection. Unlike many young poets, Bogan was her own most ruthless editor, choosing to exclude poems that had already been published in reputable magazines. Some of these appeared in *Poetry* as part of a group of five poems called collectively "Beginning and End"—out of the five, only "Knowledge" was chosen for *Body of This Death,* although the other titles certainly explored the same themes to which the book was committed. One of these, "Leave-Taking," is more explicit in setting than Bogan's other poems treating the end of sexual intimacy. It begins physically in bed and emotionally in an unexamined relationship: "I do not know where either of us can turn / Just at first, waking from the sleep of each other." While many poems in *Body of This Death* imply this scene, with their mention of "passion" and invocation of "chastity," this one is more direct. It is also, I think, less stoical in its conclusion:

So let it be the same
Whether we turn to the dark or to the kiss of another;
Let us know this for leavetaking,

That I may not be heavy upon you,
That you may blind me no more.[13]

Here Bogan resorts to rhetoric; she *knows*, or hopes to know, rather than *feels* the "realization" in the last two lines of this poem. These words sound like wistful rationalization; Ridgeway calls them "a sad attempt to be philosophical about a painful separation."[14] Bogan prefers, in her collections, to combine rhetoric with tight rhyme and meter, as if intellectual "knowledge" must be earned through formalism; emotional "knowledge" must be earned through imagery—and may in turn, earn a freer form.

The poem titled "Knowledge," the only one from the 1922 *Poetry* to appear in her book, reveals these preferences.

Now that I know
How passion warms little
Of flesh in the mould,
And treasure is brittle,—

I'll lie here and learn
How, over their ground,
Trees make a long shadow
And a light sound.
     (*The Blue Estuaries*, 9)

Bogan placed "Knowledge" after "Ad Castitatem," whose speaker longs to renounce sexual passion, saying "I invoke you, / Chastity." The speaker in "Knowledge" seems to be turning that invocation into action—or really an ultimate *inaction*, since she appears to be in her grave. The first stanza tells how she has intellectualized her pain: "I *know*" how unsatisfactory passion is; the second shows what she hopes to "learn" of stoical loneliness and renunciation of the life of the flesh. Importantly, *past* emotion (bitterness, unhappiness) has been translated into intellectual understanding; *future* emotion, or hoped-for stoical acceptance of loneliness remains an understanding of the body, whose language is imagery.

Another of these early poems, "To a Dead Lover," also does not appear in *Body of This Death*. It is a strong poem, certainly as strong as "Knowledge" or "Ad Castitatem," if not quite equal to "Betrothed."

13. *Poetry* 20,5 (August 1922): 250.
14. Ridgeway, *Louise Bogan*, 29.

One might call this speaker "philosophical"; she is surely a "strong woman," however tired she may be, however quietly she may speak.

The dark is thrown
Back from the brightness, like hair
Cast over a shoulder.
I am alone,
Four years older;
Like the chairs and the walls
Which I once watched brighten
With you beside me. I was to waken
Never like this, whatever came or was taken.

The stalk grows, the year beats on the wind.
Apples come, and the month for their fall.
The bark spreads, the roots tighten.
Though today be the last
Or tomorrow all,
You will not mind.

That I may not remember
Does not matter.
I shall not be with you again.
What we knew, even now
Must scatter
And be ruined, and blow
Like dust in the rain.

You have been dead a long season
And have less than desire
Who were lover with lover;
And I have life—that old reason
To wait for what comes,
To leave what is over.

This is a poem of honest achievement. Bogan explores the concept of mutability through the ways we encounter it: the changing of seasons, the diurnal passage of time, the loss of sexual desire; but she does more than simply remark on time's enactment of permutations in our lives. She projects thought forward, imagining a future time when "I may not remember." This is an important line, for it admits that the poignancy and sentiment we feel in loss is dependent upon our recognition—and later memory—of the loss. That poignancy may itself be lost. Unlike a melodramatic, Millayesque speaker, Bogan does not suggest that the pain of change will demand her own death or even a declaration of everlasting despair. She will transcend her own pain, not through any act of emotional heroism, but simply through the inevitable truth that "life" is a pattern of change—"what comes" and "what is over."

Without this poem, the dead lover's body does not appear so strongly as one of the manifold presences behind the book's title. The only remaining reference is a line from "My Voice Not Being Proud": "As you lie, I shall lie / Separate, eased, and cured." Other significances sound in the title: the death of love; the death wish of an unhappy lover; the longing for timeless, changeless, deathless/lifeless existence.

The words are taken directly from Romans, 7:24: "O wretched man that I am! Who shall deliver me from the body of this death!" Certainly the speakers and characters throughout the collection are wretched, but interestingly enough, most do not assume that anyone else—even God—is capable of delivering them from their misery. Only one speaker "invokes" aid from another source; that source is Chastity. More often, the speakers reveal their intent to endure rather than to escape. Elizabeth Frank suggests that Bogan intended another allusion to be recognized by fellow poets. From Symons's *The Symbolist Movement in Literature*, she cites this passage:

> It is the distinction of Mallarmé to have aspired after an impossible liberation of the soul of literature from what is fretting and constraining in "the body of that death," which is the mere literature of words. Words . . . must be employed with extreme care, in their choice and adjustment, in setting them to reflect and chime upon one another; yet least of all for their own sake, for what they can never, except by suggestion, express.[15]

Perhaps Bogan even hoped not to suggest a literal death, as if the presence of a "dead lover" behind these poems would be too much, too gothic. The effect of this decision is to leave the allusions in the range of the intellectual more than the personal, taken from books, not a life. Yet I believe that any reader aware of Curt Alexander would see that connection as well, and his elegiac presence would not detract from the book's achievement but would instead add to it. This elegiac enhancement is much more readily visible to scholars treating the work today than it would have been for many of Bogan's contemporary readers since we have access to critical biography. Yet Bogan need

15. Frank, *Louise Bogan*, 54–55.

not have excised his presence so thoroughly. She might better have kept the poem but changed the title which is, admittedly, a bit breathy.

We see Bogan's desire to overcome the torments of a human emotional life in two longer poems published in her second collection, *Dark Summer* (1929): "The Flume" and "Summer Wish." The first of these was later omitted from collections of her work because, Bogan explained in 1956, she "was never quite sure about 'The Flume.' It came from the right place, and I worked hard on it, and it has some nice moments—the hot stove and the no-sound of water—which were actually observed and lived with, at one period of my life. Perhaps I have the feeling that one doesn't get out of that kind of obsession so easily—the 'facts' are false, at the end."[16] The "facts" at the poem's end are a resolution of the consuming jealousy and rage that possess a young wife throughout more than one hundred lines of narrative. As we shall see, Bogan's own obsessive expectation of disappointment, what she calls in the poem a "lust for betrayal," took years to overcome and cost her emotional breakdown and hospitalization. So she may very well have come to believe that the poem itself is the kind of desire or "wish" she writes of in "Summer Wish"—one which the first voice in that poem cannot believe will be fulfilled.

The title refers to a flume remembered from her mill town childhood. In her journal she wrote of it, "My mother was afraid of the flume. It had voices for her: it called her and beckoned her. So I, too, began to fear it." In the poem, the constant sound of rushing water drives the woman, alone in the house while her husband is at work, into a frenzy. The first two lines explain, "She had a madness in her for betrayal. / She looked for it in every room in the house."[17] This madness, tantalized by the "Water as loud as a pulse pressed into the ears," urges her "to start the game / Of finding agony hid in some corner." Set in the landscape of her childhood, the poem explores Bogan's debilitating expectation of infidelity, probably instilled in her from her own mother's constant extramarital affairs and the violent fights between her parents.

Yet the "she" is not simply a portrait of her mother. Bogan also draws on the unhappiness she brought to her marriage with Raymond Holden, due to her disturbed expectation of disappointment

16. Bogan, *Selected Letters*, 8n.
17. Bogan, *Journey*, 59–60; the poem first appeared in *Dark Summer* and is available at present in *Journey*, 60–67.

and sexual betrayal; the collection *Dark Summer* was dedicated to Holden. Although the poem is in the third person, a familiar technique in her work, the narration follows the woman's fears extremely closely. In section three the couple lie in bed, the flume "roaring" in the distance, and while he sleeps beside her, the woman lies awake, "Strain[ing] out again toward ravenous memory." The narration moves closer and closer to her thoughts until there is no mediating narrator's presence between the reader and the woman's perceptions: "He is perhaps a child, / With a child's breath. He lies flexed like a child, / The strong ribs and firm neck may count for nothing." Only in the last line of this stanza does the narration pull back into some detachment: "*She* will think him a child. He is weak and he will fail *her* [italics mine]." This line hints at the complexities involved: the man is fated to fail her because he is a metaphoric child, weak. An unhappy, unresolved childhood lies somewhere within the poem at least as much as does an unhappy adulthood. To see children as "failures" perhaps reveals something about the way Bogan emerged from her own youth—many children blame themselves for their parents' marital strife.

Throughout most of the poem, the writing is very good. With the constant sound of turbulent water in the background, and the appearance in section two of a thunderstorm as it comes through "the valley," and arrives at last at the woman's house—"The spill from the long sky, over the roof, / Mounting as surely as the beats in pain"— Bogan creates a setting and story every bit as compelling as Robert Frost's disturbing narratives of rural people. She emphasizes the power of the flume, referring to the woman's grief as "a rusty wheel, revolving in fury." And the language itself in the poem's conclusion does not sound like a lie—but I think Bogan was right in deciding the peace and resolution in the final ten lines cannot have emerged so simply out of all the preceding anguished, complicated turmoil. It seems a bit too neat for this destructive "lust for betrayal" to pass so quickly so that the woman "will lie there / Hearing at last the timbre of love and silence." Again, I think Bogan's error was in abandoning the poem, rather than working to revise it, to finish it. Perhaps, in later years, she chose not to try because she had already written other poems that achieved a similar peace, such as "The Sleeping Fury." But I doubt this, since Bogan published numerous poems treating the same themes and realizations. Instead, I suspect Frank is right in attributing the poem's final exclusion from later collections to

Bogan's mistrust of autobiography since "It is perhaps Bogan's most openly autobiographical poem, and, considering her belief in the superiority of art detached from its source, obviously unacceptable to her."[18]

"The Flume" and "Summer Wish," as they appear in *Dark Summer*, are the only two poems to stand alone as numbered sections in the book (two and five, respectively). The latter closes the collection and retains that position in her later volumes of collected poems. It, too, comes to embrace inner peace, hope, and acceptance, and the despairing first voice's conversion happens no less swiftly than does the wife's in "The Flume." But "Summer Wish" is a much more formalized, less clearly personal poem, and Bogan clearly preferred it.

The epigraph is from Yeats's "Shepherd and Goatherd," an elegy in eclogue form for Lady Gregory's son Robert. Unlike Yeats's poem, however, the dialogue in Bogan's focuses not on the death of an individual person—a semi-public figure—but on the death of hope. The first voice begins with all the angst of a voice from an Eliot poem: "We call up the green to hide us / This hardened month, by no means the beginning / Of the natural year . . ." (*The Blue Estuaries*, 53). This voice expresses hope—desire, or a "wish"—as a seasonally returning set-up for disappointment, and in its spiritual weariness, it can no longer muster up the energy to wish again. "It would be no use," it says. "You cannot / Take yourself in."

The second voice moves in to try to show the first how to be more accepting of seasonal change. Instead of seeing summer as a brief respite before inevitable winter, it points out that even in chilly March each shadow "Already falls with a look of summer, fuller / Upon the snow" and advises, "Count over what these days have"— instead of what they lack, or instead of dwelling on what future days will lack. But the first voice remains unconsoled, convinced that the future will bring disappointment, and is forced to reluctantly recall the past. It asks what is the good of this: "Call back in anguish / The anger in childhood that defiled the house / In walls and timber with its violence?"

This section suggests Bogan's keen identification with the first voice, as she implies that the first voice's hatred of memory is similar to her own hatred for poetic confession, for "the rough and vulgar

18. Frank, *Louise Bogan*, 117.

facts."[19] "Now must you listen again / To your own tears[?]" asks the voice, with the kind of helpless knowledge Cassandra holds in an eponymous poem from *Body of This Death*. The first voice disparages the body's vulnerability, its lack of defense against

>            delight that changes
> Upon the lips that taste it, to the lash of jealousy
> Struck on the face, so the betraying bed
> Is gashed clear, cold on the mind. . . .

These are the same concerns that plague the wife in "The Flume," here housed in a poem even less directly personal, where the jealous and unhappy figure is not even "she" but a genderless and disembodied "voice" that still does not speak of its own sadness, but relies in turn on the second person ("You cannot take yourself in") and the definite article ("the raped defense of the body").

Ridgeway sees the first voice as "human experience" and the second as "nature" in a dialogue where the second "reflects" the first "in a working through by the poet of old fears and a loss of hope to a point where they can be seen as a part of the universal cycle with the same promise of renewal."[20] Certainly the second is less despairing and less mired in the agonies of the self than the first. It "answers" the first only indirectly, presenting the natural world: light, shadow, season, plants. At one point the second voice is nearly Christ-like, urging the first to consider "lilies / Returned in little to an earth unready." While the first voice imagines retreating from reality ("The mind for refuge, the grain of reason, the will"), the second continues to present the external world, not merely a nature independent of human beings, but also the way "Fields are ploughed"—the way work can produce change.

As Ridgeway points out, the first voice finally escapes despair and determines to take up "the wish" once more.[21] Its last words are a natural image, as if it has truly adopted the vision of the second voice: honeysuckle blooming beside granite. Thus, what is obdurate and unromantic—granite—still exists, but is mitigated by the beauty of the flowering vine. Although it is understood that honeysuckle is a fragile, brief flower, the voice no longer focuses on mutability.

19. *Journey*, 72.
20. Ridgeway, *Louise Bogan*, 62.
21. Ridgeway, *Louise Bogan*, 64.

Meanwhile, the second voice has the final word, presenting a hawk in flight over a field. This image is even less idealized than that of the flower and stone: the hawk, however graceful, is a predator, a grim sort of beauty—or a symbol that what is grim can also be beautiful.

While these images suggest that hope cannot be a Pollyannaish expectation for the best of all possible worlds, the conversion of the first voice is no less sudden than that of the wife in "The Flume": again, more than one hundred lines pass before the change. Bowles similarly finds the poem to be "more wish fulfillment than real" in its sudden close. The difference is that "Summer Wish" acknowledges the continued existence of pain alongside beauty and hope, whereas "The Flume" completely transforms jealousy and thunder and rushing water to "the timbre of love and silence," which the woman lies hearing in the last two lines. It seems probable that the "wrong facts" of the ending were not insurmountable problems: Bogan learned, in writing "Summer Wish," how to achieve an ambiguous ending and could have, with slight revision, altered "The Flume" along roughly similar lines. There is biographical support for this theory: according to Frank, "The Flume" was written in the summer of 1924; "Summer Wish" was written four years later, suggesting indeed that Bogan learned how to solve a compositional problem while completing the latter poem.[22]

But perhaps the "facts" throughout "The Flume"'s development were too true, too autobiographical, and did not "break away in some oblique fashion from the body of sorrow or joy" enough to meet Bogan's disapproval toward confession. Repeatedly we find that Bogan prevented publication, or re-publication, of poems that were more detailed and more personal than those she chose to publish. Unlike H. D., she did not revise to enhance the personal classicist veil; instead, she simply cut entire poems from her opus; as a result, *The Blue Estuaries*, her last collection, emphasizes intellect over emotion out of proportion to much of her career's work.

Throughout Bogan's career, we see a determined move toward increasingly intellectual verse. From the slightly allusive "My Voice Not Being Proud" of her first collection, she progresses to the densely allusive "Hypocrite Swift" (written after reading Swift's *Journal to Stella*) and "Homunculus" (based on Goethe's *Faust, part 2*). Both of these are highly literary poems, so much so that both John Hall

22. Bowles, *Aesthetic of Limitation*, 102; Frank, *Louise Bogan*, 77.

Wheelock of *Scribner's Magazine* and Katherine White of the *New Yorker* rejected "Hypocrite Swift." White wrote that it demanded "a literary knowledge and background that most of our readers would not have and that it would not be understandable to many people." "Homunculus," however, was accepted by the *New Yorker*. Both poems appeared in her third collection, *The Sleeping Fury*.[23]

Bogan treats her own inclination toward more intellectual poetry in a poem from *The Sleeping Fury*, "Henceforth, from the Mind." The four-stanza poem is an exhortation (a mode she returned to often in her work and the title of another poem in the same collection). Here she resolves to will herself toward happiness: joy does not reside in the things of this world, she seems to imply, but is only achieved through a deliberate act of the mind. This is, in fact, a poem based on her personal experience, but little in the poem's language or details suggest this. Bogan suffered a severe depression during her thirties. In April 1931, she checked herself into the Neurological Institute in New York City, gripped by a creative despair brought on by the 1930 fire that destroyed the country house she and her second husband, Raymond Holden, had restored together. Most of their manuscripts and belongings were lost. Moreover, she was tormented by a certainty that Holden was unfaithful to her.

In an attempt to reclaim her creative and emotional stability, she applied for a Guggenheim fellowship in order to travel in Europe. When the award was granted, she left in April 1933, determined to absorb, take notes, and write poems. She returned to the States in September, certain that Holden was engaged in an affair. Bogan's fears were probably justified, according to her biographer. In November, she entered New York Hospital in White Plains, determined to heal herself with professional help. This act of will to overcome her emotional trauma—one which was largely successful, as she came to a new kind of mature peace—likely was inextricable from her creative movement toward increasingly more intellectual and less emotionally revealing poems.

*The Sleeping Fury's* title poem suggests that this is true. Taken from a relief sculpture, "L'Erinni Addormentata," which she had seen in Rome during her Guggenheim trip, the poem both addresses and describes a tormenting fury "Who, after rage, for an hour quiet, sleeps out its tears." The publisher included a line drawing of the

23. Frank, *Louise Bogan*, 250.

sculpture in the original dust jacket design. On the first worksheet of the poem, Bogan specified that the intended fury was "Megaera," the jealous punisher of sex crimes, suggesting her own torment over infidelity, reaching from her mother's behavior during her childhood to her most recent troubles with Holden.[24] The first and last stanzas reveal the speaker's composure now that the fury, "my scourge, my sister" sleeps:

> You are here now,
> Who were so loud and feared, in a symbol before me,
> Alone and asleep, and I at last look long upon you.
>
> . . . . . . . . . . . . . . . . . . . . . . . . . . . . . . . . . . .
>
> Beautiful now as a child whose hair, wet with rage and tears
> Clings to its face. And now I may look upon you,
> Having once met your eyes. You lie in sleep and forget me.
> Alone and strong in my peace, I look upon you in yours.
>
> (*The Blue Estuaries*, 78–79)

In 1935 she wrote to Morton D. Zabel, "I am happy now—happy for the first time in my life. At peace for the first time. . . . I worked and fought for 37 years, to gain serenity at 38."[25] While this peace would not last forever, and she would suffer at least one more depression in her later years, it was a very real mastery over the emotional illness that had plagued her childhood and young adulthood. She was proud of—and grateful for—this mastery, and just as her early reticence had informed her poetic technique, so this willed peace would prove important to her poetry, in both subject matter and approach. She would continue to favor acts of the mind that could contain or subdue emotions over emotional experience itself.

Another factor may have led to her growing preference for the mind over emotion. Like Virginia Woolf, she felt all her life the lack of a formal university education. She was self-taught from the age of nineteen, and although she must have appreciated that her men friends guided her, she felt a recurrent defensiveness about her educational background. In a 1932 letter to Zabel (who was writing a recommendation in support of her Guggenheim application), she wrote, "Do bear down on native quality of mind, will you? That awful

24. The poem is currently available in *The Blue Estuaries: Poems, 1923–1968*, 78–79; Frank, *Louise Bogan*, 258.
25. *Selected Letters*, 109. The letter is dated October 7, 1935; less than a year after this letter she was at work on the poem.

blank after academic honors frightens me. Tate and Adams and Tag-
gard all had degrees; Tate and Adams were Phi Beta Kappa. . . ." In
1935, describing Theodore Roethke (whom she had just met) to
Humphries, she made a point of mentioning that "he once won a
Phi Beta Kappa." Describing him to Zabel, she mentioned he had
received "a flat A under I. A. Richards at Harvard." In another letter
to Zabel, while discussing some realizations she had made about the
art of prose writing, she told him, "You probably knew these things
all along, because you were educated and I was not, although I *did* get
[an] A plus with Genung, or whatever his name was, in my one year
in college."[26]

She clearly felt at a disadvantage—as, indeed, she was. She moved
in an intellectual circle; her job as poetry reviewer at the *New Yorker*
from 1931 until her death, in 1970, depended upon critical acumen
and wide reading; and as she wrote fewer poems over the years, her
professional reputation relied increasingly upon her criticism and
university teaching rather than the publication of poetry. She was
acutely aware that for years she had needed to catch up by reading
on her own, and that, as a woman, she would need to doubly prove
her intellectual merit to some readers. In fact, she may have needed
to prove it to herself, as well, for she seems to have accepted some
sexist notions of what women were—and were not—capable of
achieving.

In her 1947 essay "The Heart and the Lyre," Bogan suggested
certain limitations with which women were faced intrinsically. The
title alludes to Elizabeth Oakes-Smith's poem "Ode to Sappho" in
which the speaker addresses the dead poet, "What has thou left,
proud one? what token? / Alas! a lyre and a heart—both broken!"
Bogan says of women writers, "They are not good at abstractions and
their sense of structure is not large. . . . women are capable of perfect
and poignant song. . . . Though she may never compose an epic or
tragic drama in five acts, the woman poet has her singular role and
precious destiny." These thoughts all point to Bogan's hesitations
about what women may aspire to; the "singular role and precious
destiny" is a condescending nod toward women's acknowledged, or
permissible, achievements. The same begrudging attitude informs a
poem from Bogan's first book, "Women," wherein women "have no
wilderness in them," and are both blind and deaf to the natural

26. *Selected Letters*, 67, 84, 95, 145.

world around them. The women in this poem are hapless characters, unable to participate appropriately with the world around them, and even possessing inappropriate emotions: "Their love is an eager meaninglessness / Too tense, or too lax."[27] How could a serious poet wish to make such emotions the clear focus of the work? Herein lies some of Bogan's antipathy toward the romantic lyric.

Bogan extended this same attitude toward women poets throughout much of her professional life: they chose subjects or means of expression that were inappropriate, given their own limitations. When asked in 1935 to edit an anthology of women's poetry, she found the idea distasteful. She explained to John Hall Wheelock, her editor at Scribner's, "As you might have expected, I turned this pretty job down. The idea and the task of corresponding with a lot of female songbirds made me acutely ill. It is hard enough to bear with my own lyric side."[28] Interestingly, Bogan associated women with lyricism—a tie to romanticism that she hoped to unknot in her own work.

I do not mean to suggest that Bogan was eccentric or overly defensive in her wish to distance herself from nineteenth-century women writers. Even a sympathetic critic like Cheryl Walker, trying to rediscover a nineteenth-century "tradition" of American women poets admits that with the important exception of Dickinson, "We may, I think, justly judge most of this poetry as amateurish." Bogan was determined not to remain an amateur, and to distinguish herself from the very gender-specific "tradition" that such an anthology would suggest. Walker discusses the period's "sentimentality," involving "an over-fondness for idealizing children or the dead, a tendency to take comfort in simplistic conceptions of life and pious platitudes."[29] Bogan wished to have nothing to do with such attitudes in literature.

By 1962, Bogan had modified her position slightly from that taken in her 1947 essay. In a talk given at Bennington College, she again lists what women must not do in their writing, but this time her list reflects an awareness of the male literary world's attitudes toward women's art as being a limitation imposed from without, not from within. She quotes a phrase from Roethke's review of her own

27. Published in Rufus Griswold's *The Female Poets of America*; Bogan, *A Poet's Alphabet: Reflections on the Literary Art and Vocation*, 429; Bogan, *The Blue Estuaries*, 19.
28. *Selected Letters*, 86.
29. *The Nightingale's Burden*, 55, 57.

work: women must not "stamp a tiny foot at the universe."[30] In his review, Roethke says Bogan avoids this danger, and in her talk, Bogan shows that this is a failure that readers of women's work will be watching for, and that to avoid censure from the largely male literary establishment, a woman must avoid gender-specific "failures" in her writing. Indeed, while a part of Bogan would surely have been gratified to be distinguished from the "scribbling horde" of women sentimentalists, another part of her—perhaps less fully conscious—could have been chilled at the way a man would so easily and offhandedly discount women writers. Roethke was her friend, had been, briefly, her lover—and had been something of a student, sending his early poems to her for advice. Her correspondence shows that she was both demanding and generous in her comments, making recommendations for his reading, urging him to get on with his work, and constantly showing that she believed wholeheartedly in his capabilities. Roethke was, in fact, complimentary toward her own work. Yet his review, although it praises her, implies something like surprise at her accomplishments, given her gender.

Bogan's talk to the young women at Bennington College does not renounce the idea of limitation specific to women's poetry; it does, however, suggest that the limitation is not solely due to shortcomings in women's character, but to the attitudes prevalent concerning "women's" poetry. As Bowles points out, Bogan and her contemporaries faced "condescension and arrogance" from the time that they began to write, and to achieve literary recognition they had to contravene through various strategies, one of which was to "dissociate themselves from the prevailing view of women poets."[31] Bogan's talk urges the young women of Bennington College likewise to dissociate themselves from women's specific poetic "failures" through careful control or veiling of gender-identified emotion, the kind of techniques she has practiced in her own poetry to win approval from the (largely male) literary world.

Roethke's words certainly did not provide the only note of caution. Bogan had begun her career sharing the themes treated by Millay, one of the most notedly personal women poets of the time, whom Bogan, with her competitive nature, must have considered

30. Theodore Roethke, "The Poetry of Louise Bogan," in *Critical Essays on Louise Bogan*, ed. Martha Collins, 87. Roethke's exact words are "stamping a tiny foot against God."

31. *Aesthetic of Limitation*, 36.

something of a rival. As an insistent romantic, Millay represented a view in opposition to Bogan's personal classicism, and in addition to the high praise she won for her musicality, she incurred the condemnation of the more conservative members of the intellectual establishment. In 1937 John Crowe Ransom published an essay, "The Poet as Woman," in which he leveled at Millay the very criticism that Bogan surely hoped to avoid for herself. In the essay, Ransom declares that women are not intellectual; "man distinguishes himself from woman by intellect," and that many of Millay's shortcomings are failures in intellect. He has much to say as well about the peculiar relationship between the woman poet and the male critic, and some extended excerpts will be useful in demonstrating his revulsion.

> She is an artist. She is also a woman. No poet ever registered herself more deliberately in that light. She therefore fascinates the male reviewer but at the same time horrifies him a little too. He will probably oscillate between attachment and antipathy . . . A woman lives for love, if we will but project that term to cover all her tender fixation upon natural objects of sense, some of them more innocent and far less reciprocal than men. Her devotion to them is more than gallant, it is fierce and importunate, and cannot but be exemplary to the hardened male observer.[32]

The reviewer, therefore, is not prepared to confront a body of work, but a bitch/goddess of the page. Here is what Ransom sees as the ensuing task for himself and others:

> A critic must be scrupulous. . . . The most general and staple questions which he has to consider will be something on the following order. Is the experience comprehensive or 'expressive' of the whole personality? (The reviewer's masculine and contemporary personality, not Miss Millay's personality, which may have to be assumed as perfectly expressing itself.) Is it up to his mental age or general level of experience?[33]

Ransom has defined an impossible tautology, wherein women are fundamentally different from men, in experience and intellect, and the reviewer will attempt to judge literary work only according to his own exclusively male standards. Voices such as these may have reinforced Bogan's own hesitations to "confess" distinctly female experience, even

32. "The Poet as Woman," 784.
33. "The Poet as Woman," 785.

though some of her male associates repeatedly urged her to return to her past, in autobiographical fiction or poetry, as a source of power.

Bogan's mistrust of her own lyric side, her beliefs in the necessity of poetic control, particularly, as she said, "for some temperaments," and her continuing concern to intellectualize pain and present acts "from the mind," all appear to be a mixture of both conscious decision and inner compulsion. In 1953 she wrote, "And open confession, for certain temperaments (certainly my own), is not good for the soul, in any direct way. To confess is to ask for pardon; and the whole confusing process brings out too much self-pity and too many small emotions in general." It is significant that she was concerned about avoiding "small emotions," since that phrase is similar to the kind of failings Roethke cites in women's poetry in his review. He mentions "lack of range" in "emotional tone"; "the embroidering of trivial themes"; "carrying on excessively about Fate, about time; lamenting the lot of woman; caterwauling" among many others.[34]

Also in 1953, she wrote more specifically about herself, "For people like myself to look back [through confession] is a task. It is like reentering a trap, or a labyrinth from which one has only too lately, and too narrowly, escaped."[35] These words suggest that Bogan herself felt it psychically necessary that she not return too vividly to the powerful events from her past for source material for poetry. The autobiographical reminiscences in *Journey Around My Room* took years to write, and while she occasionally wrote autobiographical fiction for the *New Yorker*, Bogan found it difficult to overcome her aversion to "confession." For years she hoped to pull her memoirs together in the form of fiction, to be titled *Laura Daley's* [or *Daly's*] *Story*, but although she returned to the project intermittently, she could never finish it.

Her fears call to mind A. Alvarez's suggestion, made some years later, that the continued, close scrutiny of dark emotions proved destructive to Sylvia Plath. "Poetry of this order is a murderous art," he wrote in 1963, shortly after Plath's death, and when he later clarified his remarks in 1966, he continued to assert that for Plath, death was "an unavoidable risk in writing her kind of poem."[36] Bogan's

34. Bogan, *Journey*, 10; Roethke, "The Poetry," in *Critical Essays*, ed. Martha Collins, 87.
35. *Journey*, 10.
36. "Sylvia Plath," in *The Art of Sylvia Plath: A Symposium*, ed. Charles Newman, 56–68.

life, as well, was fraught with recurring bouts of mental and emotional depressions, and more than once she spent time in the New York Hospital for psychiatric treatment. She wrote about these experiences, but carefully, guardedly, privately—and only briefly. For her, the techniques I call personal classicism are related to both a conscious method through which to avoid the denunciation of male readers like Ransom or even Roethke, as well as a less conscious desire to not reexamine the pain, disappointment, and betrayal of the past. While the poetic effects from each impetus may be roughly the same, they come from very different sources. And it is this peculiar mixture of conscious decision and unconscious desire that is of particular interest to the feminist critic seeking to distinguish between men and women writers of the twentieth century. To see real differences we may need to look behind effect to the efficient cause, and causes are bound up with gender-specific restraints.

"Evening in the Sanitarium," with its setting clearly indicated in the title, was written and published in 1938. It began as a parody of W. H. Auden, as if the only way Bogan could begin to write about her hospitalization in the early 1930s was to try to write like someone else, since she felt *she* certainly couldn't write such a poem. The poem is very strong, however, and avoids being merely derivative. It elegantly and sympathetically presents a scene with many characters, all of whom are safely distanced by the third-person pronoun or occasionally, when the speaker addresses the women, the second person, never the first. In long, graceful lines, Bogan adds explanation to the poem's presentation of place and persons:

> The period of the wildest weeping, the fiercest delusion, is over.
> The women rest their tired half-healed hearts; they are almost well.
> Some of them will stay almost well always: the blunt-faced woman
>     whose thinking dissolved
> Under academic discipline; the manic-depressive girl
> Now leveling off; one paranoiac afflicted with jealousy.
> Another with persecution. Some alleviation has been possible.
>                                        (*The Blue Estuaries*, 111)

Another piece, apparently written in December 1933 and intended for the *New Yorker*, treats the same material. Unpublished during Bogan's lifetime, "The Long Walk," also set in the omniscient third person, describes an evening walk of women in a sanitarium.

At this moment of the walk Miss Andrews heard again inside her heart her father's voice; he admonished her; he looked at her with love. Little Mrs. Harburg felt the fear that nothing could happen again; that everything was over; that life had closed up against her. Mrs. Shields saw again the face of her husband, that denied her, and felt his shoulder, turning strongly, unhurriedly away from her arms. The young girls felt a flood of wildness and fear go over them; the older women saw the monotonous afternoon light recede away from them, like a tide going out that reveals the ugliness of the beach. At this point Miss Gill heard the voice that told her she must run away. Her plan, to get rid, forever, of her sagging and unused body. Some heard or saw nothing, but felt again that pang, nameless and cen-tered below the throat, of sorrow which had become part of them, like an organ in their flesh. Some began to listen to the old story of suspicion and thwarted love, always told in the same words, always ending in a question and an answer they could not bring themselves to acknowledge. Over and over, in the groove worn into their minds, the terrible certainty loosened and moved. That which could not happen, but had happened; that which could not be borne, but which they were bearing.[37]

Such examples illustrate the way Bogan continued to distance herself from personally difficult subject matter when she chose to treat it at all. The examples are few. Although she includes some childhood memories—intended to become *Laura Daley's Story*—in the journals that make up *Journey Around My Room*, the memories are often only glimpses, hints, rather than sustained, direct investi-gation. One brief memory suggests that very early on Bogan found protection through not investigating, not even seeing, and perhaps through forgetting. "The secret family angers and secret disruptions passed over my head, it must have been for a year or so. But for two days, I went blind. I remember my sight coming back, by seeing the flat forked light of the gas flame, in its etched glass shade, suddenly appearing beside the bureau. What had I seen? I shall never know."[38] The word choice implies loss—"I shall never know"—but also safety. Whatever dreadful, violent thing she witnessed and then lost through temporary blindness does not now haunt her conscious life. Instead, Bogan has achieved stasis, rather like that sought in so many of her

37. *Journey*, 88–89.
38. *Journey*, 26.

poems and perhaps best depicted in the recurring image of the Medusa. And Bogan, unlike H. D., seems not to have believed that discovery and recovery of her childhood experiences could contribute to her artistic development. Her staunch stand that autobiography in the form of confession is destructive for people with her temperament was a form of self-protection against the discovery of darkness and chaos.

Bogan articulated the matter in a letter to Zabel in 1934, during the period following her hospitalization when she worked so hard to repair her psychic and emotional health.

> Morton, I produced two poems, and sold them both for bread and shoes. I shall produce two or three more, if only to keep my promises to *Poetry* and to you. But thereafter the fountain will be sealed for good, I'm thinking. . . . I can no longer put on the 'lofty dissolute air' necessary for poetry's production; I cannot and will not suffer for it any longer. With detachment and sanity I shall, in the future, observe; if to fall to the ground with my material makes me a madwoman, I abjure the trade. Having given up alcohol and romantic dreams, having excised my own neurosis with my own hand, having felt the knife of the perfectionist attitude in art and life at my throat. . . . [39]

Perhaps she was referring to difficulties like these in her remarks, mentioned at this chapter's outset, about the "terror" in writing poetry. She certainly suggests so in an unpublished poem, "Portrait of the Artist as a Young Woman." Here is the first stanza:

> Sitting on the bed's edge, in the cold lodgings, she wrote it out on
> her knee
> In terror and panic—but with the moment's courage, summoned up
> from God knows where.
> Without recourse to saints or angels: a Bohemian, thinking herself
> free—
> A young thin girl without sense, living (she thought) on passion
> and air.[40]

"Portrait" concerns a young writer, a young woman, who writes in "terror and panic"; the poem moves closer into her head after this first stanza, and allows something of the panic into the poem. It in-

---

39. *Selected Letters*, 79, ellipsis Bogan's.
40. *Journey*, 54–55.

sists on the artist as woman—the artistic development in youth of a young woman living "on passion and air"—rather than on the woman as artist. This poem is not about "tension" within a conscious, measured search to create form or meaning, but rather the "terror" that is involved in the woman's embarking on the poetic quest in the first place. To write is terrifying, the poem suggests. It is one Bogan chose not to include in her collections.

For Bogan's contention that emotion and the past must be not only veiled in poetry but—further—carefully controlled extends more specifically to women than to men. It is interesting to note that her protégé and lover, Theodore Roethke, went on to become one of the more extreme romantic poets of the century, against whom this study defines the personal classicists. In a letter to him, not long after they met, Bogan urged Roethke to pursue very romantic directions. "The difficulty with you now, as I see it, is that you are afraid to suffer, or to feel in any way, and that is what you'll have to get over, lamb pie, before you can toss off the masterpieces . . . 'To My Sister' is a swell poem, because, as I said, you are right in it, mad as hell, and agonized as hell, and proud as hell."[41] Her advice to Roethke contrasts sharply with what she proposed for her own work and for the work of other women writers. If we turn again to her prose, we see arguments with which she supported such a distinction.

In 1945, one such exchange took place between Bogan and William Maxwell, her close friend. In distress, she wrote to him about the difficulty she had with her prose memoirs: "I don't want to confess; I want to create; and the hatred of confessing has been one thing that has held me up all these years." Maxwell urged her to continue: "What is this reluctance to confess? . . . my own experience has been that confession leads straight lickety to creation, if you are of a certain temperament, and creation, as you have pointed out . . . is inevitably confession."[42] Bogan was not convinced by such coaching; she continued to believe that her own interior hesitations about frankness were correct, and there was no lack of exterior corroboration such as that in Ransom's essay. For a woman who never fully overcame insecurities over her own lack of formal education, the kind of objective detachment from her personal concerns that I call personal classicism probably seemed the safest method to mediate

41. *Selected Letters*, 96.
42. Frank, *Louise Bogan*, 334.

between her own romantic tendencies and the demands for control popular among the literary establishment—first the moderns, then the new critics.

Many critics discussing Bogan's work mention not merely her aesthetic technique of poetic control as it appears in her poems, but also this attitude toward subject matter and approach. Although the methods I identify with personal classicism may have seemed to Bogan a prudent approach, one appropriate to her temperament and sensibility, according to Ruth Limmer, Bogan's friend and literary executor, "her reticence . . . had the effect of circumscribing her talent" and "dignity, taste, and a belief in the (qualified) sacredness of art—*but which may also be called a fear of revealing oneself*—kept her from full creative freedom."[43]

Gloria Bowles agrees. She calls Bogan's aesthetic one of "limitation," produced by the complex combination of Bogan's life circumstances, including "her precarious psychological balance" and "her idea of the innate limitations of the woman poet." She sees Bogan's work as that of a woman who "had taken the modernist aesthetic to its extreme in order to disprove what she had also internalized from her culture, the notion that women poets could not control their emotions."[44] Bogan had something to prove as well as something to say, and Bowles is right to say that Bogan allowed the expectations and condemnations of too many other people—writers, readers, critics, even her friends and lovers—to shape her relationship to her own art.

At one point Bogan expressed fear that she would be "the woman who died without producing an *oeuvre*. The woman who ran away." She did, in fact, produce her "*oeuvre*," and her work exhibits courage and dedication. But it also reveals that she allowed herself, if not to run away, to stop short. Poems were begun, but all too often they were abandoned rather than completed. Moreover, Bogan chose to exclude many strong poems from her final "*oeuvre*" rather than take the last steps toward final revision because, it seems, they were decidedly personal—too personal for a personal classicist like her. She continually pushed herself to achieve greater "objectivity," even writ-

43. Jacqueline Ridgeway suggests that Bogan's metaphysical tendencies are closely linked to her desire to remove any element of her conscious personality from her work, placing her poetic emphasis on metaphor and concrete imagery. See *Louise Bogan*, 17; Limmer, "Circumscriptions," in *Critical Essays*, ed. Martha Collins, 172, 171.
44. *Aesthetic Limitation*, 126, 137.

ing a note to herself during the compilation of poems for *The Sleeping Fury* to write ten more poems, "and they must be as objective as possible."[45]

This urge to achieve objectivity—what Bowles explains as "distance"—leads to her presenting a veiled version of her authorial self, a carefully selected image, which suppresses the more romantic poems from among those to appear in *Poems and New Poems* (1941). She wrote Wheelock that she intended to omit "A Letter" due to "something sentimental or unfinished or mawkish." Similarly, she wished to omit another poem, explaining, "It isn't that I'm turning on my early self. But the girl of 23 and 24, who wrote most of these early poems, was so seldom mawkish, that I want her not to be mawkish at all."[46] One hears behind this explanation a hint of overprotestation: although *many* women poets might be hopelessly sentimental romantics, mawkish through and through, Bogan would shape her literary self with utter emotional control and understatement.

As Gloria Bowles demonstrates throughout her study, Bogan's continual self-editing, until her final collected edition contains only 105 poems, amounts eventually to a kind of self-silencing. Alicia Ostriker's discussion, in *Stealing the Language*, of what she calls the "impermeable tone" practiced by many women writers is precisely to the point:

> The woman poet who adopts an impermeable tone is less in danger of being dismissed as sentimental or overemotional by critics. . . . To approach the strategy of this style from another angle, we need look no further than Laing's observation that an ontologically uneasy person may adopt, to the point of caricature, the personality of his oppressor. Control, impersonality, and dispassionateness are supposedly normative masculine virtues in any case, and are favored by the contemporary literary climate. The cooler the voice, the warmer the reception is a good rule of thumb. An intelligent woman poet may have every reason in the world to construct, as her fortress, a perversely exaggerated version of an acceptable style.[47]

Bogan's creative career stretched from the rise of high modern-

---

45. *Journey*, 103; Bowles, *Aesthetic of Limitation*, 132. Bowles writes, "Louise Bogan's manuscripts at Amherst reveal many poems begun but unfinished, many lines started but not pursued"; Bowles, *Aesthetic of Limitation*, 114.

46. *Selected Letters*, 222.

47. *Stealing the Language*, 88–89.

ism to that of confessional poetry. Contemporary critics, as those mentioned above, may find that Bogan's insistence on reticence actually diminishes her overall achievement, and there is certainly some validity to such claims. Bogan herself expressed this danger, this destructiveness, when she wrote to Zabel of "the knife of the perfectionist attitude in art and life at my throat."[48] Although what I call "reticence" and what Bogan called "a perfectionist attitude" are not interchangeable terms, the latter—a personality trait—can lead to the former—a kind of behavior or an artistic technique. Finally, psychoanalysis of writers through their artistic work is an interesting activity and may even sometimes yield helpful approaches to the work, but I do not intend to reduce what a writer employs as a part of art to a symptom or indication of some—however related—psychological trait.[49]

Similarly, Bogan's poetry needs to be judged for what it is, not merely for what it is not. After all, the more repellant feature of Ransom's essay is his insistence on reading Millay's poetry not on its own terms, but rather only according to Ransom's particular kinds of experience and expectations. The poetry of Louise Bogan demonstrates the emergence of a personal classicism independent from the imagist movement, retaining, as I have pointed out, elements of lyric romanticism in her continual insistence on emotion as the source for poetry, while adopting elements of control from a classical aesthetic. Her approach is a response to her own inner drives and opinions as well as those from the literary—and socio-political—world around her. Unfortunately, we also see in her poetry the danger to be faced in trying too hard to suppress personality, biography—the "rough and vulgar details."

48. *Selected Letters*, 79 (July 27, 1934).
49. John Muller gives such an interesting discussion of Bogan's work, applying Lacan's and Erikson's ideas of the Self and the Other to Bogan's biography. While his essay pays little attention to actual poetic technique, he does say that "[I]n giving voice to her desire, Bogan's poems seem to enable her to contain her lack, her want, and to do so precisely by affirming it as unsatisfiable." Muller might argue that personal classicism is a psychological response to emotional deprivation in childhood. Bogan's biography certainly suggests such a theory, but I find that it does not adequately discuss the structure of poetry. See Muller, "Light and the Wisdom of the Dark: Aging and the Language of Desire in the Texts of Louise Bogan," in *Memory and Desire: Aging—Literature—Psychoanalysis*, ed. Kathleen Woodward and Murray M. Schwartz, 90.

# 4

# Mastering Disaster

## Elizabeth Bishop's Tonal and Formal Understatement

Until recently, the popularity of Elizabeth Bishop's poetry with diverse critics has been based primarily on two aspects of her work that tie her directly to the two previously discussed personal classicists: her detailed description and her distinctive tone. Description, that quality through which she gives us the objects and places that are so fundamental to her poems, links her to the imagist/modernist preference for implying meaning through concrete particulars, effacing the role of the poet as narrator or explicator, as in some of H. D.'s early work. Her tone, that natural, spoken voice which so often mutes or withholds the real emotional intensity of the poems, again relying on implication rather than direct explanation or high rhetoric, links her to Louise Bogan's development of a stoical, courageous understatement.

As I will argue, these two elements are finally inseparable. She renders her descriptions *through* her tone, and it is this combination— this voice articulating her vision—that advances her beyond the modernist miniatures and parables of Marianne Moore, to whom she clearly owes much. For Bishop, description and tone combine in pursuit of what she calls "truth": truth is neither simply overt and detailed autobiography, nor the impersonal arena of world events and politics. Instead, it is a little of both, combined into a search for human experience—experience that encompasses the author's own, of course, but may be more readily seen to bespeak something closer to universal truth.

In many of her poems, description insists upon the literal, often autobiographical, basis of the work; in her surreal poetry the description insists upon the life of the subconscious or the emotions. Yet

104

although this description usually provides the major structure for the poems, Bishop so carefully selects her descriptive details as to mute the most personal autobiographical elements in the work. Likewise, her tone is usually relaxed and conversational, even confiding at times, but not so confiding as to become confessional. Instead, Bishop relies on casual understatement, in which the tone hints at the poem's personal center but refuses to dwell on it. Both description and tone embody her balance between revealing and concealing.

And both these aspects surely helped her win approval from critics and from her fellow poets early on. She was called modest, delicate, balanced—the kind of praise that critics seem to reserve primarily for women poets. She was, therefore, demonstrating what were considered a woman poet's virtues, although her consistent disdain for classifying poets according to sex suggests this result did not follow conscious effort on her part. Mastery of a balanced tone also places her as an important architect in the development of personal classicism, and it is from these accomplishments that subsequent practitioners have perhaps most to learn. However, more recently she has drawn the attention of critics interested in feminist and lesbian issues in her work. These studies often seem more interested in subject matter than technique; even if taking a formal approach, they do not often explore what is Bishop's greatest lasting achievement: a tone that imparts an understated personal intensity—a much more complicated effect than can be summed up by the term "modesty."[1]

I want to look at the way imagery and description—ostensibly objective presentations of the subject matter—function within the recognizable tone of Bishop's poetry and how these elements combine to make her particular contribution to personal classicism. I also want to examine her most lyrical poems to see to what extent understatement—or indeed, omission—combines with what Moore extolled as "accurate" description to forge her own particular form of the reticent lyric. Unlike H. D., Bishop does not create allusive mythological veils to express anger and sadness toward lovers in her life; she does not attempt to demonstrate some kind of archetypal, historically repetitive quality in most of the situations she depicts.[2] Instead, as

1. Joanne Feit Diehl is a fine exception to this trend. In *Women Poets and the American Sublime* she discusses Bishop's tone of "passionate reserve." See esp. p. 91.
2. An arguable exception to this assessment lies in "Brazil, January 1, 1502," in which the first lines equate the current age with one from the past. The poem extends

I've already suggested, the way she both reveals and conceals personal subjects is more like the tonal quietness of Louise Bogan. Indeed, she voices a dislike for emotionally extreme poetry in words very like Bogan's disparaging comments about "oh-god-the-pain girls" in a letter to her biographer. She explains that she admires Emily Dickinson for "having dared to do it, all alone," but that some of Dickinson's poems she simply does not like. "I still hate the oh-the-pain-of-it-all poems," she says.[3]

In spite of similarities, both stylistic and temperamental, however, I find she is finally a more original poet than Bogan. She is also set apart from Bogan by the very nature of her autobiographic subject matter: Bogan's "secrets" include her mother's violence throughout her childhood, her own disappointments in love and marriage, and her bouts with depression. Bishop's secrets likewise include experiences from early childhood—her mother's madness—but her lesbian romantic life marks her much further as a kind of outsider and may be supposed to affect the nature of her reticence. My pursuit will entail drawing on biography, confronting some issues raised by gender and lesbian studies; it will require a look at Bishop's relationships with other writers, particularly Moore and Robert Lowell; but most important it will demand a careful look at the poems themselves and the way they demand to be read—indeed, the tone of voice with which they read themselves to us.

Bishop's first and longest-lasting poet friend was Marianne Moore, inevitably something of a mentor, whose early influence contributed greatly to her description and restraint. Moore, often considered the leading woman in the modernist movement in poetry, combines scientific and quirky exactness in her work, and she continually avoids romantic, emotional appeal. As Bishop recounted in "Efforts of Affection: A Memoir of Marianne Moore," their friendship began with both formality and ease.[4] Bishop kept private her own growing interest in writing, and had the good luck or foresight at the time of

---

one possibility—rape, exploitation—as the outcome from the preceding poem, "Arrival at Santos," dated January 1952. But this is, indeed, an exception, and in no way approximates the insistence for actual reincarnation of experience in H. D.'s work.

3. David Kalstone, *Becoming a Poet: Elizabeth Bishop with Marianne Moore and Robert Lowell*, 32. I note that Bishop does not mention her contemporaries who might also write "oh-the-pain-of-it-all" poems; she was reluctant to publicly give specific disapproval of living poets, not unlike Bogan's reluctance to give negative book reviews of women poets who were her contemporaries.

4. See Elizabeth Bishop, *The Collected Prose*, ed. Robert Giroux, 121–56.

their first meeting to invite Moore to a circus. As it turned out, they both loved these events. Thus they met without an uncomfortable sense of The Art underlying all their comments and activities. This probably allowed Bishop greater freedom to learn from Moore as she chose—without a constant, constraining imitation of the older poet.

Even so, Moore became Bishop's literary sponsor soon enough. Bishop asked her to write the introductory note accompanying her 1935 appearance in the anthology *Trial Balances*, edited by Ann Winslow. In 1946 the *Nation* ran Moore's review of Bishop's first full collection, *North & South*: "Elizabeth Bishop is spectacular in being unspectacular. Why has no one ever thought of this, one asks oneself; why not be accurate and modest?"[5] In her first two sentences, Moore introduced the two main approaches critics would take toward Bishop's work for years: accurate detail and modesty in presentation. And, of course, critics would continue to notice Moore's influence on Bishop even as they defined how the younger poet departed from her older model. Bishop herself encouraged such attention, perhaps, with her penultimate poem in *A Cold Spring*, "Invitation to Miss Marianne Moore," which is shallower in its emotional impact than most of the other poems in the collection, and seems to be almost an occasional poem, an indulgent exercise in cataloguing detail.

Yet Bishop's attention to detailed description receives notice beyond the comparison to Moore. Bishop was not merely engaging in an apprentice's imitation of a favorite expert's style, but instead she felt committed to much more than the use of description. The technique reveals important assumptions about subject matter, too: the subject matter so often is an example of "truth," realism—an encapsuling of daily existence illuminated with understanding. As Lee Edelman has shown, Bishop herself repeatedly remarked that her work is predicated by the very set of facts and details each poem presents: "Bishop undertakes to authenticate her work, and she does so, tellingly, by fixing its origin on the solid ground of literality—a literality that Bishop repeatedly identifies as 'truth.' "[6]

Yet another example of Bishop's insistence on the literal "truth" of her work deserves fuller quotation than it receives in Edelman's

5. "A Modest Expert: *North & South*," in *Elizabeth Bishop and Her Art*, ed. Lloyd Schwartz and Sybil Estess, 177.

6. "The Geography of Gender: Elizabeth Bishop's 'In the Waiting Room'," 179.

essay. Wesley Wehr, a former student of Bishop, recounts another such protestation:

> I *always* tell the truth in my poems. With "The Fish," that's *exactly* how it happened. It was in Key West, and I *did* catch it just as the poem says. That was in 1938. Oh, but I did change *one* thing; the poem says he had five hooks hanging from his mouth, but actually he only had three. I think it improved the poem when I made that change. Sometimes a poem makes its own demands. But I always *try* to stick as much as possible to what *really* happened when I describe something in a poem.[7]

Such disclaimers seem to absolve the poet from all blame—or praise—in reducing her role to one of recounting, retelling, rather than shaping. I agree with Edelman that Bishop's insistence on her fidelity to historical fact is a conscious method of demystifying the poet's power—it is, as Edelman says, a "strategy of evasion." The questions that Edelman poses follow naturally, and are important: "for what is such an appeal to literality a figure? Against what does it defend?"[8] These are questions about the structure and essence of personal classicism, about the mode's tension between revealing and concealing. If Bishop makes an "appeal" to the literal quality of her work, she is creating a "figure," a mask, for something behind the simple matter-of-fact accretion of details. In a sense, she is hiding the personal interest she takes in her subject matter behind the mirror she is holding. Why? What is the impulse here to veil or shroud?

Edelman's questions—and basic argument—would seem to support my own definition of personal classicism, showing that Bishop "reveals" homoeroticism while she "conceals" it through careful evasive strategy. But I believe the ultimate conclusion Edelman draws—that Bishop's poems are sly studies in homoeroticism—is too reductive. While there is a quiet, even suppressed presence of homoeroticism in some of Bishop's work—most notably in some uncollected poems—for the poem Edelman examines in greatest detail, "In the Waiting Room," a study of lesbian awakening does not appear to be the most fruitful reading of this poem. I want to quote the poem more fully than Edelman does and point out that what the speaker, Elizabeth, reads in the copy of *National Geographic* is more than the

7. "Elizabeth Bishop: Conversations and Class Notes," 324.
8. "Geography of Gender," 182, 179–80.

pictures and descriptions of naked women, but also the possibility of cannibalism and decoration of babies through mutilation.

> Osa and Martin Johnson
> dressed in riding breeches,
> laced boots, and pith helmets.
> A dead man slung on a pole
> —"Long Pig," the caption said.
> Babies with pointed heads
> wound round and round with string;
> black, naked women with necks
> wound round and round with wire
> like the necks of light bulbs.
> Their breasts were horrifying.
> I read it straight through.
> I was too shy to stop.
> And then I looked at the cover:
> the yellow margins, the date.
> 　　　　(*The Complete Poems*, 159)

Certainly the poem shows gender awareness here and later when Elizabeth says

> Why should I be my aunt,
> or me, or anyone?
> What similarities—
> boots, hands, the family voice
> I felt in my throat, or even
> the *National Geographic*
> and those awful hanging breasts—
> held us all together
> or made us all just one?
> 　　　　(*The Complete Poems*, 161)

Yet the gender awareness is tied up with the larger awareness of humanity in general; the young Elizabeth is not really discovering her sexuality so much as she is discovering her own participation in the human race—including her gender identity. The result, therefore, is an epiphany on a larger order than awakening of sexual orientation, and the poem's subject is larger than a careful encoding of lesbian identity. It does not exclude the connections among human beings that are homosexual in nature, nor does it those that are heterosexual. In fact, the poem does not seem interested in excluding human relations at all but rather on noting their peculiar, "unlikely" ten-uousness. The poem does not close, after all, focusing on those breasts but rather on a deadly political issue:

> The War was on. Outside,
> in Worcester, Massachusetts,
> were night and slush and cold,
> and it was still the fifth
> of February, 1918.
> (*The Complete Poems*, 161)

This is quite unlike, for example, Adrienne Rich's poem "Trying to Talk with a Man," where the imagery of nuclear bomb-testing is not the major issue at stake but is rather a trope for understanding the combative relations between the sexes. For Bishop, World War I sug-gests a danger, as does nuclear testing for Rich. But that danger is not one that arises because of gender-identification or sex roles, unlike the "danger" Rich specifically mentions. Instead, it is the possibility of violence done by any human being to another, on an individual, tribal, or global level: a woman to her baby, a man to another man, etc. Bishop wishes to make a large suggestion about the perplexity—the "unlikeliness"—of being human. And she wants to be sure to make it through the perception of an individual, an "Elizabeth."

Much more convincing examples of poems with homoerotic ele-ments are the love poems in *A Cold Spring*, which I want to return to later, or the uncollected, joking "Exchanging Hats," which begins

> Unfunny uncles who insist
> in trying on a lady's hat,
> —oh, even if the joke falls flat,
> we share your slight transvestite twist
>
> in spite of our embarrassment.
> (*The Complete Poems*, 200)

"In the Waiting Room" is full of gender awareness, as well as rec-ognition of each individual's participation in humanity, but if it is not merely a carefully concealed proclamation of homosexuality—the kind of careful concealing of the personal that we noted in H. D.'s work—how do we satisfactorily answer questions like Edelman's? Is Bishop hiding something, and if so, what is it? Is the act of hiding the point of the poem? If not, what is?

One answer lies in the moral implications of Bishop's use of detailed description, what Carolyn Handa calls "Bishop's vision, her acute, unflinching, pressuring gaze." Handa departs from the critical judgment of Bishop as miniaturist and explains that a poet's devotion to literal detail has philosophical, perhaps even political, undertones. "For Bishop . . . vision does not simply mean close and careful observation. Vision is directly connected with morality." Bishop herself expresses this connection in a letter to her biographer Anne Stevenson, which Handa quotes at length: "Lack of observation seems to me one of the cardinal sins, responsible for so much cruelty, ugliness, dullness, bad manners—and general unhappiness, too."[9] We might be reminded of Richard Wilbur's poem "Love Calls Us to the Things of This World" and William Carlos Williams's constant determination to reach the universal only through the particular. In this context, Bishop's reliance and even insistence on the literal descriptive detail of her poems allow her to make implications about morality without waxing didactic, or as Theodore Roethke would have it, without "stamping a tiny foot at God." She is able to craft the environment in which the statement can make itself, and so can remain a poet of understatement or as Moore said, "modesty."

There are examples to support this view throughout Bishop's collections; one notable poem is "Roosters," from her first book, in which the relentless rhyming triplets present a landscape raw and ready for the violence that occurs. Even the rhythm of the lines themselves, increasing from two to three to four beats per line, adds to the mounting restlessness and anxiety:

At four o'clock
in the gun-metal blue dark
we hear the first crow of the first cock

just below
the gun-metal blue window
and immediately there is an echo

off in the distance,
then one from the backyard fence,
then one, with horrible insistence,

grates like a wet match
from the broccoli patch,

9. "Vision and Change: The Poetry of Elizabeth Bishop," 19–20.

flares, and all over town begins to catch.
                    (*The Complete Poems*, 35)

Another is "Faustina, or Rock Roses" (*A Cold Spring*) where the close, detailed description reveals a discomforting and confusing picture of relations between a wealthy white woman and her servant. Absent entirely from the poem is the kind of accusing, declamatory, moralistic rhetoric that would have led critics to instantly label the poem "political." Yet another is "Brazil, January 1, 1502," (*Questions of Travel*) in which the detailed description of the Brazilian jungle, likened to rich tapestry, implies the immoral destructiveness of the Christian explorers, who are "hard as nails" and who "ripped away into the hanging fabric, / each out to catch an Indian for himself."[10]

Bishop's insistence on the literalness of her poems adds weight to the moral message—or moral "conundrum," to quote "Faustina"— and by disarming the reader, ensures that their moral implications deserve serious consideration. Writing of *North & South*, Randall Jarrell says, "All her poems have written underneath, *I have seen it.*"[11] The next implication is that the reader will have seen it, too, and must have understood.

Another interesting aspect of her work not to be neglected in this context—especially since it differentiates her from Moore—is her experimentation with surrealism. Surrealism, too, can be a "strategy of evasion," a way to both reveal and conceal aspects of the self because surrealism does not accept the kind of rational structures of selfhood or reality that we usually recognize. Bishop uses visual imagery to achieve rather surreal effects, especially in poems from her first collection, most of which were written during a time when she was living in Paris, had met a few surrealist painters, and was interested in the artistic movement. Most notable among these are "The Monument," based directly on Max Ernst's frottage technique in *Histoire Naturelle*, and "The Weed."

As Richard Mullen has pointed out, "Bishop rejects the shapeless poetics accompanying the derangement of consciousness" of French surrealists such as Andre Breton.[12] She insists upon the power of poetry to shape, but she also hints that such shaping does

10. *Complete Poems*, 92.
11. "On *North & South*," in *Elizabeth Bishop and Her Art*, ed. Schwartz and Estess, 181.
12. "Elizabeth Bishop's Surrealist Inheritance," 64.

not truly penetrate the surface of our experiences. To be human is to long for order, identity, human connection—to long to be at home in the world. Yet, as many readers have noted, Bishop's poetry repeatedly reveals a profound sense of homelessness, traceable to the uprooted and traumatic childhood we read about in her autobiographical fiction. Her use of surrealism reflects this tension between the urge toward poetic order and the near-horror at the world's inhuman refusal to become easily domestic, easily graspable.

In "Casabianca" language itself becomes a surrealist tool, wherein the poem turns back upon itself and seems to lose distinction between the reference to Felicia Hemans's poem and reference to its own narrative situation.[13] But primarily she relies upon manipulation of images to achieve a romantic eruption of the subconscious, or unconscious, even while the language and syntax of the poems classically affirm the existence of logic and conscious control.

In a letter to Anne Stevenson, Bishop writes, "Dreams, works of art (some) glimpses of the always-more-successful surrealism of everyday life, unexpected moments of empathy (is it?), catch a peripheral vision of whatever it is one can never really see full-face but that seems enormously important." As Mullen explains, "images are an element common to both the waking and sleeping states."[14]

Thus Bishop's use of imagery finally functions not unlike Pound's definition of the image when "a thing outward and objective transforms itself, or darts into a thing inward and subjective." In that "glimpse" the image seen is fraught with the "inward" awareness of what seems "enormously important," yet precisely because it is a glimpse, it remains somewhat at a distance and therefore not overpowering. Indeed, at times the visual details themselves become so numerous, so thoroughly filling her poems that, as Mullen says, "the created settings also seem oddly dream-like because they radiate with a disturbing ambiguity similar to the manifest content of dreams."[15]

13. See Lloyd Schwartz's discussion in *That Sense of Constant Readjustment: Elizabeth Bishop's 'North & South'*, 21–23. As Schwartz points out, in this poem, "The atmosphere is also literary—'Casabianca' is the title of Felicia Hemans' famous poem about Louis Casabianca, whose son refused to abandon his dead father in the Battle of the Nile and went down with the burning ship. Miss Bishop plays on both the poem itself and the fact that the poem became a common classroom exercise in recitation. Of course, the real subject of the poem is the tenor of the Casabianca metaphor, a kaleidoscopic definition of love" (21).

14. Stevenson, *Elizabeth Bishop*, 66; Mullen, "Elizabeth Bishop's Surreal Inheritance," 64.

15. Pound, "Vorticism," in *Literary Essays*, 467; Mullen, "Elizabeth Bishop's Surreal Inheritance," 65.

Just so, if one stares long and hard enough at an ordinary, familiar object or a word, it will seem to detach itself from the surrounding context and become, somehow, very strange. Jean-Paul Sartre, for example, relied on this same effect in *Nausea*, as Roquentin is constantly surrounded by a world whose physical presence confounds and disgusts him in the associational way each thing appears as something else, detached from a rational context. Surrealism at work in Bishop's poetry is usually a subtle force, suggesting dislocation, but never fully achieving it, and so at times might be seen as the work of "fancy" rather than the serious—even moral—undertaking that it usually is.

"The Weed" is a fine example of the way Bishop uses surrealist techniques and principles to her own advantage, since the occasion of the poem is a "glimpse" at the emotional life of the speaker, achieved through a "dream" or perhaps a dream-vision. In the disembodied, fractured way of dreams, the speaker feels distanced from her own self, referring to "the heart" and "the breast" with the definite article, not a possessive pronoun. From her point of strange detachment, she watches the drama of the weed splitting open the heart:

> The rooted heart began to change
> (not beat) and then it split apart
> and from it broke a flood of water.
> Two rivers glanced off from the sides,
> one to the right, one to the left,
> two rushing, half-clear streams,
> (the ribs made of them two cascades)
> which assuredly, smooth as glass,
> went off through the fine black grains of the earth.
> (*The Complete Poems*, 20)

Bishop narrates this remarkable event in fairly simple, declarative phrases, matter-of-factly, with the added confidence of "assuredly." What is assured here? The manner in which the cascades went off? Or the fact that they did? Either way, the adverb's presence in the midst of a surreal dream-experience works to enforce the speaker's quiet, controlled logic in telling the tale. Toward the poem's end this safe distance is slightly lessened, when "A few drops fell upon my face / and in my eyes," bringing the speaker into physical contact with the turmoil taking place in her heart. Her "glimpse," articulated parenthetically—as is so often the case in Bishop—reveals that the stream is all a series of images:

> (As if a river should carry all
> the scenes that it had once reflected
> shut in its waters, and not floating
> on momentary surfaces.)
>
> (21)

The suggestive symbolism here is rather complex. The speaker lies "dead, and meditating" until she is prodded from "desperate sleep" by the motion of the weed. The weed has a "graceful head" and moves "mysteriously," with no body of light apparent for it to grow toward; these strange tropisms suggest the attractions that regularly affect, and often divide, or rend, the heart. Are those waters tears? "My own thoughts" appear a few lines later, when the heart is broken, and "reflect," as water usually does, what passes above it. Yet the images are not mere reflections, since those many scenes are not merely "on momentary surfaces" but actually comprise the very matter of the stream. We see that what grows from, and so must be nourished by, also breaks the heart, and all the images that the heart contains will be brought forth by the continued growth and change that takes place.

Bishop addresses attraction, heartbreak, depression—in short, the human emotional condition and the stuff of many a romantic poem—through such detached and surreal metaphors that the speaker herself is distanced from her pain, carefully observing it. Norma Procopiow reads the poem as a homoerotic defense, where "rejoining two parts of the split heart has clear connotations."[16] I think such a reading deliberately misses the point of the very distancing methods we have seen at work. The entire human race is familiar with the notion of broken-heartedness, which forms the major trope for this poem. Moreover, no "rejoining" takes place. Rather, the poem closes with the weed still standing "in the severed heart" replying to the speaker's question, "I grow . . . but to divide your heart again,": "again" implying surely that the "severed" heart may be subdivided through further heartbreak, leaving it in even more fragmented sections.

The point is not, I think, a clever and surreptitious set of codes specifically for lesbian love, but a poem which attempts to create a picture of all human emotional experience. The poem avoids specif-

---

16. "Survival Kit: The Poetry of Elizabeth Bishop," 10.

icity among those images racing away; no catalogue exacts them, nor defines the speaker's emotional experience as romantic love, either heterosexual or homosexual. Amid all the gorgeous, frightening detail, there is a remarkable lack of specificity, even in a surreal "glimpse" of the unconscious. Thus, while Bishop indicates neither kind of relationship as the impetus for heartbreak, neither does she suggest that one kind of romantic or erotic grief might be nothing more than a symbolic trope for another. She is careful to remain more inclusive than exclusive in her depiction of human relations. As Joanne Feit Diehl explains of the poems in general, often Bishop "distinguishes between eroticism and sexual identity, a distinction that allows her to deflect sexual identification while simultaneously sustaining a powerful erotic presence."[17]

In fact, the last poem Bishop wrote continues just this kind of careful inclusion. "Sonnet" is a fourteen-line poem of entrapment and release, or according to the usual understanding of the form, it is a problem and a solution. But it does not look much like the sonnets that once made the form ubiquitous; most lines carry only two stresses, from one to four words. Bishop seems to suggest that the pattern of problem/resolution is still an important one in poetry and that the "sonnet" form itself had better be rendered more flexible to allow for greater expression.

Robert Dale Parker calls this a poem of "explicit homosexuality," focusing on Bishop's contemporary use of the word "gay." But another poet, Jean Valentine, doesn't see the poem as being "explicit" in its indication of any single kind of constricted life. She calls "Sonnet" "a redemptive poem for *any* particular guests on this earth who start up 'caught' and end up 'freed.'"[18] Here is the entire poem:

Caught—the bubble
in the spirit-level,
a creature divided;
and the compass needle
wobbling and wavering,
undecided.
Freed—the broken

17. *Women Poets*, 92.
18. Robert Dale Parker, *The Unbeliever: The Poetry of Elizabeth Bishop*, 142; Jean Valentine, from *Field* 31 (Fall 1984): 44–45, italics mine. The issue contains many essays in recognition of Elizabeth Bishop.

thermometer's mercury
running away;
and the rainbow-bird
from the narrow bevel
of the empty mirror,
flying wherever
it feels like, gay!
    (*The Complete Poems*, 192)

While I certainly think the poem can be seen to express the kind of joyful freedom that oppressed homosexuals can feel when they are finally able to throw off societal prejudice and taboo and live openly according to their own decision, I hardly think the poem can be read as an expression of only that particular achievement; it cannot be said to be "explicit." Instead, Bishop's images present a pattern of caught/ freed corresponding to an old poetic form that would instead imply a plethora of experiences, all variations on a more general theme.

Moreover, the last word, which Parker takes as proof of the poem's sole subject, is as old as the form Bishop invokes: it has meant "joyful" and "merry" for hundreds of years, and has been connected to poetry through the Provençal term for the art of poetry, *gai saber*, or gay science.[19] While in 1988 and 1979 (the dates of Parker's and Bishop's respective publications), the word clearly does in conversational English connote "homosexual," in the context of Bishop's poem, it *also* partakes in a larger, literary vocabulary, which stretches back to antedate our most modern usage. From Bishop's choice of images, including a level, a compass, a thermometer (hardly erotic symbols—except, perhaps, the compass, recalling John Donne's famous poem), and her lack of metaphorically charged language as she presents them, I think we can conclude that she wanted her poem to invoke a pattern of constriction and release that, while including freedom of sexual identity, does *not* explicitly say so and implies much more than just that. Considering the fact that it is Bishop's last published poem, it can be read as "about" being no longer compelled to write poetry—no longer obliged to measure and describe and mirror the world, as Bishop did with poetry throughout her life. It can, therefore, also be read as "about" death—the release of the soul, that caged bird. Bishop engages in an exploration of the humane, but not the candidly

19. I rely here on the entries for "gay" in the compact edition of the Oxford English Dictionary (Oxford University Press, 1971).

personal; while she does not, in this poem, extinguish or disguise a lesbian reading, she does not specify one, either. As one of her poet friends, May Swenson, wrote of her poems in general, "Their brilliance is inside, and not on the surface. And they are subtle—not obvious."[20]

Clearly, there are boundaries to the kind of specific emotional detail Bishop wishes to delineate in her published work. For Bishop, both the "moral vision" of imagistic detail and the "peripheral vision" of surrealism focus attention on the personal, lived quality of a poem, but they also keep the technique careful and controlled, so that the personal does not become the private, occluding the genuine inclusion of any given reader.

Bishop's reliance on detailed description, accompanied by her insistence upon the literal basis for her work, suggests that she is a self-effacing presence in her poems, "modest," understated, subdued, and nondidactic. All these elements she shares with other personal classicists. Closely related to her unpretentious use of details is her distinctive tone, and it is the importance of tone developed as a kind of formal tool in free verse poetry that makes Bishop such a significant figure in the development of personal classicism.

Initially readers and critics noted the naturalness, the spoken quality of her tone, which tended to differentiate her work from that of Moore. As Robert Lowell said in his 1947 review, "[Unlike Moore] Bishop is usually present in her poems; they happen to her, she speaks, and often centers them on herself." Similarly, Arthur Mizener wrote, "But Miss Bishop's poems are primarily accounts of states of mind, not of objects about which they crystallize, much as she respects these objects and insists upon their importance." John Ashbery made the same distinction in his 1969 review of the first *Complete Poems:* "Miss Moore's synthesizing, collector's approach is far from Miss Bishop's linear, exploring one." In a letter, May Swenson admitted to an admiring envy of Bishop's tone: "I would like to find the casual and absolutely natural tone that you have in your poems—they are never over-colored or forced the least little bit—they are very honest, and never call attention to their effects."[21]

20. Letter to Elizabeth Bishop, July 12, 1963. Elizabeth Bishop Collection, Olin Library, Washington University, St. Louis, Missouri. Unless otherwise identified, all quotations from correspondence are taken from this collection.

21. Robert Lowell, "From 'Thomas, Bishop, and Williams,'" in *Elizabeth Bishop and Her Art,* ed. Schwartz and Estess, 188; Arthur Mizener, "New Verse: *North & South,*" in Schwartz and Estess, 191; John Ashbery, "*The Complete Poems,*" in Schwartz and Estess, 201–2; Swenson to Bishop, July 12, 1963.

It is not a new idea to suggest that twentieth-century poetry, dominated as much of it has been by free verse, has needed to discover and develop new formal methods with which to distinguish itself. Free verse is not, after all, merely the absence of certain traditional properties of verse in practice since the late sixteenth century; it is also the embracing of new properties. Charles O. Hartman's discussion of "counterpoint" as a vital new definition for formal meaning in the free verse line lays out ways of approaching the line prosodically without reliance on the concepts of strict meter or end rhyme. Jonathan Holden raises the possibility of replacing the traditional shapes for poems (sonnet, villanelle, ballad, and so on) with nonliterary "analogues"—forms like the letter, the conversation, the confession.[22] One need only look back to the free verse in Whitman's *Leaves of Grass* to see the development of the image as a formal element of transition. In Whitman, the image becomes as surely a tool for composition—and not merely an accident of expression—as the familiar shapes of meaning in the Shakespearean sonnet's octet of problem and sestet of resolution.

Tone is yet another important new element of form and becomes especially important in the work of the personal classicists. While Bishop is by no means primarily a free verse poet, we see in her work a keen interest in tone as a formal element: seconding the understatement implied in her descriptions, working as surely as rhythm or meter to develop a visceral mood within a poem, and occasionally asserting itself visually on the page as the controlled articulation of powerful feeling bracketed in parentheses, as in "One Art" or "Five Flights Up." Both of these poems reveal the emotional intensity even while concealing how much is at stake. Similarly, the casual, conversational tone throughout "One Art" combines with description of mundane losses: keys, an "hour badly spent." Here, the relaxed tone formally embodies the trivial subject matter, analogous to the way William Carlos Williams allows trimeter to embody meaning in "The Dance":

> In Breughel's great picture, The Kermess,
> the dancers go round, they go round and
> around, the squeal and the blare and the
> tweedle of bagpipes. . . .[23]

22. See, for a brief perspective of the historical development and importance of accentual-syllabic verse in its relation to free verse, Roger Mitchell's "The Fifteenth Century Again," 23–25; Charles O. Hartman, *Free Verse: An Essay on Prosody;* Jonathan Holden, *Style and Authenticity in Postmodern Poetry.*
23. *Selected Poems of William Carlos Williams,* 116.

At the poem's conclusion, the speaker, still trying to keep devastating sorrow at bay, can hardly bring herself to name what she is feeling; only in the hidden, contained space of the parentheses does she even raise her voice, through italics and exclamation point: "though it may look like (*Write* it!) like disaster." The sudden shift, although muffled in parentheses, works not unlike a metrical variation to emphasize a sudden shift in meaning or intensity; here Bishop uses a tonal substitution to achieve the "even bolder relief" one might expect from a spondaic substitution amid regular iambs.[24]

As he begins to account for what is "personal, even quirky, about her apparently straightforward descriptive poems," David Kalstone defines tone as "the kind of authority a single voice will claim over the material included in a poem." He mentions Bishop's own manner of reading aloud: "How flat and modest her voice is, how devoid of flourish, how briefly she holds her final chords and cadences and allows a poem to resonate."[25] This kind of discussion assumes the author's reading voice is not an accident or mere decoration, but that it offers some element of illumination about the literary "tone" itself, about the formal power of understatement or simple syntax. Bishop clearly shared this interest in tone, as evidenced by remarks she made in her rare interviews.

In 1966, Bishop explained that what she admired most about George Herbert was "the absolute naturalness of tone," which led her to reread Herbert "a great deal." Later in the same interview she discussed the way very different poets—Hopkins, Browning, Cummings—employ "the use of the present tense [that] helps convey this sense of the mind in action."[26] A poetics interested in depicting the mind in action has something in common with Olson's and Creely's pursuit of composition in the field, or "projective verse." Of course, Bishop's lifelong interest in closed, traditional forms, and her mastery of them that led to such excellences as "One Art," places limits on the usefulness of discussing her in conjunction with the Black Mountain poets or the projectivists. Even so, her keen interest in creating poetry that suggests natural, human perception and voice as

24. See Paul Fussell's *Poetic Meter & Poetic Form* (New York: Random House, 1979), 41, for his discussion of how Wordsworth employs such substitution in "A Slumber Did My Spirit Seal"; *Complete Poems*, 178.

25. "Elizabeth Bishop: Questions of Memory, Questions of Travel," in *Elizabeth Bishop and Her Art*, ed. Schwartz and Estess, 5.

26. Ashley Brown, "An Interview with Elizabeth Bishop," in *Elizabeth Bishop and Her Art*, ed. Schwartz and Estess, 295, 298.

its source seems to relieve her of some of the limitations that Bogan imposed upon herself, and leaves her poetry with a rich achievement in tone that can prove very useful to later free verse writers.

Eavan Boland, an Irish poet, describes the strong impact she felt from reading Bishop, finding some kind of kinship with a writer who "defines her country—as so many good Irish writers do—by her absence from it." Bishop, she says, is "the one un-Romantic American poet of her generation" even though "self-discovery [is] at the heart of her work, however occluded." In her short essay, Boland touches on various aspects of the way Bishop's reticence is a kind of articulation, the way her refusal to base her poems solely on her own subjectivity becomes an embrace of humane perception of the world. Interestingly, Carolyn Handa calls Bishop a "post-Romantic poet," explaining that even in regard to nature itself, Bishop's perceptions were "no longer part of the idealistic, expansive nineteenth century."[27] This movement away from a romantic "expansiveness" is by no means confined to personal classicists in this century, and in fact constitutes one of their primary links with the modernist movement itself; certainly it exhibits an uneasiness with the self as the unfettered center of poetry that leads them to eschew autobiography as confession.

A mind pursuing such goals in poetry is not interested in "explicit" homosexual poems, but rather poems that are, through their own understatement, more generally inclusive and less glaringly personal. Robert Pinsky, too, addresses the way Bishop's tone combines the seemingly contradictory elements of the personal and the objective in her own "idiom": "And most essentially, it is utterly personal and individual, yet under a surface of detached, traveler-like anonymity. That anonymity of the tourist is a defense of the private self. . . . Its neutrality, or simulacrum of neutrality, keeps us at a distance."[28]

Michael Ryan begins his 1984 essay "A Dark Gray Flame," with consideration of how tone functions in Elizabeth Bishop's work: "Reticence, which is first a character trait of the poet, is made to serve a formal function in the poetry. It becomes the guiding principle of technique. It pervades the tone and, transliterated into decorum, even defines the range of style and subject within which technique

---

27. "An Un-Romantic American," 90, 75, 78; "The Poetry of Elizabeth Bishop," 126.
28. "The Idiom of a Self: Elizabeth Bishop and Wordsworth," in *Elizabeth Bishop and Her Art*, ed. Schwartz and Estess, 58.

can be employed."[29] Ryan's words help in defining and examining personal classicism at work, especially in poetry from the second half of the twentieth century; in the prosody we develop to discuss such poetry, reticence "pervades" the tone and "serves a formal function."

Yet if reticence is a formal element of poetry, to what degree can its formalism also be simply a "character trait" of the poet? Louise Bogan seems to have had a deep aversion to self-disclosure, which, reinforced constantly by the critical and social world in which she lived, pervaded her work to the point of limiting her final achievement. And what Lynn Keller and Cristanne Miller call elements of "indirection" are prevalent throughout both the speech and the literature of women. These critics compare Elizabeth Bishop to Emily Dickinson, noting that both poets employed "tools traditionally used by women in speech to control situations without appearing to control, to hide strength while exercising it, complement the more conventional poetic tools that express shades of emotion." Their comments suggest that indirection in conversation is a result of socialization; in literature, indirection is perhaps more a consciously selected device, the product of choice, not necessity. Yet they suggest that the choice itself is necessitated "because of the great risks women have faced in expressing their aspirations or powers openly."[30] To what extent was the control, reticence, modesty, and reserve found throughout Bishop's work similarly a mixture of "character trait," deliberate formal concern, and a way of conforming to critical expectations for a woman writer? We can gain a sense of the answers to these questions by examining further Bishop's own use of autobiography and her attitude toward confessional poetry.

It will be useful for comparison to recall with what reluctance, even horror, Louise Bogan regarded autobiography—which she equated with confession. Even in the form of prose, Bogan found it very difficult to bring herself to recount her childhood and her past, although her male friends urged her to do so. Elizabeth Bishop, despite her shyness toward reading aloud in public, seems not to have shared Bogan's attitude. Carole Kiler Doreski examines the autobiograph-

---

29. "A Dark Gray Flame," 518.
30. "Emily Dickinson, Elizabeth Bishop, and the Rewards of Indirection," 534. Keller and Miller cite these forms of indirection in poetry: "reliance on connotative or implicit meanings, wordplay, manipulation of understatement, qualifiers, or slight shifts in tone." It is important to mention that they note these forms are not exclusively the domain of women writers.

ical writings of both Lowell and Bishop, illuminating some interesting similarities between the male confessional poet and the female personal classicist. She quotes a letter of 1955, in which Bishop explains to Lowell the excitement, challenge, and attraction of writing autobiographical prose.

> Do please write an autobiography—or sketches for one, the two or three stories I've managed to do of that sort have been a great satisfaction somehow—that desire to get things straight and tell the truth—it's almost impossible not to tell the truth in poetry, I think, but in prose it keeps eluding one in the funniest ways—.[31]

As we found Bogan urging Roethke to put more of himself into his poems, encouraging him toward the poetic approach that would bring him his greatest recognition, we find Bishop urging Lowell toward the technique that would bring him his. She is essentially suggesting he undertake *Life Studies*. The great difference, of course, is that Bogan suggests for Roethke something she cannot bring herself to try, whereas Bishop testifies that it has already been useful for her in "two or three stories I've managed to do."[32] Clearly, autobiography was not the anathema for Bishop that it was for Bogan.

With the 1965 publication of *Questions of Travel*, she even included "In the Village," the autobiographical account of her mother's final mental breakdown in Nova Scotia, after which the woman was permanently institutionalized, never to see her daughter again. The story moves slowly toward its emotional center: it begins with a distant, detached, almost surreal description of a scream that has become a timeless, inescapable presence, pictured as "a slight stain in those pure blue skies." Throughout the entire introductory paragraph, only one sentence links the scream with the author: "Its pitch would be the pitch of *my* village."[33] In the next two and a half pages, the connection is absent as the narrator refers to the woman and "her child" or "the child," not identifying the little girl with the narrator through the first person.

In fact, the prose has something of the feeling of Virginia Woolf's writing in the way the point of view hovers above the action, then

31. "Robert Lowell and Elizabeth Bishop: A Matter of Life Studies," 91.

32. For a look at Bishop's and Lowell's relationship during the years when both were exploring autobiography, see Kalstone's *Becoming a Poet*. Pages 135–221 focus most directly on the issues under examination here.

33. "In the Village," in *Collected Prose*, 251, italics mine.

darts down as if to enter someone's consciousness—but the someone remains unnamed. Indeed, the last line of the second section seems to settle into the dressmaker's consciousness: "Now the dressmaker is at home, basting, but in tears. It is the most beautiful material she has worked on in years. It has been sent to the woman from Boston, a present from her mother-in-law, and heaven knows how much it cost."[34] But immediately after, as the third section begins, the story is in the first person, as the little girl—the madwoman's daughter— tells her story.

The story, then, combines the immediate, first-person narration of autobiography with distancing methods. It deals with painful, frightening material: the madness and loss of a mother, the only living parent for the child. She is, therefore, rootless in a certain sense, and that fact resonates within the title poem of *Questions of Travel*: "Should we have stayed at home, / wherever that may be?"[35] With the inclusion of the story in her collection, Bishop followed Lowell's example of placing "91 Revere Street" within *Life Studies* as a way to complement, or even to explicate, the poems in the book. In this way the two poets encouraged each other to explore and use autobiography in their work.

But "In the Village," while the only story to appear in a collection with her poetry, is not the only autobiographical story Bishop wrote. "Gwendolyn" was published in the *New Yorker* in 1953, six months after "In the Village" appeared in the same magazine. "Gwendolyn" corresponds in many details with the earlier story: the narrator lives with her grandparents, and her family life is defined by relatives other than parents and siblings. In "Gwendolyn," however, the sense of distancing is much less present, from the way characters are not merely shadowy "aunt" or "older aunt" but named specifically: "my Aunt Mary." The story focuses on the narrator's friendship with Gwendolyn, a beautiful and "delicate" girl afflicted with diabetes, and Gwendolyn's eventual death. To the young narrator, the disease itself is "attractive" because of her grandparents' explanation that it is caused by "too much sugar": "as if she would prove to be solid candy if you bit her, and her pure-tinted complexion would taste exactly like the icing-sugar Easter eggs or birthday-candle holders, held to be inedible, except that I knew better."[36]

34. Ibid., 254.
35. *Complete Poems*, 94.
36. "Gwendolyn," in *Collected Prose*, 216.

Running throughout "Gwendolyn" is the hint of physical attraction between young girls. The narrator's interest in Gwendolyn is not primarily emotional; she is drawn to the other's beauty, and that attraction seems to manifest itself with oral, taste-centered imaginings. Even Gwendolyn's last name is suggestive: Appletree. I think it would be a mistake, however, to read this story primarily as an exposé of early homoerotic awakenings, just as it would "In the Waiting Room." Loss, this time through death, is the center of this story as well as "In the Village." "Memories of Uncle Neddy," published in the *Southern Review* in 1977, is likewise about loss, this time through the gradual dissipation, or disease, of alcoholism rather than insanity or diabetes. The art of losing is practiced by very young narrators in Bishop's work, corresponding to her own young losses of father, mother, and then maternal grandparents when she was taken to Boston to stay with her father's family. Bishop herself was quick to acknowledge that her stories were autobiographical, in letters to Anne Stevenson during the preparation of the Twayne edition on Bishop. "'In the Village' is accurate—just compressed a bit. 'Gwendolyn' is, too."[37]

In spite of Bishop's interest in autobiography, however, I do not mean to equate her work with Lowell's confessionalism; rather, I mean to demonstrate the extent of the "personal" in her quiet work and to suggest the degree to which reticence is a consciously chosen formal element, not a mere accident of personality. To be fair, I must point out that Bishop *was* a private person and a shy one, granting few interviews, giving infrequent public readings, and she suggests in her interview with George Starbuck, "Sometimes I think if I had been born a man I probably would have written more. Dared more, or been able to spend more time at it."[38] Whether she is blaming society's perception of women or some feminine disposition for any self-imposed limits is unclear here. She does, however, acknowledge limitation.

Advice from Bishop to her former student Sandra McPherson reveals more about the way Bishop viewed the relationship between gender and poetry. As late as 1970, she wrote to congratulate McPherson on the publication of her first book, but also to issue a warning:

One thing I feel I should warn you against . . . do be careful of the *female* element . . . ! It's fine up to a point, but shouldn't be stressed,

37. Letter to Anne Stevenson, October 2, 1963.
38. "The Work! A Conversation with Elizabeth Bishop," in *Elizabeth Bishop and Her Art*, ed. Schwartz and Estess, 329.

I feel—the beauty of pots and pans, simple household tasks (that are really neither simple nor beautiful), babies' smiles, that are really just reflexes, and so on . . . MEN don't talk about being MEN all the time, in their poetry, & I don't think women should either.[39]

Here Bishop rejects poetry that might, in its selection of details, be construed as exclusive, only pertaining to the private experience of one of the sexes. Many would take exception to her justification that men don't write about being men all the time—much of Western literature has, indeed, remained exclusively male in its perspective. I sense that Bishop's argument is more inductive than deductive and that regardless of what male authors may have done, she believes that one simply shouldn't base one's poetic vision solely on gender-defined experience—especially that of women. It is also surely tied to her distrust of compartmentalizing poetry according to sex or gender. As she explained in a letter to May Swenson, "I have always refused to be in any collections, or reviews, or special numbers, etc., of just women. *Always*—this has nothing to do with, or at least, didn't start with, the present Women's Lib. Movement (although I'm in favor of that, too, of course). . . . Literature is literature, no matter who produces it."[40]

Moreover, she professed a great dislike for confessional poetry, although she never specifically targeted Lowell for public attack. In response to a student's comment that he was trying to read "some of the 'confessional' poets lately," she answered with some force, although she mentioned no names. "I *hate* confessional poetry, and so many people are writing it these days. Besides, they seldom have anything interesting to 'confess' anyway. Mostly they write about a lot of things which I should think were best left unsaid."[41] Interestingly, an implication remains that *some* confessional poetry might very well be worthwhile, if it were "interesting."

But her proscription against what is "best left unsaid," although vague, might suggest the same kind of discomfort with subject matter that M. L. Rosenthal himself voiced when he first reviewed Lowell's *Life Studies.* Reportedly, she also disliked Roethke's poetry focusing on mental illness. Sandra McPherson suggests that Bishop may have come to this predilection because of her own mother's breakdown

39. Postcard to Sandra McPherson, September 2, 1970, made available to me by Sandra McPherson. I thank her for her help.
40. Letter to Swenson, November 7, 1971.
41. Wehr, "Conversations and Class Notes," 327.

when Bishop was a small child. In a 1967 *Time* article focusing on Robert Lowell's achievement, Bishop is reported to distinguish among him and his "confessional imitators"; of the latter she said, "The tendency is to overdo the morbidity. You just wish they'd keep some of these things to themselves." Moreover, in her 1966 *Shenandoah* interview, what she praised in *Life Studies* was not Lowell's subject matter but his tone, which, she suggested, may have a new moral strength: "Poets have to change, and possibly the more subdued magnificence of his later tone is more humane."[42]

In spite of her possible concern for whatever deleterious effect the project of confessional poetry might have on Lowell due to his own mental instability, her real concern seems to be rather different from that of Rosenthal. Instead, her letters to Lowell discuss how poems—confessional poems, primarily—might affect *others*—the people who appear in them or who know those who appear in them. As early as 1948, she wrote to Lowell in disapproval of William Carlos Williams's incorporation of letters from a woman poet into *Paterson*. Bishop thought them angry, unhappy, and inappropriate to the poem since "they are too overpowering emotionally . . . so that the whole poem suffers." Moreover, Bishop identified with the young woman, and seemed to be imagining how she would feel if those were *her* letters appearing in somebody else's poem.[43]

Nearly ten years later, Lowell was writing a flurry of poems about Bishop, even rendering a poem version of her story, "In the Village." In one early draft he included a stanza about her mother, including lines, supposedly spoken in Bishop's voice, recalling the mother's declaration that she wants to kill her daughter. Bishop wrote back asking him to change that "remark" if he ever decided to "do anything" with the poem. "She never did make it [that remark]; in fact I don't remember any direct threats, except the usual maternal ones. . . . Poor thing, I don't want to have it any worse than it was."[44]

Bishop does not want the "truth" to be distorted in Lowell's poem. Her fear is not that it would hurt her mother directly, since the woman has been long dead; she cannot be afraid the poem will lead to psychic distress for Lowell himself since he is "confessing" a fiction-

42. Sandra McPherson, January 11, 1989, letter to the author; "Poets: The Second Chance," 68; Ashley Brown, 300.

43. Kalstone, *Becoming a Poet*, 137. See 137–38 for fuller quotation of this June 30 letter.

44. Ibid., 181.

alized version of Bishop's life, not his own. Instead, she is vehement that, however unhappy her childhood may have been, it will not be portrayed in an exaggerated poetic version; it will not be exploited. However disingenuous some of Bishop's remarks may be concerning her own strict adherence to fact ("I *always* tell the truth in my poems . . . that's *exactly* how it happened"), she will not approve Lowell's distortion of fact concerning her own biography.

In 1972, when Lowell was preparing to publish *The Dolphin*, Bishop seemed to feel he had gone too far with his own subject matter. The book would include in its fourteen-line poems bits of letters, phone calls, and cables, all chronicling the sad break-up of Lowell's long marriage to Elizabeth Hardwick. The prospect of including Hardwick's words in this way troubled many of Lowell's friends, as Ian Hamilton shows in the Lowell biography. Hamilton includes a letter Bishop wrote to Lowell urging him not to go ahead with publication.

Clearly the letter was difficult for her to write, and she begins with firm, repeated protestations of the excellence in the book's poetry: "Please believe I think it is wonderful poetry. . . . It's hell to write this, so please first do believe I think DOLPHIN is magnificent poetry." Her caution to him begins, "Because I love you so much I can't bear to have you publish something that I regret and that you might live to regret, too." The regret might not be strictly a matter of conscience, she suggests. "The worldly part of it is that it—the poem— parts of it—may well be taken up and used against you by all the wrong people—who are just waiting in the wings to attack you." She goes on to quote Thomas Hardy on the "mischief" of mixing fact and fiction; Hardy feels that the presence of facts among fictional elements can imply that truth applies to the fictional elements, as well—"a horror to contemplate" since it could be a way of "getting lies believed about people."[45]

Bishop's letter takes on a more urgent tone, with more frequent italics, as she begins applying Hardy's quotation to Lowell's own situation: "One can use one's life as material—one does, anyway—but these letters—aren't you violating a trust? IF you were given permission—IF you hadn't changed them . . . etc. *But art just isn't worth that much.* . . . It is not being 'gentle' to use personal, tragic, anguished letters that way— it's cruel."[46] Her main concern here, even more

45. Ian Hamilton, *Robert Lowell: A Biography*, 422–23.
46. Ibid., 423.

than her prudent thought for his career, is for Hardwick and their daughter. She is concerned for what is right—speaking of trust, of permission—above and beyond the demands of art. Her desire, as she describes it here, to see personal, private detail excised from the poem is one arising from morality, not aesthetics, not shyness, not temperament. However much personality may incline her toward reticence, however much she may see understatement as a fine poetic tool, in the final argument it is careful moral conclusion that leads her to advise Lowell as she does.

Elizabeth Bishop, then, insistently strives in her work to tell the "truth" and to do so "accurately"—as we have seen, she relies largely on detail and imagery with which to depict the "truth." Her attention holds firmly to the exterior world, only implying the interior one. She was not a writer who loathed autobiography, but neither was she by any means a confessional poet. As her letter to Lowell suggests, her final criticism against confessional poetry was not aesthetic but rather moral, since she felt the poems in *Dolphin* are good poetry. And it would appear that she defined the limits between truth-telling and confession very precisely for herself, allowing in her fiction a more expansively personal voice and a greater sense of autobiographical detail. In her love poems, we find an interesting combination of expression and restraint.

From among the poems collected during Bishop's lifetime, I find that nine seem to touch most closely upon her personal romantic life. Seven of these are from *A Cold Spring*: "A Cold Spring," "A Summer's Dream," "Insomnia," "Varick Street," the series titled "Four Poems," "Argument," "The Shampoo."[47] The other two are from *Geography 3:* "One Art" and "Five Flights Up." It is interesting that *A Cold Spring* roughly corresponds with the flurry of autobiographical fiction Bishop undertook; the volume was published in 1955, two years after "Gwendolyn" and "In the Village" appeared in the *New Yorker* and the same year that she was recommending to Robert Lowell that he should write some autobiography, too. There may have been some connection between the personal scrutiny Bishop gave her childhood, through her short stories, and that she gave her adult life, through the poems of *A Cold Spring*.

47. I am indebted to Alan Williamson's insightful essay "*A Cold Spring*: The Poet of Feeling" in *Elizabeth Bishop and Her Art*, ed. Schwartz and Estess, although our projects differ significantly.

Norma Procopiow has noted the relative preponderance of "veiled sexual" poems throughout *A Cold Spring*, observing that even the order of poems within the book parallels "the burgeoning and decline of a love affair." Her point is well taken, although Bishop herself said that the order was not chronological. The book proceeds from the opening title poem's tentative promise, through the disquieting "Varick Street," the two letters that seek some kind of diversion, "Letter to N.Y." and "Invitation to Miss Marianne Moore," to the poignancy of "The Shampoo" with its final image of the moon, both "battered and shiny." Yet the movement is subtle, and not without digressions such as the well-known "Over 2,000 Illustrations and a Complete Concordance." The poems themselves are subtle, too, full of the understatement that is fundamental to personal classicism. Their clustered presence in *A Cold Spring* is unusual; as Alan Williamson says, they are "Bishop's one sustained attempt at a passionately personal kind of lyric."[48] I wish to point out, however, that they are not the only examples of Bishop's personal classicism; instead, they represent a concentration of her personal classicist effort.

"A Cold Spring," the dedication for which reads "For Jane Dewey, Maryland," takes its epigraph from Hopkins, but its opening imagery recalls William Carlos Williams's "Spring and All" rather than the lushness and exuberance of Hopkins's "Spring." Personal classicism, as already evidenced through H. D.'s work, relies heavily on imagery rather than explicit narrative to create an emotional setting. The close attention to natural detail in both Bishop's and Williams's poems emphasizes spring's hesitant, tentative beginning. From Bishop:

> For two weeks or more the trees hesitated;
> the little leaves waited,
> carefully indicating their characteristics.
> > (*The Complete Poems*, 55)

From Williams:

> Now the grass, tomorrow
> the stiff curl of wildcarrot leaf
> One by one objects are defined.

48. Procopiow, 14; Bishop to Stevenson, letter, March 20, 1963; Williamson, "Poet of Feeling," 96.

Both poems retain the chill traces of winter even amid spring's arrival; from Williams, "All about them / the cold, familiar wind—" and from Bishop, "One day, in a chill white blast of sunshine." Williams's poem is an occasion of birth, all those plants entering the new world, with language suggestive of mammalian, human birth, as, surely, the speaker drives to the hospital to deliver a woman's baby. Bishop's poem contains in the first stanza the birth of a calf, but the poem's language is suggestive of something else. As Alan Williamson points out, there is a kind of eroticism in the description of "your big and aimless hills," those hills that "grow softer" when the "new moon comes."[49] Of course, there is some levity in this moonlit moment, since those hills are literally "where each cow-flop lies," and the erotic suggestions are interrupted. But they begin again almost immediately, with the beautiful moths that "flatten themselves" against "your white front door," clearly drawn, through that fascinating attraction to light, to the home of the "you." For the "you" is the center of the poem—owner of the land, the home, the very occasion of the spring.

The poem draws to a close with the beautiful mating dance of the fireflies, until again there is a moment of levity that interrupts the building effect of the imagery. The line, "—exactly like the bubbles in champagne," is slightly amusing in its overstated insistence on the unusual comparison. But there is a shift back to understatement in the next line: "—Later on they rise much higher," returning to the rather erotically charged atmosphere, preparing for the entendre in the last sentence. The poem closes with all the rich potential assigned to the you:

> And your shadowy pastures will be able to offer
> these particular glowing tributes
> every evening now throughout the summer.
> (*The Complete Poems*, 56)

"A Cold Spring" moves beyond that chilly beginning into a poem that, for all it has in common with Williams's poem, finds its metaphoric power in the suggestion of a romance, not procreation. Yet through the two carefully timed interruptions, the poem prevents itself from becoming overly sentimental, and hedges its expression of passion. Bishop maintains a reticent control not only through what

49. "Poet of Feeling," 102.

Richard Hugo calls "writing off the subject" in her use of imagery, but also through humor.[50] This is a love poem, but one that is kept carefully quiet.

Williams's poem, of course, depends on the author's own experience to inform its imagery: Williams was the good New Jersey family doctor, and so the "contagious hospital" and all the birth imagery come from his own life, his own sensitivity. But the poem, for all its celebration of individual life, is much more public than Bishop's. What is at stake emotionally for Williams is of a different tenor from that for Bishop; essentially he is noticing the particular enactment of a universal—birth—and he emphasizes the particular in order to support the universal; whereas she is noticing the universal symbols that surround her own personal subject—*this* love—and she emphasizes the universal in order to contextualize and curtail the personal. This technique is a bit more pronounced than it was in "In the Waiting Room," which, if placed on a continuum of personal/universal emphasis, would slightly be closer to "Spring and All," although clearly on Bishop's end of the spectrum.

"The Bight" is another instance where Bishop barely allows the personal to enter her descriptive poems. Parenthetically, as a kind of epigraph, the poem confides: "(on my birthday)" and so whatever personal importance is attached to the busy scene—the beach littered with boats that resemble "torn open, unanswered letters," those "old correspondences"—and the dredge with its "dripping jawful of marl" (the sediment of the past) is revealed only in the most sparing way.

By "A Summer's Dream" we have left the chilly inauguration of the opening poem and have entered a strange, isolated community where "few ships could come." In this seclusion, the "we" are set against the other inhabitants, five misfits of one sort or another. This "we" then, is a small unit of outsiders within a community of outsiders, who lie awake listening for a horned owl. Even the light of the lamp appears "horned," as if this oddly removed existence is always threatened—and summer dreams usually are, in one way or another. The "we" is a couple who are

> . . . wakened in the dark by
> the somnambulist brook

---

50. See *The Triggering Town: Lectures and Essays on Poetry and Writing*, esp. the first two chapters, "Writing off the Subject" and "The Triggering Town."

nearing the sea,
still dreaming audibly.
(*The Complete Poems*, 63)

Their position is both intimate and precarious: "The bedroom was cold, / the feather bed close." In this reading, the strange resort to which this couple has come holds the qualities of a dream, since it is indeed peopled with strange inhabitants, and focuses on the night-time oddities that are intriguing and vaguely threatening—or threatened. This poem is indicative of what Adrienne Rich has called "the eye of the outsider" in her essay by that title, and it hints only slant-edly, almost absurdly, at the private life shared by the "we." Again, Bishop hints at the personal life and the sexual relationship of the couple, but it only reveals glimpses; the poem's surrealist qualities prevent it from divulging much.

"Insomnia" is another of these veiled love poems, not so veiled as some. It is a sad and poignant piece, almost seeming to indulge in self-pity. Yet the pity is diverted from the speaker to the moon: "By the Universe deserted, / *she'd* tell it to go to hell," so that the speaker's feeling of desertion is implied rather than stated directly. The entire poem relies on the kind of close-knit symbolism and suggestion that seem almost metaphysical until one tries to pin them down precisely— and then it becomes apparent that the comparisons are not finitely explicable. According to Procopiow, in this poem "homoeroticism is defiantly asserted,"[51] presumably because the world is "inverted" and presided over by feminine imagery—the moon, water, a bureau mirror. But the "inverted world" described in the last stanza has another level of connotation, one that is sad rather than defiant:

where left is always right,
where the shadows are really the body,
where we stay awake all night,
where the heavens are shallow as the sea
is now deep, and you love me.
(*The Complete Poems*, 70)

It is difficult to read a poem titled "Insomnia" as a defiant defense of lesbian love; staying awake all night may very well be a pleasurable activity, especially with one's lover, but if so it does not warrant the term "insomnia," a definitely unpleasant, unwanted condition. More-

51. "Survival Kit," 14.

over, the "inverted world" is introduced with a nursery-song resolution: "So wrap up care in a cobweb / and drop it down the well"; this is a world wished for against harsh reality. The "inversions" are rejections of reality, not merely of the "norm"; since last in the wish-list of the last stanza is "and you love me" the firm implication is that the you does *not* love the speaker.[52]

This, then, is foremost a poem of unrequited love, of desertion, and so is another example of Bishop's continued studies of loss. As Carolyn Handa explains, "The speaker's world is not this mirror world. And therefore she must live where she remains unloved by the person she cares for."[53] The feminine details already cited in the poem do imply that the failed love affair was lesbian; it is nonetheless failed, not defiantly asserted, and the promise and excitement of the volume's opening have come to melancholy, not joy. They have done so quietly, however; the yearning for love is imbedded within— and therefore partially concealed by—the various wishes expressed. Thus the poem, while deeply personal in conception, avoids the kind of explicit detail that one would expect in a confessional poem, or in one with a strong message. Only in the last line does the speaker's situation come clear, and it does so with syntactical gracefulness: rather than announcing openly, "You don't love me," the speaker's loss of love is implied since all the wishes—including the last— are unmet.

The setting for "Varick Street" also is a long way from the pastoral opening of this collection, and has none of the wistful freedom of movement felt in "Over 2000 Illustrations and a Complete Concordance." In the dingy, dirty picture of the city with its factories that "struggle awake" and its "wretched uneasy buildings," its "Pale dirty light," the poem is reminiscent of Eliot. But the couple's private life, figured in the last stanza, is not fully Eliotic, lacking his characteristic disgust with sexual love. The picture here is one of the lovers threatened by the surrounding grime, not one of an intrinsically sordid relationship. Still, betrayal is certain, with the refrain "And I shall sell you sell you / sell you of course, my dear, and you'll sell me." But the refrain seems to come out of the surrounding atmosphere of the squalid city, as it follows the preceding two stanzas

52. See Williamson, "Poet of Feeling," p. 97, for a reading of "Insomnia" similar to mine.
53. "The Poetry of Elizabeth Bishop," 134.

of description as well, and intrudes into that desperate sanctuary. The inescapable perfidy is a result of the sick, mechanical world described throughout the poem, and though the lovers' bed "shrinks" from such contamination, love is not safe. Bishop creates this feeling through the extensive use of grimy imagery and the formal repetition of the refrain; the vital, personal moment, first introduced by the natural, immediate "I suppose" and then reified by "Our bed," significantly arrives at the poem's end. Bishop buries what is at stake personally and emotionally toward the poem's end—thus muting the personal or confessional tendency throughout the poem's development, a formal and tonal approach that is perhaps best used in "One Art."

"Argument" again presents strife within a relationship, in which "Days" and "Distance" "argue argue argue with me / endlessly / neither proving you less wanted nor less dear." The poem confronts "the intimidating sound" of the voices that both days and distance may be supposed to have; once again the "we" are threatened from without. Yet they expect to be victorious, so that the voices, with all their intimidation, "can and shall be vanquished," while the poem itself has the formal comfort and closure of quietly rhyming the first and last lines in each seven-line stanza. The balance achieved through form offsets the discord with which the poem begins, so that argument becomes something more abstract, more distant; rather than emphasizing the personal pain involved at the heart of that argument, the poem uses "argument" as a formal element to precede resolution.

The sequence "Four Poems" is surely among the most difficult and obscure of Bishop's work. Each of the separate pieces seems to rely more on oblique suggestion with a touch of surrealism than on an underlying connective narrative. Yet I think they must be read in connection in order to find their meaning; Bishop clearly intended them as a unit, originally publishing them together as a series in the *Partisan Review* in 1951. In that initial publication, only the section "Rain Towards Morning" was titled; it appeared first, followed by what now bear the titles "Conversation" and "While Someone Telephones." "O Breath" was not included in the sequence. Although Bishop later expanded the series to its final form in *The Complete Poems 1927–1979*, from the initial publication of the poems, she conceived them as a group, and they should be read collectively to discern their full effect. What emerges from this reading is not a strong narrative connection but a thematic one; the poem's organization is by accretion.

"Conversation," more than most of Bishop's poems, is largely abstract, with little of the imagery and precise detail with which Bishop usually establishes her subjects.

> The tumult in the heart
> keeps asking questions.
> And then it stops and undertakes to answer
> in the same tone of voice.
> No one could tell the difference.
>
> Uninnocent, these conversations start,
> and then engage the senses,
> only half-meaning to.
> And then there is no choice,
> and then there is no sense;
>
> until a name
> and all its connotation are the same.
> (*The Complete Poems*, 76)

Instead of Bishop's usual vividness and visual specificity, the poem is comprised largely of abstract nouns and copulae; although the title is "Conversation," what she describes sounds more accurately like an internal debate; it is "The tumult in the heart." The self-searching is described as "Uninnocent" and without either choice or sense, and seems to be viewed with a kind of depressed resignation. The form Bishop uses for this poem is significant; the poem works not unlike a sonnet in handling its argument. Two five-line stanzas state the dilemma—the state of internal debate—and a final rhyming couplet, while offering no real solution, brings the debate to a close. These stanzas rhyme roughly abcde, abfde, with the couplet closing on a rhyme of gg.

Surprisingly, although the poem has been "about" an internal conversation and has come to a conclusion ratified through poetic form, we learn nothing specific about the topic of conversation, nor what the "name" and its various "connotations" finally are. All the personal matter is veiled in obscurity, and what is given to the reader is not specificity but mood; a rather dreary, fatalistic one. Bishop has "confessed" nothing and has revealed little. We must hope to learn more from the surrounding context of the poems that follow.

"Rain Towards Morning" is more typical of Bishop's work, since

it returns to imagery, a wonderful description of the last hours of
a thunderstorm. But even so, it is a difficult poem to read; Lloyd
Schwartz has called it a "cryptic love poem." In spite of the offhand
insertion of "I think," which both adds to a sense of spoken imme-
diacy and suggests, as Bishop so often does, that knowledge is at best
uncertain, the poem is rather aloof. It is more markedly iambic than
many of her poems, and although varying from tetrameter to pen-
tameter, it has few metrical variations. The most notable of these is
in the second line, where "freeing, I think" allows a trochaic inver-
sion to emphasize that break to freedom. Lorrie Goldensohn discusses this poem in a way I think is helpful, though not definitive.
She sees the "pale" face in line six as an allegorical figure, "the fabu-
lous 'face' of heaven"; yet even though the face is in some ways other-
worldly, "the kiss a quite august affair," Goldensohn insists that
"Bishop doesn't entirely rule out erotic stimulus" because the freckled
hands and the poem's "alit" ending seem much more "humanly
present."[54]

Goldensohn is interested in drawing comparisons between this
poem and an unpublished manuscript using similar imagery, to which
I shall return later, but at present I want to emphasize that this poem
is obscure when read as a distinct unit. Is it an extended personifica-
tion of the heavens, full of the power of a passing storm? Or is it, as
Goldensohn says later, about "something simpler than heaven and
earth . . . being released from its problematic prison"?[55] Again, the
poem should be read as part of its sequence: it follows a poem about
stymied conversation, about a senseless, inevitable, (therefore im-
prisoning) situation. Moreover, Bishop does not generally indulge in
metaphysical comparisons merely for the sake of artifice. Whenever
a fanciful comparison is made—I am thinking here of Goldensohn's
suggestion that the pale face is that of heaven—it is through a personality's perception. Never merely decorative, metaphor reveals
something about the speaker's emotional state, or perhaps that of
a character within the poem. There is, for example, that moon in
"Insomnia," or the description of the moose blocking the road in her
often-anthologized poem, "The Moose": "high as a church, / homely
as a house / (or, safe as houses)" which reveals so much about the bus

54. Lloyd Schwartz, "Annals of Poetry: Elizabeth Bishop and Brazil," 86; Lorrie
Goldensohn, "Elizabeth Bishop: An Unpublished, Untitled Poem," 39.
55. "Unpublished, Untitled Poem," 40.

passengers' feelings. This poem frees us from the unhappy stasis of "Conversation"—and so the breaking storm with its electrical and emotional charge may very well be heaven sent—and that "unexpected kiss" is indeed terrestrial, human, and erotic.

Bishop remains interested in a pattern of entrapment and release even to the time of her last poem, "Sonnet," discussed earlier. "Rain Towards Morning" is a more tantalizingly specific poem, hinting further at possible personal meaning than does "Sonnet"; both poems, however, ultimately avoid any direct personal or autobiographical divulgence. Both show personal classicist tendencies, the earlier through reticent treatment of emotions and emphasis on imagery rather than direct statement; the later through embracing a general principle (release) without implying specific situational embodiments. Thus, the earlier poem is slightly more "personal," the later more "classicist."

"While Someone Telephones," the third of "Four Poems," takes us to another glimpse of a moment within a personal relationship. It has moved away from the serendipity in "Rain."

> Wasted, wasted minutes that couldn't be worse,
> minutes of a barbaric condescension.
> —Stare out the bathroom window at the fir-trees,
> at their dark needles, accretions to no purpose
> woodenly crystallized, and where two fireflies
> are only lost.
> Hear nothing but a train that goes by, must go by, like tension;
> *nothing*. And wait:
> maybe even now these minutes' host
> emerges, some relaxed uncondescending stranger,
> the heart's release.
> And while the fireflies
> are failing to illuminate these nightmare trees
> might they not be his green gay eyes.
>
> (*The Complete Poems*, 78)

Here, too, Bishop has included the kind of detailed imagery we might expect from her, in addition to the occasional abstraction. The fir trees seen through the bathroom window, for example, appear "woodenly crystallized"; they are "accretions to no purpose." Fireflies, recalling the lovely dancing lights of promise in "A Cold Spring," are here "only lost," and they "are failing to illuminate these nightmare trees." These images create a mood extending that of the more abstract language, "minutes of a barbaric condescension," or "a train that goes by . . . like tension." In the rhythmic shift of this poem sequence, "Telephones" moves us back into a static, unhappy moment, but the narrative context is still obscure.

Carolyn Handa reads the poem as an internal meditation conducted while the speaker has been kept waiting, her host talking to somebody else on the telephone. Handa explicates the fourteen-line poem as another sonnet, in which the tension built in the first eight lines is released in a sestet, where the host himself does return: "Now, however, this other person can cause her heart's release."[56] This seems to me a plausible enough reading except for a few important points. That sestet of release is uncertain, beginning "*maybe* even now [italics mine]." Moreover, the "other person" of whom Handa speaks is not introduced to us properly; he is an abstraction, really, host to "these minutes," and not properly the speaker's host, seeming to be more a construct of the speaker's own tension than a real person. And what about that bathroom window of line three? That seems to suggest the privacy of one's own home, rather than the place one would await one's host. The final image remains rather powerless; the fireflies "are failing to illuminate these nightmare trees" and the equation of them to "his green gay eyes" is no more certain than the earlier emerging of the host: "*might* they *not* be his green gay eyes [italics mine]."

All these enigmas show how a narrative situation is difficult to discern in this poem; mood and theme emerge more clearly. And the few revisions Bishop made from the time of initial publication to its collected form do not clarify the narrative obscurity but rather help solidify the shared texture among all four sections. In the *Partisan Review*, the eleventh line reads "a soul's release," not "the heart's release." The revision works to recall the "tumult of the heart" from "Conversation." In 1953, commenting on a certain "mysteriousness" in "The Shampoo," which Bishop had just sent her, May Swenson recalled "While Someone Telephones": "I remember a poem of yours about 'his green gay eyes' that seemed even more mysterious in the same kind of way. I felt the emotion or impression being expressed but couldn't seize an outline of what was behind it—what was engendering it." Later, when *A Cold Spring* was published, Swenson wrote

56. "The Poetry of Elizabeth Bishop," 145.

a long letter discussing the book, all of which she thought was "excellent" except for "Varick Street" and the "Four Poems."

> I don't understand the Four Poems, that is I get their *mood*, but I can only imagine what they're talking about—my imagination goes pretty wild and comes back with strange answers, none of which fit exactly. . . . I have to furnish them with "meanings" from my own experiences because you've left yours out (their labels)—you had to, I suppose, to get them said at all.[57]

"O Breath" is an interesting formal experiment with the line, which Bishop began as an attempt to reflect her asthma in the very rhythm of the lines.[58] It is, then, an attempt to achieve something similar to what the Black Mountain poets sought: the shape of the line defined by the writer's own rhythms of breathing. The caesura space within each line creates that effect. Yet the verse is not unrhymed, as is most poetry of the Black Mountain School, and the poem is not merely "about" the speaker's/poet's own breath. Unlike "Telephones" this poem specifically mentions "I," addresses a "you," and refers to a "we." It begins by describing "that loved and celebrated breast" of the other and suggesting a kind of wonder about how the interior life of the other (what "grieves, maybe lives and lets / live") is finally beyond real sharing and comprehension. "I cannot fathom even a ripple," the speaker says. Yet "what we have in common's bound to be there," she continues, and the poem closes in a triplet rhyme hoping for some kind of meaningful connection.[59]

I think it is clear that all these poems are "about" what is tentative and changing within relationships, and although each one individually is, as Handa says of "Telephones," "difficult and opaque for the most part,"[60] taken together they reinforce one another thematically. Their difficulty and opaqueness seem to be protective measures against their own subject matter. As lyric studies of mood, they are deeply rooted in the personal but they eschew the kind of details that would reveal an overtly autobiographical narrative. I am reminded of Gloria Bowles's suggestion that Bogan's self-censuring led at last to artistic silence, a self-defeat rather than artistic control. While Bishop certainly avoids such an extreme consequence for her

---

57. Swenson to Bishop, September 14, 1953, and August 24, 1955.
58. Handa, "The Poetry of Elizabeth Bishop," 146.
59. *Complete Poems*, 79.
60. "The Poetry of Elizabeth Bishop," 143.

career, and while the temporal texture and use of sound in all of these poems is quite lovely to read aloud, I think the work is damaged in this instance by her own obscuring of the personal element which lies behind these lyrics. Her obscurity is rather too great, and they are interesting experiments in personal classicism more than successful, lasting poetic achievements.

"The Shampoo," openly addressing the "you" as "dear friend," is as well a very private poem, but more easily understood. It is tender and wistful as it seems to try to stop what has been both "precipitate and pragmatical" in a relationship. What has been the paradoxical decision or action on the part of the you? Again the specific information is withheld, whereas it would be the primary basis in a confessional poem. Yet the fact of the personal situation is the very heart of Bishop's lyric. She focuses on an almost metaphysically symbolic texture of lichens and the heavens, both harbingers of time, and brings all this symbolism home as the shooting stars (gray hairs, perhaps?) seem to flock in the "dear friend's" black hair. The poem closes with a specially feminine intimacy, an invitation or command: "—Come, let me wash it [your hair] in this big tin basin, / battered and shiny like the moon."[61]

Again, the narrative details are left out and only the lyrical understatement of feeling is present. Yet about this poem, Swenson has a great deal of praise, coming to its defense after both *Poetry* and the *New Yorker* had rejected it. "I like it very much," she continues, "but can't really grasp it—that is, it feels like something has been left out—but this makes it better, in a way." Bishop replied that the poem "is very simple:—Lota has straight long black hair.—I hadn't seen her for six years or so when I came here and when we looked at each other she was horrified to see I had gone very gray, and I that she had two silver streaks on each side, quite wide."[62] "The Shampoo," as an example of Bishop's contribution to the mode of personal classicism, is quintessential: the poem's heart—its fundamental essence—is personal, lyric emotion, yet its manner of presentation does not emphasize the personal, but rather hushes it. Elizabeth Bishop, great cataloguer of the natural and physical world in the settings of her poems, is quite reticent with the details of story within her personal poems.

---

61. *Complete Poems*, 82.
62. Swenson to Bishop, September 14, 1953; Bishop to Swenson, September 19, 1953.

This reticence is even more pronounced in her later books; only two poems from *Geography 3* appear to touch upon her inward life with the intensity of those discussed above.

This same hushed emphasis informs a poem from *Questions of Travel*, a volume dedicated to Lota de Macedo Soares, Bishop's long-time lover in Brazil. The collection's epigraph is from a love sonnet by Luis de Camoes (1524[?]–1580). Bishop quotes only the final couplet; the lines do not form a syntactic whole, but rather follow a very important line from the preceding quatrain, "Porque é tamanha bem-aventurança." Together the three translate roughly, "Because it is such a bliss / To give you as much as I have and as much as I can / That the more I pay you, the more I owe you."[63] Of course, to dedicate a book to someone is in a sense to "give" it to her or him. This dedication draws its epigraph from a Portuguese love poem, yet omits all but the final couplet, so that even the fact that it is indeed a love sonnet is obscured. Even in her dedication, Bishop is simultaneously making and veiling a passionate gesture.

"One Art" is Bishop's one example of a villanelle, a form she admired and tried to work with for years.[64] It is widely considered a splendid achievement of the villanelle.

> The art of losing isn't hard to master;
> so many things seem filled with the intent
> to be lost that their loss is no disaster.
>
> Lose something every day. Accept the fluster
> of lost door keys, the hour badly spent.
> The art of losing isn't hard to master.
>
> Then practice losing farther, losing faster:
> places, and names, and where it was you meant
> to travel. None of these will bring disaster.
>
> I lost my mother's watch. And look! my last, or
> next-to-last, of three loved houses went.
> The art of losing isn't hard to master.
>
> I lost two cities, lovely ones. And, vaster,
> some realms I owned, two rivers, a continent.

63. I thank Professor Heitor Martins of Indiana University for translating this passage.

64. Letter to Swenson, November 4, 1955: "I've tried for years to do a villanelle, I like them so much."

I miss them, but it wasn't a disaster.

—Even losing you (the joking voice, a gesture
I love) I shan't have lied. It's evident
the art of losing's not too hard to master
though it may look like (*Write* it!) like disaster.
(*The Complete Poems,* 178)

Loss is its subject, but the poem begins almost trivially. The first line, casual and disarming, returns throughout the poem. The natural-sounding contraction helps to create the semblance of real speech even within this complex form, and the details and examples that follow immediately do not, indeed, seem like great losses. Door keys, a wasted hour, even forgotten names certainly do not warrant the term consistently invoked by the rhyme: "disaster." But the poem builds, until "cities" and "realms"—of great import to this geographically inclined poet implied by this and all her books—have been lost.

Not until the final quatrain, bringing the villanelle to the completion of its required form, does the real occasion of the poem appear. Here the loss is very personal, a person, "you."[65] Yet the details and attributes here too are muted. Only parenthetically does Bishop reveal the importance of the you: "(the joking voice, a gesture / I love)," yet love is evident through the speaker's difficulty in revealing herself. There is a slight change, too, in the refrain line: "the art of losing's not too hard to master," qualifying that original assertion that loss "isn't hard to master." And in the final line the speaker must even exhort herself to complete the rhyme—"(*Write* it!)—since disaster looms very large indeed. Yes, says the poem, this is a great loss, which I am still working to master. After the suicide of Macedo Soares, Bishop returned to the United States, and so the loss of lands and love compound one another.[66] At least in part, "One Art" is a

65. Thomas J. Travisano, in *Elizabeth Bishop: Her Artistic Development,* identifies the "you" as Lota de Macedo Soares throughout the poem (148–151); Brett Candlish Millier, however, in "Elusive Mastery: The Drafts of Elizabeth Bishop's 'One Art'" asserts that at the poem's end, the "you" refers to Alice Methfessel: "While [the poem's] method is the description of the accumulation of losses in the poet's life, its occasion and subject is the loss of Alice" (122). Lloyd Schwartz, in "Annals of Poetry: Elizabeth Bishop and Brazil," concurs with Millier (95).

66. In *Becoming a Poet,* Kalstone quotes a letter from Bishop to Robert Lowell in which she touches on these losses, and her sense of them in the context of a new possible loss—the emotional breakdown of a young woman with whom she began living after Macedo Soares's death. Her concern for the young woman is colored with past concerns: "I lost my mother, and Lota, and others, too—I'd like to try to save somebody, for a

deeply felt elegy, but Bishop uses both a strict and difficult form and a casual, conversational tone to hush the emotional intensity. In this fine poem, her attempt to mute serves also to heighten the poignancy.

"Five Flights Up" is another of these poems with a strong personal center that reveals itself only quietly—and in this case, parenthetically. Bishop withholds emotion until the last line, as in "One Art," and the preceding body of the poem seems casual, even humorous at times. The animals and the physical world receive all the detailed description, and seem to be the focus of attention. But really at stake in the poem are consciousness and existence. "Still dark," the poem begins. And in that darkness, in the sleeping states of the dog and perhaps the bird, we find inquiry:

> Questions—if that is what they are—
> answered directly, simply,
> by day itself.

The little narration of the dog's master who admonishes his pet and the dog's apparent lack of shame is told simply, with a hint of understated humor.

> He [the dog] bounces cheerfully up and down;
> he rushes in circles in the fallen leaves.

> Obviously, he has no sense of shame.
> (*The Complete Poems*, 181)

We see the dog's delightful, almost cartoonlike behavior, described in a line full of consonance, the liquid "r" and "l" and the sibilant "s" sounds hinting at the loveliness of the dog's innocent state.

The poem's speaker comments on the scene before her while "Enormous morning" unfolds, and the tone is—if not precisely light—cheerful, as if she is trying to convince herself of her own observations. "—Yesterday brought to today so lightly!" she exclaims, and only in the last line does the interior pain she has been fighting off break through: "(A yesterday I find almost impossible to lift.)" Her own life, obviously, is in sharp contrast to the simple scene she has watched and considered this morning; clearly for her, *not* "all is taken care of," and the attractively naive, uncomplicated existence of the animals is finally different from her own.

change," 232.

Yet the pain, even the bleakness of this situation does not dominate the poem; Bishop does not allow her speaker, nor her poem, to wallow in misery. Again, as is so often the case in her work, the disclosure of an emotional crux, even a crisis, appears only at the poem's end. Moreover, Bishop uses the white space of the page to help formally extend her quietness. She makes her simple admission of pain, and then stops altogether, not even allowing herself the small drama of saying, "I will not speak further of this," nor the comfort of changing the subject—she just stops talking.

Often in her work, Bishop, like Moore, allows animals to suggest human characteristics. Perhaps the clearest example is her prose poem series, "Rainy Season; Sub-Tropics" in which the speakers are "Giant Toad," "Strayed Crab," and "Giant Snail." Each animal presents a kind of extended metaphor for human behavior and emotion, and in their monologues they offer nuggets of wisdom or belief, such as Strayed Crab's "I believe in the oblique, the indirect approach, and I keep my feelings to myself." Yet in "Five Flights Up," the animals contrast with human life; however the speaker might long for the philosophical comfort of a simple life in which daily existence is essence, and is sufficient, she cannot share it.

Instead, she lives an examined life, not one merely experienced, and must carry the burden of her own past. Since the poem specifically makes a point of the dog's lack of shame, we might reasonably assume that part of the past's weight is indeed shame. The specific nature of that shame would be the basis for a more confessional poem; here it is merely the fact of the shame's existence that matters. At any rate, it is a very heavy burden, perhaps on the same scale as that in "One Art"; it is not, however, utterly beyond the speaker's capacity to cope. She says "almost impossible." Here, as throughout Bishop's poems, the speaker does not present herself as being helpless in the face of her own life. Instead, she remains in emotional control, a recurrent goal among the speakers we find in poems of personal classicism. What Jarrell said of Bishop's first book remains true: "Instead of crying, with justice, 'This is a world in which no one can get along,' Miss Bishop's poems show that it is barely but perfectly possible—has been, that is, for her."[67]

Before closing, I want to return to the unpublished manuscript Lorrie Goldensohn discusses. Found among some of Bishop's papers

67. "On *North & South*," 181.

in Brazil, the poem is undated, but Goldensohn speculates, due to its position among drafts of poems from the Florida years, that it was written in the 1940s previous to Bishop's 1951 voyage to Rio. I reproduce the poem as it appears in the *American Poetry Review* article.

> It is marvellous to wake up together
> At the same minute; marvellous to hear
> The rain begin suddenly all over the roof,
> To feel the air clear
> As if electricity had passed through it
> From a black mesh of wires in the sky.
> All over the roof the rain hisses,
> And below, the light falling of kisses.
>
> An electrical storm is coming or moving away;
> It is the prickling air that wakes us up.
> If lightning struck the house now, it would run
> From the four blue china balls on top
> Down the roof and down the rods all around us,
> And we imagine dreamily
> How the whole house caught in a bird-cage of lightning
> Would be quite delightful rather than frightening.
>
> And from the simplified point of view
> Of night and lying flat on one's back
> All things might change equally easily,
> Since always to warn us there must be these black
> Electrical wires dangling. Without surprise
> The world might change to something quite different,
> As the air changes or the lightning comes without our blinking,
> Change as our kisses are changing without our thinking.

This is not confessional poetry in the sense of poetry that tells something terrible or reprehensible or really even shameful about the "speaker," supposed to be the author. Nor does it abuse confidences, combining fact with fiction so as to "get lies believed about people," Bishop's complaint about Lowell's *The Dolphin*. But it does present a sexual situation with a precision, while hardly graphic, that Bishop does not exercise in her published work. Goldensohn sums up the matter quite well.

> Bishop did not publish or title "It is marvellous to wake up together" because it seems clear that the meaning of the poem lay too close to

the bone for public exposure. This poem has a cargo of explicitly sexual feelings. . . . With the consistent reticence of a lifetime behind her, Bishop seems to have felt that the subjects and objects of her sexual pleasure were no one's business but her own.[68]

Bishop herself had some firm opinions about the effect of explicit physicality in poetry. As she explained in a letter:

It's a problem of placement, choice of word, abruptness or accuracy of the image—and does it help or detract? If it sticks out of the poem so that all the reader is going to remember is: "That Miss Swenson is always talking about phalluses"—or is it phalli—you have spoiled your effect, obviously, and given the Freudian-minded contemporary reader just a slight thrill of detection rather than an aesthetic experience.[69]

I think that this poem is not as strong as much of her published work; the tone is less fully developed than that in many of her poems, and the feminine rhymes in the couplets of the second and third stanzas especially seem to be unintentionally humorous. For comparison, we might remember the wonderful couplet in "Cootchie": "I saw him walking with Varella / and hit him twice with my umbrella." There the poem does poke gentle fun at its own speaker, and does so quite consciously.

Goldensohn mentions that the typescript is clean, "without deletions or additions, and conspicuously unadorned with any of those boxed or questioned alternative words or phrases with which the writer usually indicates unfinished work."[70] Goldensohn seems to imply that because the draft is not marked up like most unfinished poems, Bishop must have considered it finished. But it is also logical to assume that Bishop not only did not choose to title or publish the poem; she decided not to finish it, not to bring it to the level of her own high standards. Instead, it would seem, she used some of the same imagery and themes—the changing world and the changing of relationships—in the much more obscure "Four Poems." She chose not to pursue a much more divulgently erotic poem, and instead focused some of that draft's images and energies into much more private and obscure examples of personal classicism.

68. Goldensohn, "Unpublished, Untitled Poem," 40.
69. Letter to Swenson, July 3, 1958.
70. Goldensohn, "Unpublished, Untitled Poem," 35.

Other poems that have recently surfaced also show less personal, sexual reticence, as does the draft of "It is marvellous to wake up together." Lloyd Schwartz has located two unpublished love poems which are more openly physical in their language, and more warmly embracing of passion than is her published work. As Schwartz says, we find here "quite the opposite of the distance and disconnection between lovers in most of Bishop's pre-Brazilian love poems." Both poems involve lovers in bed, finding knowledge of one another, and the language is playful but clear: in the final stanza of one, the lovers retire to bed in the cold, but not to simply "keep warm." It is fascinating to read this side of Bishop, sounding like herself—Schwartz says it is the "unmistakable voice of Elizabeth Bishop"—but like more than herself, too. And yet, although she finished these poems, illuminating one with watercolor illustrations and giving the other as an engraving to a friend for a wedding gift, she did not publish them. Their role was clearly personal and private, and they were not to be shared with a national (or international) readership during Bishop's lifetime.[71]

Bishop remarked about her own propensity for reticence in a letter to May Swenson. Here she seems to be echoing Eliot when he spoke of "thinking through feeling," and she emphasizes the personal classicist belief in the inescapable quality of the personal— what one has control over is the way one sounds, one's tone. And although her manner does not approach manifesto, her words sound as if they could have been spoken by any of the writers I call personal classicist.

> I am puzzled by what you mean by my poems not appealing to the emotions. . . . What poetry does, or doesn't? . . . And poetry is a way of thinking with one's feelings, anyway. But maybe that's not what you mean by 'emotion.' I think myself that my best poems seem rather distant, and sometimes I wish I could be as objective about everything else as I seem to be about them. I don't think I'm very successful when I get personal,—rather, sound personal—one always is personal, of course, one way or another.[72]

---

71. "Annals of Poetry: Elizabeth Bishop and Brazil," 90, 86.
72. Letter to Swenson, September 6, 1955.

# 5

# Louise Glück

## The Ardent Understatement of Postconfessional Classicism

We have seen three different manifestations of the personal classicist mode undertaken by three very different women. H. D. worked to develop the persona poem as a means to present a palimpsest of personal and mythic experience, and to embed autobiography within a timeless continuum of countless women's experiences. Even while declaring certain subjects taboo for women artists, Louise Bogan tried to perfect the lyric as a modernist form for women, a possibility for understated personal expression in a time when the high moderns often moved toward longer, disjunctive narratives and a greater reliance on irony. Elizabeth Bishop continued to enhance the possibilities for a tone emphasizing the emotional importance of personal details that are themselves muted or even omitted.

The mature work of the contemporary poet Louise Glück represents a kind of postconfessional personal classicism—one in which the voice of the self is muted by an amplified sense of the mythic, the archetypal (somewhat like H. D.), without losing the compelling presence of an individual, contemporary "I," a personal voice addressing the reader. She continues the search for personal expression in a poetry that nonetheless relies on silence and omission and eschews extreme statement or merely private disclosure. In this respect she is more like Bogan than any of the others treated so far, yet she extends beyond Bogan's achievement in bringing women's poetry into a new kind of feminist awareness; one editor, Carol Rumens, has termed Glück a "post-feminist" writer. She explains, "'Post-feminist' expresses a psychological, rather than political, condition, though its roots are no doubt political. It implies a mental freedom which a few outstanding women in any age have achieved, and which many more, with increasing confidence, are claiming today." Classification according to Elaine Showalter's historical examination would tend to support such a view. Showalter sees a "female" phase of literature following a "feminist" one; in the "female" literature that has emerged throughout the twentieth century, writers "turn . . . to female experience as the source of an autonomous art, extending the feminist analysis of culture to the forms and techniques of literature."[1]

While such statements seem to imply that feminist intent is no longer applicable to many contemporary writers, and that the sexist forces that have shaped and even distorted women's work in the past have ceased to function, Glück must be understood as a transitional poet. She moves, with many of her contemporaries, further along the path toward psychic freedom and—yes—equality. But as Rumens cautions, "The term [post-feminist] is certainly not meant to suggest that utopia has arrived, and that all is now milk and honey for the once-oppressed."[2] Instead, transitional writers such as Glück continue to turn with the "increasing confidence" Rumens mentions to an inner reliance in their pursuit of formal exploration. Glück has developed the poem sequence as a means for extended expression built upon reticence, and she has introduced a startling (and apt) metaphor for women artists of the late twentieth century, likening her poetic attitude—what I call personal classicism—to anorexia nervosa. Because her work is less widely known than that of her predecessors, and because few autobiographical details are available for public scrutiny, my examination of her contribution will rely more upon close readings of the poetry itself than upon biographical background.

I add the modification "postconfessional" to distinguish Glück's particular contribution to the mode of personal classicism because, unlike the other authors in this study, she first began to write during the heyday of confessional poetry, and her earliest influences most clearly included the well-known confessional poets of the time. Her movement into personal classicism was therefore a deliberate choice to abandon the dominant mode, unlike the eschewal of explicit detail practiced continually by her predecessors. In this, Glück's

1. Carol Rumens, "Introduction," *Making for the Open*, xvi; Elaine Showalter, "Toward a Feminist Poetics," in *The New Feminist Criticism*, ed. Elaine Showalter, 139.
    2. "Introduction," xv.

shift was similar to Louise Bogan's; Bogan also began her career writing her most nearly confessional—certainly her most personal—poems and then chose to become more modernist and more reticent. To fully comprehend the ardent understatement of Glück's mature work, we must first understand in greater depth her debt to the elements that have contributed to the movement literary historians continue to identify as confessional poetry.

Admittedly, the term "confessional" is itself controversial, and many critics, including M. L. Rosenthal—who first introduced the term in his 1959 review of Robert Lowell's *Life Studies*—express their uneasiness about the precision and usefulness of such a label. This study is not the place to launch another extensive definition of "confessional poetry." Yet the importance of agitated, relentless imagery and language—including the rhythms of syntax itself—among the work of the confessional poets is certainly vital to the texture of Glück's early work, and it is her deliberate discontinuation of those angry rhythms that ushers in her postconfessional stage.

Of course, the age of confessional poetry has not drawn fully to a close. The presence of a long-running debate over terminology, form, intent—damaging or not—and the presence of the poetry itself continue to help shape the work of contemporary writers. One need only open practically any literary magazine to find these confessions. In general, though, much contemporary confessional poetry doesn't make the kind of connection between the personal and the social, exploring the personally lurid or hidden in order to bring the hypocrisy of the social order under indictment, as many critics have claimed the first confessionals wanted. Many poems today divulge pathetic, graphic details in slack, post-deep-image diction, as if confession alone—"facts" alone—made poetry.

And although arguably the first confessional poets were males—W. D. Snodgrass and Lowell—the specter of a confessional school is largely a feminine haunt due to the immense popularity of Anne Sexton and, most especially, Sylvia Plath. Throughout the 1970s, critical as well as popular interest swelled around Plath as a feminist/confessional martyr; her suicide in 1963 sensationalized the discussion of her writing, even to the point of psychoanalysis of Plath's "problem," in studies like David Holbrook's *Sylvia Plath: Poetry and Existence*. Graduate students focused dissertations on her poems while the general public bought her novel, *The Bell Jar*. The novel was the subject of a television movie and a lawsuit. Such popularity saw to it that for some years the anthologies showcased confessional poets as women, and correspondingly, they showed confessional women poets to be among the most noticeable of contemporary women poets.

Alan Williamson has pointed out that "the very success of 'confessional' modes posed a threat to younger poets."[3] I would further suggest that the threat was greater for women since they had relatively fewer visible alternatives to function as models. "Threat," as Williamson uses it, entails not personal danger from the risks of "murderous art," as Charles Newman and A. Alvarez suggest, but rather a greater probability that the poet will work within almost preordained limits to the poetic modes and styles available to her. With so few female precursors as role models, it remains all the more difficult for a writer to learn from her influences and then move beyond them; she may very likely remain imitative rather than original. Thus we find the first book of Louise Glück, a very talented young writer, mired in imitation of the confessional mode; although technically accomplished, it remains work in apprenticeship to the popular style. Indeed, upon the publication of *Firstborn* (1968), most critics immediately commented on Glück's affinities with the confessional poets; reviewers saw traces in her work of Lowell, Snodgrass, Plath, and Sexton. These influences are apparent everywhere in her first collection of poems.

Something in her sensibility throughout the collection recalls Snodgrass's pronouncement from "To a Child": "Without love we die; / With love we kill each other." The speakers in *Firstborn* seem all to be dying for love and yet simultaneously to be trapped in stifling relationships that are killing something in the spirit. The speaker in "The Lady in the Single," for example, is caught in a death-in-life existence, unable to overcome the sense of absence following the loss of her sailor-lover. Although she tries to think she has left behind the "memory,"

> . . . his ghost
> Took shape in smoke above the pan roast.
> Five years. In tenebris the catapulted heart drones
> Like Andromeda. No one telephones.
>                                    (*Firstborn*, 25)

---

3. Alan Williamson, *Introspection and Contemporary Poetry*, 149.

Repeatedly, the speakers make clear that romantic and familial relationships are destructive; unlike Snodgrass or Plath, however, Glück
includes no character for whose sake she attempts to find redemp-
tion. There is no daughter, no needle-in-the-heart who must believe
that love is "possible," (Snodgrass), nor any son who is "the one /
solid the spaces lean on, envious" (Plath).[4] Indeed, much of the book
centers on an abortion, while several poems in which children do
appear show the speaker not to be the parent, but rather a slightly
removed relative ("My Cousin in April") or merely a kind stranger
entering the child's life only briefly ("Returning a Lost Child"). The
poems are more consistently stoical, more bleakly existential, than
those of either Snodgrass or Plath, despite similarities of subject and
theme. This stoicism is the seed of Glück's postconfessional classicist mode.

Like Plath and Sexton, she writes with angry bitterness about
female sexual or romantic experience in a world where women remain primarily powerless. Poems like "The Egg," "Hesitate to Call,"
and "The Wound," center around the event of an abortion in which
the woman is not an active figure, exercising her right to choose and
to take control of her life, but rather is one who is acted upon by
others, such as a lover or a doctor. As in Plath's work, Glück's poems
rely on an inventive, even pyrotechnical implementation of metaphor, frequently evoking landscapes that are in fact mindscapes.
Also like Plath, Glück sometimes allows this inward-gazing use of
metaphor—this melding of tenor and vehicle—to get out of control
and become an impediment to the poetry, something merely clever
or exclusively private. For example, lines from "The Egg," in *Firstborn*, one of these poems about unwanted pregnancy and abortion,
seem forced elements only of the suffering but ingenious will: "A
week's meat / Spoiled, peas / Giggled in their pods."

The formal technique employed throughout *Firstborn* is akin to
that of Lowell. In the words of Williamson, Glück uses Lowell's "tense
iambics and emphatic rhymes; his apostrophes and choked sentence
fragments." Glück herself refers to the book's "bullet-like phrases,
the non-sentences."[5] This kind of intense, relentless syntax is typical of confessional poetry. But it is not merely the sentence structure

---

4. Snodgrass, *Selected Poems*, 67; Plath, "Nick and the Candlestick," *Collected
Poems*, 242.
5. *Introspection*, 151; Glück, "Descending Figure: An Interview," 118.

that is bulletlike; there are the syncopated line breaks, where en-jambment is disjunction; the uneasy use of rhyme; even the breaking of words in the middle, to suggest the mockery or choppy dissolution of harmony. In the false pastoral scene of "Early December in Croton-on-Hudson," the landscape prepares for what must be a terrible, inescapable sexual attraction voiced in the last line:

> Spiked sun. The Hudson's
> Whittled down by ice.
> I hear the bone dice
> Of blown gravel clicking. Bone-
> pale, the recent snow
> Fastens like fur to the river.
> Standstill. We were leaving to deliver
> Christmas presents when the tire blew
> Last year. Above the dead valves pines pared
> Down by a storm stood, limbs bared . . .
> I want you.
>
> (*Firstborn*, 13)

The attention to craft that many reviewers noted is evident throughout the book's many variations on fixed forms: there are, for example, half a dozen near-sonnets, poems using four-line ballad stanzas, even rhyming couplets. Glück uses these forms the way she does enjambment and rhyme in general: to emphasize disjunction and dis-ease. Just as she often selects slant rhyme to produce a more unsettling feeling in her poems than that which true rhyme gener-ally suggests, Glück alters the elegant stability of the sonnet to suit her vision of life either threatened or already out of balance.

The most formally traditional of these near-sonnets is "My Neigh-bor in the Mirror." It is shrewdly appropriate to use this form to pre-sent the subject, an affected academic, whom she calls "M. *le pro-fesseur* in prominent senility." Most of the lines have five stresses and the rhyme scheme is roughly Shakespearean—the piece is certainly recognizable as a sonnet. Yet a Shakespearean sonnet's form tradi-tionally poses a problem and then reaches, perhaps after some slight musing, a resolution. Even Bishop, in her variations of the form, maintains that basic pattern of meaning. But such implications have nothing to do with Glück's task in this poem. Instead, the "prob-lem," an encounter on the apartment building stairway during which the neighbor ridiculously preens before a mirror, is simply followed by what-happens-next information that is simultaneously banal and, therefore, pathetic. This conclusion is not confined to the final couplet, but rather to the last three lines: "At any rate, lately there's been some / Change in his schedule. He receives without zeal / Now, and judging by his refuse, eats little but oatmeal."

The couplet itself rhymes with a dying fall, linking stressed "zeal" (what is lacking in the senile man's present existence) with the unstressed syllable in "oatmeal." Thus, Glück's poem suggests that there is no solution, no resolution; there are only pathetic consequences. Indeed, that suggestion pervades the entire book as she moves from one static or degraded situation to another.

Glück's use of clever metrics rivals that of Plath or Lowell and reveals a clear difference between her work and that of Sexton, whose use of traditional form and rhyme is much less sophisticated, much less thoughtful. In other near-sonnets, the stanzaic shape is not so recognizably precise, and the number of lines may be thirteen or fifteen; however, the general movement and sense of timing is like that in "My Neighbor in the Mirror." The poems' endings, although not always confined to the final couplet, arrive with swift viciousness.

Glück also reveals her debt to confessional poetry in the collection's persona poems. The persona poem has been a literary tool in personal classicism throughout the century, as I have shown, since it can allow a writer to unite personal, autobiographical material—tales of the self— with a mythological, allusive mask—tales of an other—and to finally seek shelter behind that mask. Yet persona poetry has played an important role in the work of the confessionals, as well. Its precise importance seems to vary from poet to poet—or from critic to critic, according to what particular definition each one ascribes to confessional work.

For those who maintain that confessional poetry must eventually transcend the solely personal in favor of the public, the persona poem's role is in the actual collection of poems, the book: through careful placement of persona poems among more personal ones, the poet builds a bridge out of the confines of the self and into the wider historical or sociological realm. A. R. Jones is representative of this attitude in his discussion of Lowell: "His most characteristic and successful effects have been achieved by his use of an escalating imagery that moves with easy assurance from personal experience into public and metaphysical meaning." Not only imagery, but entire poems, such as Lowell's "The Banker's Daughter" or "A Mad Negro Soldier Confined at Munich" effect this movement into "public and metaphysical meaning." Indeed, the whole arrangement of *Life Studies*, with Lowell's insistence upon history, reinforces such an appraisal. For the critic who sees confessional poetry as extremist, a term A. Alvarez favors, the persona poem may be a way to shock the reader, a kind of ultimate metaphor that implies something of psychosis, a splitting of the self. To probe into the thoughts—or pain—of the persona becomes another way to pursue disaster for the sake of new experience, another way to achieve what Alvarez called at one time "a murderous art."[6]

In each of these cases, it would seem that what distinguishes the persona poem by the confessional artist from that by any other writer is not primarily an attribute of the poem itself but rather the fact that the writer also composed "real" confessional poems. Critics therefore see whatever thematic connections exist among the poems of both genres, and emphasize that thematic heart as the confessional interest. Robert Phillips includes among his characteristics of confessional poetry, "It is therapeutic and/or purgative,"[7] and he might also have sought to establish a unity among a confessional writer's "autobiographic" and persona poems with this postulate.

But other critics and writers would probably discount such an intentional fallacy as a poor way to approach the confessional mode—the point of real art is not to provide an alternative to analysis or medication, although in meeting their own drives to create, to make, artists may, consequently, experience catharsis or purgation. Perhaps one of the best formulations is Williamson's description of the way "a subtle tissue of implicit psychological preoccupations links the impersonal poems to the personal ones, and helps give the impersonal ones a delicate complexity of feeling we have missed in some of the ontological lyrics that try to leave the specific self too completely behind."[8] Williamson emphasizes the continued interest in the personal, or interior, even while framing that interest amid the impersonal, or social—this is the heart of Glück's postconfessional personal classicism. What links the persona poems with the others in *Firstborn* is certainly theme but also tone. Like Plath's "Lady Lazarus,"

6. "Necessity and Freedom: The Poetry of Robert Lowell, Sylvia Plath, and Anne Sexton," 18; "Sylvia Plath," in *The Art of Sylvia Plath*, ed. Charles Newman, 67.
7. *The Confessional Poets*, 16.
8. *Introspection*, 154.

the speakers are almost out of control, full of wild energy or anger. They do not participate in the understatement and calm tone of the later work any more than the early autobiographical poems do.

The book's second section, titled "The Edge," contains most of the clearly identifiable persona poems in the collection. These speakers range from a race car driver's widow to a photojournalist of the Vietnam War; yet the diversity is introduced slowly, beginning with the section's title poem. This speaker is not very different from those in most poems throughout the book: she is a woman trapped in a destructive relationship with a man. A dramatic monologue, "The Edge" is full of imagery from other poems in the collection. Domestic yet discomforting, the setting includes bed, table, and house with all the attributes of success: lace table linens, roasts, bouquets. Yet the speaker remains "crippled," her life a "waste." What sets her apart from the speaker in poems of section one, "The Egg," and section three, "Cottonmouth Country," is that she is married; the destructiveness of her relationship with a man is now trapped in the ostensible tranquility of marriage. Glück chose this poem to open the section, seeming to imply quietly that all the speakers to follow, and their various troubles, are not really too different from those of anyone else. Thus Glück advances the personal themes found elsewhere from a slightly different perspective.

"My Life Before Dawn" is a striking example of a radically different perspective: the male narrator discusses the manner in which he jilted his lover, saying, ". . . I told her Sorry baby you have had / Your share. (I found her stain had dried into my hair.)" Yet he remains haunted by her memory, and at the poem's close she appears in his nightmares with all the vindictive power of Plath's "Lady Lazarus." In the man's terrifying dreams, he has not been able to so easily cast her off.

One critic, attempting to argue a strictly confessional reading of the entire book, and likening Glück throughout to Sexton, sees in this poem a strange struggle between a female narrator and her mother, "a vampire risen from her childhood."[9] Yet this reading of the poem is insupportable, since the speaker begins

Sometimes at night I think of how we did
It, me nailed in her like steel, her

---

9. "Women in Transition: The Poetry of Anne Sexton and Louise Glück," 136.

Over-eager on the striped contour
Sheet (I later burned it) . . .
                    (*Firstborn*, 24)

The opening obviously suggests violent sex, not childbirth. Certainly it demonstrates the danger in labeling a poet "confessional" and then attempting to apply to her work the rules Robert Phillips sets forth in his book-length study, the first of which is that "the emotions [confessional poets] portray are always true to their own feelings."[10] Such critics miss the point.

Glück portrays emotions that are *not* her own in order to *imply* the ones with which she sympathizes. Clearly, the male speaker is a voice representative of a type: men who use women. There is nothing about the poem that suggests what we usually consider to be confession in poetry. Even though the male speaker is, in fact, "confessing" his own macho boorishness and demonstrating that he cannot escape the result of his own actions, only a careless or contorted reading could lead one to assume that the poet identifies herself with the speaker. This poem lacks the insistent sense of witnessing, sharing, speaking from the central recesses of the self—what some critics call sincerity—that we find in some of her poems, such as "Easter Season." It is, instead, a cunning—if not always well done—variation on the book's primary subject matter.

"My Life Before Dawn" employs the same compositional techniques as the other poems in *Firstborn*, however, and its tone reinforces its unity within the collection. In this poem we hear the same jerking, spiky enjambments, the same violent images that appear in the more autobiographical personal pieces. It is a kind of companion piece for "Hesitate to Call," one of the first section's abortion poems, in which the poem's speaker is addressing a former lover who has left her pregnant. The title forms a bitter circular sentence with the final line, "Love, you ever want me, don't"—playing off the phrase, "don't hesitate to call."

Both these poems—like all the poems in *Firstborn*—speak abruptly, both in their actual sentences and their use of the line. They are nearly all joyless, comfortless. They speak of the body and sex in terms of use, violence, and decay—without renewal— while syntax, diction, and lineation combine not merely to speak of pain, but to create its rhythms.

The great difference between *Firstborn* and Glück's later books

10. *Confessional Poets*, 1.

lies largely in the tone Glück creates as she develops into a personal classicist. In his 1981 review of Glück's third book, *Descending Figure,* Calvin Bedient touched on this important change: "Glück's importance lies more and more in her stringency, which is an earnest of her truthfulness and courage. . . . What has grown upon her, insidiously and strengtheningly, is an 'infamous calm.' " Yet this "infamous calm" actually began some years earlier with Glück's second collection, *The House on Marshland* (1975), a body of work that is simultaneously a break from her earliest style and a continuation of the same themes. As Helen Vendler wrote of the second collection, "Now, though a violent perception has not ceased, violent language has." Three years later, Vendler expanded her description of Glück's tone, pointing out that the new poems' tone "owes nothing to Plath; it is not Lawrentian or clinical (Plath's two extremes.)"[11] Glück is clearly leaving behind her early debt to the language of the confessionals.

The new tone is subtle and ubiquitous; the calmness emphasizes tone as a way to embody stoicism and endurance, not suffering and victimization. It frequently employs understatement rather than the exaggerated metaphoric comparisons of Plath's confessional poetry or the angry insistence on lived detail of Adrienne Rich's. While some very personal autobiographical/narrative detail is important, each poem's strength seems built out of how very little detail is really allowed and how quietly the information is conveyed. Her understatement seems different from the kind of careful encoding earlier women writers relied upon. Glück does not appear interested in telling a carefully "slanted" truth; rather, she concentrates on bearing a quiet, though straightforward and honest, witness to the world—and to the world of selfhood. It is this ardent understatement in Louise Glück's mature poetry that constitutes her major contribution to the mode of personal classicism.

In a 1981 interview, Glück discussed these issues, revealing how she attempted to change the "mood" of her poetry.

> When I finished the poems in [*Firstborn*], it was clear to me that the thing I could not continue to do was make sentences like that. The earliest poems in *The House on Marshland* were responses to a dictum I made myself, to write poems that were, whenever possible, sin-

11. Calvin Bedient, "Birth, Not Death, Is the Hard Loss," 168; Helen Vendler, review, *New York Times Book Review,* 37; Vendler, "The Poetry of Louise Glück," 34.

gle sentences. I tried to force myself into latinate suspensions, into clauses. What it turned out to do was open up kinds of subject matter that I had not had access to.[12]

Her remarks reveal assumptions that fiction writers as well as poets have held for years: syntax creates a personality in the work, a distinctive mood or atmosphere. Thus Glück is focusing on an element even deeper in composition than the line—although the line is usually considered the primary unit of poetry—to effect real change in her work. She continues to explain that she wanted an effect in which "the sentences won't snap down like that, hard upon each other. The atmosphere of deadendedness will go."[13]

Yet she also suggests a slight variation on the familiar wisdom offered by Charles Olson and Robert Creely—that form is only the extension of content. In changing her voice, her tone, Glück could "open up kinds of subject matter that [she] had not had access to." Here the relationship is reversed in the process of composition, so that content does not merely demand its proper outward expression, but modes of expression can even suggest new possibilities of subject matter. There is not a great distinction between "form" and "mood" in this context; in many of Glück's poems, the "mood" is in fact the poem's subject, much the way the Objectivists and others see a poem's embodiment of material as its real subject. In the era of nonliterary analogues to form like the letter, the conversation, the dream, such as Jonathan Holden has suggested, choices in tone or mood can replace those of stanzaic form.[14] While the choice between, for example, sonnet and sestina once established nuances of meaning about the world, such nuances are predominately established in contemporary poetry by other means.

What new subject matter was opened up by changes in syntax? Glück does not say, but I suggest it is the presence of the mythic, the archetypal, the legendary in our lives. It is once again a way to use the personal as a means to explore beyond the lonely, quotidian existence of the self; the personal is somewhat subordinated to the overarching world of myth. She shares this desire with many poets— H. D., of course, but there are also countless writers who are neither personal classicists nor confessional poets, yet who appeal to myth in

12. "Descending Figure: An Interview," 118.
13. Ibid.
14. Ibid. See *Style and Authenticity in Postmodern Poetry*, chapter 1.

their writing. A difference in Glück's later work is that even while the personal is placed within the mythic, the tone of the poem and the structure of the book suggest that the personal remains the point of the poetry, its heart or center, rather than simply providing a means to achieve the more imposing and important mythic. As I have shown, the same impulse remains true to some extent in H. D.'s work as well; her poems "about" mythic characters still focus privately on her. But Glück goes to less elaborate means to mask her own experience behind recognizable mythic characters, though the two share a common interest.

In the opening poem of *Marshland*, "All Hallows," pacing, details, and vocabulary all bespeak something ancient, as out of Old World folktale.

Even now this landscape is assembling.
The hills darken. The oxen
sleep in their blue yoke,
the fields having been
picked clean, the sheaves
bound evenly and piled at the roadside
among cinquefoil, as the toothed moon rises:

This is the barrenness
of harvest or pestilence.
And the wife leaning out the window
with her hand extended, as in payment,
and the seeds
distinct, gold, calling
*Come here*
*Come here, little one*

And the soul creeps out of the tree.
(*House on Marshland*, 3)

This poem embodies precisely what Robert Bly talks about in his discussion of the image as *arm*, or that through which the non-human universe enters the human by way of an image. It is also indicative of what he calls the metaphor of "forgotten relationships": "Ancient man stood in the center of a wheel of relations coming to the human being from objects. The Middle Ages were aware of a relationship between a woman's body and a tree, and Jung reproduces in one of his books an old plate showing a woman taking a

baby from a tree trunk." Indeed, Glück seems to have learned something from the deep imagist poets like Bly and James Wright which
shows in her introduction of the mythic into her work.[15] Deep imagery allows preservation of the personal quality, the personal voice,
even where the rational self disappears in a moment of psychic or
mythic revelation. Glück has a similar goal for her work as she moves
away from confessionalism and toward personal classicism.

In a grossly reductive sense, there is little difference between the
subject of "All Hallows"—the creation of children—and that of the
domestic, familial poems in *Firstborn*. But such an equation would
belie the poem's actual achievement. In Anna Wooten's words, "The
topical matter of the two volumes is similar; the treatment is not."[16]
"All Hallows" is explorative and, if not exactly celebratory, at least
full of awe. The destructive anger throughout *Firstborn* made both
these qualities impossible; instead, the volume remained mostly
assertive, declarative.

In the 1981 interview, Glück says, "My tendency—as is obvious—
is to very promptly build mythic structures, to see the resemblance of
the present moment to the archetypal configuration. So that almost
immediately the archetypal configuration is superimposed."[17] Although I do not mean to imply that Glück consciously took the earlier personal classicist as an influence—Glück herself never has suggested such a connection—her description of her own method sounds
very like what we have seen in H. D.'s work. One subtle difference,
however, is that, for Glück, the "almost immediate" superimposition
of the archetypal takes place within the poem itself, whereas within
H. D.'s shorter poems, the connection seems more often to take
place earlier, within the writer's earliest conceptions of the poem—
even before the writing begins—and so the superimposition appears
in the poem as a *substitution* of the archetypal for the present moment.
The process Glück describes may be applied more accurately to H. D.'s
longer poems than to those under discussion in chapter 1.

Glück's tendency is, in fact, not "obvious," perhaps not even real-
ized, until the poems in the second book. Before *Marshland*, Glück
did not really achieve what her teacher Stanley Kunitz maintains is
his own goal in poetry: "to use the life in order to transcend it, to

15. Robert Bly, "What the Image Can Do," in *Claims for Poetry*, ed. Donald Hall,
42; Williamson implies this possibility, too, 151.
16. "Louise Glück's *The House On Marshland*," 5.
17. "An Interview," 123.

convert it into legend." Her achievement, beginning with *Marsh-land,* is the "fusion" of both the "personal and mythical," thereby "rescuing the poems from either narrow self-glorification or pedantic myopia."[18]

Some critics—perhaps most notably Judith Kroll—argue that Sylvia Plath's goal is actually to transcend her own biography, to create an entire legend or mythology of her own self.[19] This is indeed one way to approach her poems, and one that would seem to equate Glück's aim with that of Plath, but it is a critical stance concerned only with imagery and symbolism, not with tone. As most readers of Plath will surely concede, one of the most striking aspects of her most well-known poems is their development of a tone that is extreme—almost out of control—in its mood. It is as if in order to transcend, Plath feels she must create a runaway roller-coaster of language that will finally hurl the self to a larger plane of existence. Nothing could be further from a personal classicist approach. Glück's shift to postconfessional classicism is initially a way to leave behind the extremist sound of her earlier poetry.

A poem from the second half of *Marshland* is a fine example of the way Glück fuses the personal with the legendary in pursuit of a thematic goal similar to that of Plath but using the postconfessional language of ardent understatement. "The Letters" focuses upon the ending of a romance between a man and a woman, full of symbolic imagery (the time of year is almost autumn) but in a voice that is not that of Everywoman but of a single, profoundly personal individual.

> It is night for the last time.
> For the last time your hands
> gather on my body.
>
> Tomorrow it will be autumn.
> We will sit together on the balcony
> watching the dry leaves drift over the village
> like the letters we will burn,
> one by one, in our separate houses.
>
> Such a quiet night.
> Only your voice murmuring
> *You're wet, you want to*

18. *Next to Last Things,* 89; Wooten, "Louise Glück," 5.
19. See, for example, *Chapters in a Mythology.*

and the child
sleeps as though he were not born.

In the morning it will be autumn.
We will walk together in the small garden
among stone benches and the shrubs
still sheeted in mist
like furniture left for a long time.

Look how the leaves drift in the darkness.
We have burned away
all that was written on them.
                    (*House on Marshland*, 40)

The stately pronouncements of the first lines suggest an utter finality
that is reinforced by the coming of autumn and by the comparison of
the way "the child" sleeps—he is given no proper name, not even the
identification "our" or "my" son—to a state of nonbeing, not even
born. Yet the world is not merely defined by primeval portents: the
familiar shapes in the yard appear in language firmly of the present
age, "like furniture left for a long time."

The poem even comments upon the calmness that informs it.
"Such a quiet night" sounds natural, like real inner thought; gently
trochaic, it ends in a stressed syllable that, like everything else about
this poem, implies finality and restraint. It is useful to compare this
poem to one of Plath's on a similar subject to see and hear the real
difference in tone and execution. Here are the last few lines of "Burning the Letters":

Warm rain greases my hair, extinguishes nothing.
My veins glow like trees.
The dogs are tearing a fox. This is what it is like—A red
    burst and a cry
That splits from its ripped bag and does not stop
With the dead eye
And the stuffed expression, but goes on
Dyeing the air,
Telling the particles of the clouds, the leaves, the water
What immortality is. That it is immortal.[20]

These two poems depict quite different emotional states: Plath

20. *The Collected Poems*, 204.

sees the event's loud, terrible violence, and both her imagery and syntax reveal this, while Glück sees the silence, the understatement, the stoically controlled sadness to be the appropriate setting for such an activity as burning a lover's letters. The bitter anger or jagged grief we might have expected had "The Letters" appeared in *Firstborn* has been sublimated into a reticent willingness to simply bear, to endure, which is, perhaps, a path to greater reflection and understanding. Yet the language of endurance becomes even more pronounced in Glück's next collection, *Descending Figure*. Indeed, this path leads forward through most of Glück's subsequent work, including her most recent collection, *Ararat*, which continues to examine calmly what it means in a human life—a woman's, specifically—to abide and survive the losses that comprise life, even while the book moves toward a greater biographic inclusion.

Although Glück herself says that she consciously worked to alter the way she wrote sentences, her second collection reflects a different use of the poetic line, as well. In these later poems, enjambment usually works to pull the poem naturally forward, in the rhythms and breaths of speech dominated not by anger, but by meditation. The use of sound throughout the line is more delicate, more musical, relying on the inner texture of assonance and consonance, and where rhyme is present it is generally internal—a marked change from the earlier poems' heavy reliance on end rhyme. Here are a few indicative lines from the first section of "The Shad-blow Tree":

It is all here,
luminous water, the imprinted sapling
matched, branch by branch,
to the lengthened
tree in the lens, as it was
against the green, poisoned landscape.
(*House on Marshland*, 9)

This language is a pleasure to read aloud, in a way none of the poems in *Firstborn* are. Glück places liquids throughout, sounds appropriate to this landscape of water and plant. The repetition of the "a" sound, with its accompanying internal near-rhyme "matched" and "branch" on the same line, creates a structure of connectedness, not the interruption Glück calls "deadendedness." Even the small technical matter of initial capitalization has changed in order to emphasize flow. Throughout *Firstborn*, the only occasions where the first word of each line was not capitalized were those words that were themselves divided by the line break ("photogen / ic"); yet in Marshland, it is the sentence, not the line, that determines capitalization. Such a change is not really radical, and may appear to be only cosmetic, but it is clearly a deliberate part of the new "mood" Glück wanted to create.

Of course, there are still some traces of the abruptly syncopated rhythms and angers in the second book; the transformation in mood continues throughout the two subsequent collections, rather than appearing immediately as a *fait accompli*. For example, "The Murderess" strikes one as a poem that could have been included in *Firstborn*. This is a dramatic monologue whose speaker addresses the commissioner, explaining why she has murdered her daughter. Like the many persona poems in the first collection, its language and imagery reveal the psychic workings of the speaker. The rhythm here is both rocking and self-interrupting, as in the opening lines: "You call me sane, insane—I tell you men / were leering to themselves; she saw."[21] The caesura before the last two words enhances the emphatic end to the sentence, an end punctuated in anger and wild perception. "The Murderess" uses longer lines to let the phrases build an energy other than simply friction, and the implication for the entire poem is that language is not at the verge of combustion, as it is in the earlier poems. Still, there are remnants of slant rhyme in the poem's twelve lines, never so abrupt as those in the poems of *Firstborn*, but still exerting their disquieting force: "men/brain"; "saw/grew"; "pare/Fear"; "talked/lent"; "day/body." This poem stands out as a link between Glück's early and later styles.

Glück's publishing record reveals further the process of transition as she worked to develop her personal classicist style. Some of the poems from *Marshland* appeared in periodicals prior to their collection in slightly different forms, including initial capitalization of each line, less modulated diction, and different line breaks. "Gretel in Darkness," for example, appeared first in 1969, six years before the book's publication. The initial published version retains her early style of capitalizing the first word in each line. This practice imparts an added sense of interruption to the pause introduced by the line break. Glück shifted to lowercase initial letters in *Marshland*, emphasizing her abandonment of the choppy anger in *Firstborn*. Another change toward the poem's end reveals Glück's movement toward

21. *Marshland*, 11.

greater understatement. In the version in *New American Review*, Gretel addresses her brother emphatically, calling him to remember their shared past:

> But I killed for you.
> I see armed firs,
> The spires of that gleaming kiln—
> come back! come back!
>
> Nothing changes. Nights I turn to you to hold me
> But you are not there.[22]

In *Marshland*, Glück deletes the melodramatic "Nothing changes," and makes the first line longer, a more extended unit of speech. She also has removed the wild exclamation and ominous explanation:

> But I killed for you. I see armed firs,
> the spires of that gleaming kiln—
>
> Nights I turn to you to hold me
> but you are not there.
> (*House on Marshland*, 5)

The changes in the final version published in *Marshland* are specifically intended to alter the voice—or rather the tone of voice—of the speaker, and to lead to a quieter, calmer mood throughout the entire collection. That calm is "infamous" in part because it is not an easy calm; instead, it is achieved through an effort of will, a deliberate attempt at stoicism. We have seen versions of this calm in the work of other personal classicists: while I have already pointed out the similarity to Bogan's stoic stance, I should call attention as well to the quiet courage in Bishop's work where she seems to steel herself into personal statement, in poems like "One Art." In spite of similarity, however, Glück's tone is distinctive; in contrast to her earlier heavy reliance on influences, she works to develop syntax and timbre that sound like no one but herself. We see that through a deliberate change in her work, she is overcoming the "threat" Williamson suggested that the popularity of confessional poetry posed for younger writers.

In addition to these revisions, Glück decided to omit certain poems published in periodicals during the years between *Firstborn* and the appearance of *Marshland* from the second collection. Glück's deci-

---

22. "Gretel in Darkness," *New American Review*, 7 (1969): 171.

sion seems to have been guided by her stated desire to take the new book in a truly new direction from that which she had already traveled. The following poem appeared in *Antaeus* in 1975, next to "Here Are My Black Clothes," which was later included in the book.

### Jukebox

You hot, honey, do she bitch and crab,
her measly and depriving body holding back
your rights? How many years? You chicken, upright
in your suit. You starve, you starve.
Here the night fill with howling, mister,
all those dreams come true in O
the sweetest sound, you say the word, you stuff
one dollar in the slot.[23]

Read aloud, "Jukebox" is certainly "bullet-like," like the spiky persona poems in *Firstborn*'s second section, such as "The Islander." Whereas transitional poems like "The Murderess" or "Here Are My Black Clothes" earn their inclusion, perhaps, due to their clear allusions to mythic implications of our lives, "Jukebox" is a lesser poem—merely startling in its street-tough language—and so it seems appropriate that it is excluded from *Marshland*.

It might be useful here to draw a comparison from a discussion of prose narration. In *The Rhetoric of Fiction*, Wayne C. Booth uses the term *implied author* to refer to the picture a reader creates of the author, based on a particular novel. Each novel a writer creates will imply a different "version" of the author, and these "versions" are to be distinguished from the terms *persona, mask,* and *narrator,* each of which refers to only one of the elements of the entire work, and not that concentration of the writer's creative self that lies behind the finished whole—plot, characters, timing, and all. Why bother to distinguish the implied author at all, when there are so many terms much easier to distinguish that account for the mechanical, technical, and rhetorical strategies in the novel? Because, explains Booth:

> It is only by distinguishing between the author and his implied image that we can avoid pointless and unverifiable talk about such qualities as 'sincerity' or 'seriousness' in the author. . . . we have only the work as evidence for the only kind of sincerity that con-

23. "Jukebox," *Antaeus* 17 (Spring 1975): 67.

cerns us: Is the implied author in harmony with himself—that is, are his other choices in harmony with his explicit narrative character?[24]

Here we see a rather New Critical-style reliance on the text itself, in Booth's emphasis on the "version" of the author implied by, even contained in, a novel. And even though a collection of poetry is different from a novel in its presentation of so many "complete" units—the poems—it is similarly helpful to consider the implied author of *Marshland* as distinct from the speakers of the lyrics, as well as from each persona present in the collection (Jeanne d'Arc, Abishag, the Murderess, etc.). Thus one can avoid unverifiable discussions of "sincerity" that would rely on Robert Phillips's premise: "The emotions [confessional poets] portray are always true to their own feelings."[25] Instead, the important aesthetic consideration of sincerity in a collection of poetry like *Marshland* is this: does each individual poem sound as if it is the truth? This question shouldn't imply a cynical situation where it sounds like truth but is not; another way to phrase the question might be: does each poem convince a reader that it is intended to present truth? "Myth," of course, has unfortunately come to mean "untruth" or even "lie" in contemporary vocabulary, but mythology has always been full of psychic, cultural truth, and I mean to include that level.

A follow-up question would paraphrase Booth: Is the implied author of the entire collection in harmony with herself? Does a resonant coherence link the various individual poems? Such questions belong to a study of a *book* of poetry, distinct from examinations of individual poems. They will help shape my discussion of *Descending Figure, The Triumph of Achilles*, and *Ararat*, all of which are fully mature works. I find that they do meet the aesthetic criteria abstracted from Booth. And while *The House on Marshland* is less strikingly unified in this manner, it introduces, in dramatic contrast, Glück's beginnings to achieve a harmonious sincerity that is both mythic and personal.

*Descending Figure* (1980) continues to develop a postconfessional idiom, classically interested in circumfusing the self with the archetypal. With her third book, Glück shows a keen interest in the book itself as a form which, because it allows for repetition of imagery and theme as one poem follows another, can permit the poet even greater

24. *The Rhetoric of Fiction*, 75.
25. *Confessional Poets*, 1.

reticence and understatement in individual poems. The collection as a whole may make clear what a single poem may leave obscure. Thus, a poet need not create the commanding presence of explanation typical of confessional poems. Williamson finds confessional poems to be essentially "a kind of true dramatic monologue."[26] Such monologues are finally intent upon explaining—even justifying—the speaker's point of view in a way the personal classicist poem is not.

This third collection received more critical notice than had her two previous books and for good reason: it is a solidly crafted book, with a greater inner unity than *Marshland* and much more maturity and depth than the precocious *Firstborn*. Many reviewers noted the collection's interest in art—not merely poetry, but the visual and plastic arts as well. As Dave Smith wrote, "*Descending Figure* is a book about art before it is about anything else because art is the answer to 'the cries of hunger' which myth wants to systematically accommodate. Poem after poem addresses the aliases of art (illusions, perceptions, qualities) and is a ceremony which attempts to fix both the known and the way of knowing."[27]

Smith touches on another important aspect of the book—the interest in hunger, especially the willed hunger of anorexia—as a way to pursue "perfection." It is also, of course, a way to deny or suppress the physical self and to seek a sterner, leaner participation in the world that Glück calls "the dying order." More than one reviewer remembered Pound's phrase about poetry "where painting or sculpture seems as if it were just coming over into speech," because of the spareness of her work, the deliberate quiet, the intense concision. Yet all this emphasis on order is not an avoidance of complexity in favor of the quotidian, but rather, as Steven Yenser points out in a review, a commitment to "linguistic torsion."[28]

Glück creates this complexity through placing the collection's poems sequentially in a tightly interconnecting texture. We see in

---

26. *Introspection*, 150.
27. "Some Recent American Poetry: Come All Ye Fair and Tender Ladies," 41.
28. Barbara Antonina Clarke Mossberg discusses "The Aesthetics of Anorexia" in *Emily Dickinson: When a Writer Is a Daughter* (esp. pp. 143–46), and certainly Dickinson's use of food—whether it is being withheld or rejected—reveals a similar attitude about the female body's self-determination. But Glück's work explores further the literal and figurative levels of metaphor, bringing to bear her comparison of anorexia—not merely hunger—to poetry, another "language of the body." Dickinson, for all her shared interests in theme, remains a much more distant forbear; Steven Yenser, "Recent Poetry: Five Poets," 99.

miniature this emphasis on placement in Glück's use of the poem sequence, an important formal development largely ignored by the other personal classicists in this study: H. D. explores the possibility of long poems in *Trilogy*, but she does not achieve Glück's intensity nor her interest in articulation through silence. In 1978, Helen Vendler commented that she wished Glück would write a long poem; her hopes may have been met with some of Glück's work that followed shortly thereafter.[29] In *Descending Figure*, there are four of these longer poems comprised of subtitled sections: "The Garden," "Descending Figure," "Dedication to Hunger," and "Lamentations." I want to begin with the sequence that Glück herself singles out for discussion, "The Garden."

In Alberta Turner's *Fifty Contemporary Poets*, Glück tells something of the poem's composition. She began, she says, with the final section, "The Fear of Burial," which was written in response to a workshop assignment in her writing circle: to write a poem about fear. As the other sections subsequently came,

> my concept of the poem changed several times during the three months spent writing it. . . . Once the piece was assembled, the individual sections were pruned here and there. Initially I had wanted each section to be capable of standing on its own. After several workshop sessions I came to feel I couldn't have both independent poems and a longer coherent work . . . From this point all editorial adjustments were made in the interest of the long piece.[30]

The "long piece" has received prominent placement in Glück's work. "The Garden" was published first in *Antaeus* in 1975—the same year that *The House on Marshland* appeared—and it has undergone only the slightest change in its subsequent appearances: a chapbook published by Antaeus Editions, dedicated to Stanley Kunitz, and the title piece in the first section of *Descending Figure*. From its first appearance to its third, only tiny revisions have been made: a comma has been removed and a period changed to a question mark. Clearly Glück saw the poem as a completed whole early on and remained satisfied with its unity. She was not alone in her opinion of its importance among her work; William Doreski called it "The most ambitious poem in her new book," further describing it as "a

29. *Part of Nature, Part of Us*, 311.
30. *Fifty Contemporary Poets*, ed. Alberta Turner, 113–14.

miracle of compression, a tight allegory composed of complex metaphors that evoke both the Biblical creation myth and the modern
myth of self-creation."[31]

"The Garden," with its five subtitled sections ("The Fear of Birth,"
"The Garden," "The Fear of Love," "Origins," "The Fear of Burial"),
practically shimmers in myth, from the title, evoking Eden, to the
concluding section, "The Fear of Burial," picturing the soul after
it has left the body. It is, in spite of its generally simple syntax and
hushed language, a difficult poem, not unlike Bishop's "Four Poems"
discussed in chapter four. Yet unlike "Four Poems," it achieves an
importance of unity, setting out many of the themes and images to
recur throughout the entire book. Birth, the body and its myriad
mutabilities, fear, the fatalistic responsibilities of adulthood: all these
appear in the "The Garden"'s first section and will return throughout the book.

In talking about the poems of *Descending Figure,* Glück says, "I
realize I have a craving for that which is immutable. The physical
world is mutable. So, you cast about for those situations, or myths,
that will answer the craving."[32] In fact, "The Garden" does not
"answer"—does not, that is, provide a solution or at least a consola-
tion for—this craving so much as it simply articulates it. In the first
section, the unborn body "could not content itself / with health,"
and so is seen to have willed its fall from real "health," or safety in
the womb.

As the sequence proceeds, in the section also titled "The Garden," the speaker addresses "you," presumably a lover who has gone
into the garden that "admires you": ". . . Yet / there is still something you need, / your body so soft, so alive, among the stone animals." The human body is not self-sufficient, and its various needs or
hungers will recur in the pages to follow. Yet "The Garden" mitigates
the fear of death with its final line, in which the deathless perfection
of the stone animals—lawn ornaments that have achieved mythic
proportions—is not, finally, envied: "Admit that it is terrible to be
like them, / beyond harm."

In section three, "The Fear of Love," we do, perhaps, see the introduction of something to "answer the craving." This is surely one
of the poems Helen Vendler had in mind when she wrote, in the rear

31. "The Mind Afoot," 157–58.
32. "An Interview," 119.

cover blurb, of "the invention of religion" as a theme for the book. As this section continues to develop the imagery that pervades *Descending Figure*, the human body itself has become like stone, seemingly through its weariness, a kind of paralysis, rather than a true immutability. The lovers, no longer in the spring of the garden, imagine that they lie partially buried in the snow, escaping the earthly, mortal cast of their own shadows in a world of light. When, dressed in feathers, the gods come "down / from the mountain we built for them," they are descending figures, and are a kind of "answer" to mortal craving and fear. They come, therefore, in response to the two preceding sections as well as that in which they appear: through the poem sequence, Glück establishes the basic interconnectedness that pervades *Descending Figure*.

The next section picks up where "The Fear of Love" left off, with the speaker supposing that a comforting voice—like that of a mother or a benevolent god—has just spoken.

### Origins

As though a voice were saying
*You should be asleep by now*—
But there was no one. Nor
had the air darkened,
though the moon was there,
already filled in with marble.
. . . . . . . . . . . . . . . . . . .
And yet you could not sleep,
poor body, the earth
still clinging to you—
        (*Descending Figure*, 7)

This section continues the sequence's allusion to—or reconfiguration of—the Genesis myth; throughout these stanzas, however, the god is absent and the voice wistful and bereft. Here we find Genesis in the existentialist age, or, conversely, existentialism even from the time of origins. Glück continues her development of the idea of the body, so important throughout the collection. The body is a kind of contemporary kenning for the "you," a momentary reduction of the self to mere body, newly formed from the earth. In other poems she returns to the matter of origination, through sex, pregnancy, childbirth, motherhood, childhood; but here she relies on the details from Genesis: man wrought from the clay of the earth.

"The Fear of Burial," the sequence's concluding section, extends
the details from "Origin"'s last lines. The body, risen from the earth
into life, is now imagined after death, while Glück introduces a Car-
tesian mind/body—or Christian soul/body—dualism, yet her language continues to imply the pantheistic.

> In the empty field, in the morning,
> the body waits to be claimed.
> The spirit sits beside it, on a small rock—
> nothing comes to give it form again.
>
> Think of the body's loneliness.
> At night pacing the sheared field,
> its shadow buckled tightly around.
> Such a long journey.
> And already the remote, trembling lights of the village
> not pausing for it as they scan the rows.
> How far away they seem,
> the wooden doors, the bread and milk
> laid like weights on the table.
>
> *(Descending Figure, 8)*

Loneliness is the condition of death, and Glück imagines that
loneliness as activity of both the body and the spirit; the body must
"journey," must "[pace] the sheared field." The spirit, too, is surely
lonely, since it sits alone while "nothing comes to give it form again,"
but the section's longer stanza delineates the body's loneliness, not
specifically the spirit's. Thus Glück sets the pattern for examining
emotions through the language of the body, which she will later define as "hunger." Although *Descending Figure* is peopled with gods
and with the dead, Glück continues to write of them in sensate terms
of the body and a physical understanding of the world. She is much
like H. D. in this respect; to H. D., as to Glück, mythic subject matter is vital, alive with present meaning and embodiment.

Even while she sets a pattern early in the collection, she does not
fully reveal the metaphorical resonance of the images and language
that constitute that pattern. As Jay Parini points out, Glück's technique owes something to the symbolists: she "cannot be pinned to a
specific interpretation" since "other meanings radiate" from whatever appears to be an individual poem's subject.[33] That radiation

---

33. "After the Fall," 466.

permeates the entire collection, effectively linking each poem to all the others in a complex texture of imagery and statement. Glück uses the book as a form much as she does the poem sequence: a tightly woven tissue of connected imagery, tone, and theme which adds up to more than the sum of its individual poems. And she uses the book to a greater formal purpose than the other writers in this study. The small bound typescript of poems from "*The Islands* series" was never published during H. D.'s life. After her first two books, Bogan published essentially "new and collected" editions; Bishop was more painstaking in arranging her collections, as the inclusion of "In the Village" within *Questions of Travel* suggests, yet even she does not achieve the degree of intraconnectedness we find in *Descending Figure.*

Not all readers admire Glück's thorough intra-allusiveness. One reviewer, Elizabeth Maraffino, availed herself of an opportunity to criticize what she saw as an unfortunate direction American poetry was taking, a direction of which Louise Glück's latest work was representative. Her characterization of Glück's technique is fairly accurate, though cursory:

> Each poem is tightly constructed: lines break with hairline precision; no useless phrases litter page or mind; images are as carefully positioned within the chamber of each poem as each object within a Cezanne still life—they are in keeping with the *tessitura* of the poem, never strident and shrill, never too muted, above all never off hand.[34]

Maraffino does not care for Glück's achievement with these techniques, holding that Glück misses an important opportunity, failing to allow for any "long digression—10 pages of digression if necessary" in order to fully explore all the minute connotations and denotations implied in each element of careful phrasing.

The review occasioned some energetic letters to the editor of the *American Book Review.* John Hawkes attempted to explain the intricacies of Glück's method this way:

> Glück calls a spade a spade but not in a way that would break old-fashioned personal pride, or, for that matter, would weaken her poems as works of art. Is one an academic, 'distant,' simply because one doesn't let it all hang out?
> 
> If Maraffino went back and read these poems over word for word and, *then*, line to line, she might come to see her own 'missed oppor-

---

34. "Missed Books: Descending Figure," 12.

tunity!' Why say more than is necessary unless one is appealing to a very unimaginative audience? Children come instantly to mind as a group where one often has to repeat oneself and to take things to the very last common denominator. This more often resembling a chant than intelligent lyricism.[35]

As Hawkes makes bitingly clear, Glück's mode of postconfessional classicism by design does not load the lyric with narrative detail, emotional digression, or, simply, explanation. Instead, she allows her vision to resonate quietly, without overt signposts, among an entire collection of poems, in which each poem adds a slight variation upon the way an image or an idea has been treated elsewhere.

The book's title, *Descending Figure*, also exemplifies this approach. Glück explains that although she had several poems written for a third book, she was working with no idea of a title until she read an interview with Paul Simon published in *Rolling Stone*, in which he mentioned the musical term *descending figure*. She explains:

> I was immensely haunted by the phrase, its implications and reso-nances. I think that from the moment I had that title, I assumed it would be the title for my next book. A phrase likely to typify my work . . . there's the feeling of minor key, a kind of irrevocable dark-ening, a moving down the scale.[36]

In music, the term refers to a figure, a smaller unit of notes than a phrase, that repeats at progressively lower pitches throughout the work. It is not exactly a variation on a theme, since the pattern of notes does not change. It is more nearly a repetition of the theme voiced at a different level, in a slightly different context, so to speak. Glück has said that her preference for subtlety and context emerged in her earliest experiences of reading poetry as a child: "I liked scale but I liked it invisible. I loved those poems that seemed so small on the page, yet swelled in the mind."[37] I also find it significant that Glück chooses musical analogies to discuss her work: "minor key, moving down the scale." Her choice implies her constant awareness of sound's importance.

The "descending figure" does indeed have many implications and resonances throughout the collection. The first poem, "The Drowned

35. Letter, *American Book Review*, 6,1 (1983): 4.
36. "An Interview," 117–18.
37. "Education of the Poet," 2.

Children," speaks of the children's bodies slowly descending through the water. The descending figure is also the angel of death—or the dead sister who returns as a spiritual presence. Because of its musical definition, the phrase also emphasizes the book's interest in art. The gods themselves are descending figures, as they come down the mountain in "The Fear of Love." That descent is reversed in the book's final poem, "The Clearing," where "at last God arose, His great shadow / darkening the sleeping bodies of His children, / and leapt into heaven."

As the title resonates throughout these different contexts, some implications remain constant. The small collection of musical notes that constitute a figure are not static matter: they are sound, energy. But the power of the metaphor that names them for us gives them tangible shape—a figure, a body. Similarly, Glück's work returns repeatedly to what is noncorporeal: the spiritual, the religious, the emotional. Yet the language with which she speaks of these non-physical subjects is the language of a mortal, full of the metaphor of the body. The word "body" or its plural occurs twenty-four times; "flesh" occurs three. In a book of only forty-eight pages, some of those simply title pages bearing no poems, this means that explicit naming of the body occurs on average more than every other page, a very insistent presence.

Glück says, "My poems are vertical poems. They aspire and they delve. They don't elaborate, or amplify."[38] This is quite true of the individual poems; only through the implied connections within the collection do we see anything resembling elaboration, and even then the word more properly would be *variation*, I think. There is something of the modernist passion for juxtaposition in her method: the desire to present rather than to explain, for simple linkage rather than careful transition. All the personal classicists have ties to mainstream modernism, whether an attraction to subject matter, as in the renewed interest in classical mythology and intellectualism of H. D.'s and Bogan's work, or an exploration of new formal—or tonal—possibilities that free verse offered, as in Bishop's.

The poem sequence gives Glück a way to realize one of her earliest interests in poetry: as a child, she says, she was not interested in words themselves, but in contexts. "What I responded to, on the page,

38. "An Interview," 117.

was the way a poem could liberate, by the means of a word's setting, through subtleties of timing, of pacing, that word's full and surprising range of meaning."[39] Thus her exploration of the poem sequence—an exploration of contexts—fulfills an old interest in language.

The title sequence, "Descending Figure," consists of three titled sections that together, like "The Garden," offer spare, locally delimited occurrences of themes that pervade the entire book, most notably hunger; language and writing; the power of names; death. The first section, "The Wanderer," combines death of the sister, and the speaker's own accompanying knowledge of loneliness, with the need for names and for writing.

> At twilight I went into the street.
> The sun hung low in the iron sky,
> ringed with cold plumage.
> If I could write to you
> about this emptiness—
> Along the curb, groups of children
> were playing in the dry leaves.
> Long ago, at this hour, my mother stood
> at the lawn's edge, holding my little sister.
> Everyone was gone; I was playing
> in the dark street with my other sister,
> whom death had made so lonely.
> Night after night we watched the screened porch
> filling with a gold, magnetic light.
> Why was she never called?
> Often I would let my own name glide past me
> though I craved its protection.
> (*Descending Figure*, 11)

The setting, "ringed with cold plumage," indicates that once again we are in the world where the quotidian present merges with the world of myth. In its echo of the Old English poem, the title enhances this sense of the old, the archetypal. And out of that setting, the speaker's need to write, to name, to describe and therefore perhaps transcend loneliness erupts in a sentence she cannot even complete. The speaker's loneliness—emptiness—is not unlike that of the dead sister; the speaker actually wills herself to experience more

39. "Education," 2.

fully that terrible loneliness, earlier imagined in "The Fear of Burial": she stands in the dusk, apart from the "gold, magnetic light" at the house, and does not take refuge and comfort from her own name. Instead, she stands silent, as if she is not a living, loved daughter being called home.

"The Sick Child," the second section of "Descending Figure," also focuses on death. Attributed by epigraph to the Rijksmuseum, it is ostensibly a description of a painting. The first ten lines are simple, objective description of a child sleeping in her mother's arms and of the winter night surrounding them. Steven Yenser points out, however, that

> no painting in that museum corresponds to Glück's scene. In the one that comes closest, "The Sick Child" by Gabriel Metsu, the child looks feverishly out at the observer, while in Glück's poem "The mother . . . stares / fixedly into the bright museum." Maybe her memory is at fault; but it seems to me possible that whatever else she means, she intends to condense and to extend her complicated relationship to her dead sister.[40]

I think Yenser is quite right about the connection to the sister; the poem itself shows, in the next seven lines, that it has left the world of the painting—or entered it so completely and imaginatively as to render the placement in the Rijksmuseum unimportant. Yet the connection is not stated, only implied.

> By spring the child will die.
> Then it is wrong, wrong
> to hold her—
> Let her be alone,
> without memory, as the others wake
> terrified, scraping the dark
> paint from their faces.
>                     (*Descending Figure*, 12)

Suddenly the poem casts free from the present into the realm of foreknowledge, and from the human world of comfort and compassion of a mother for a sick child to an awful imperative that extends compassion beyond the mortal realm. The end thus urges that the child be left alone in her fated life, since she must die soon, in order that she

40. "Recent Poetry," 99.

may be "without memory," and therefore unable to fully experience her own loneliness, never having not been alone.

Yenser also points out that the final section, "For My Sister," reveals the speaker acting as a mother to the child.[41] These different contexts explore the various relationships among different generations of women; thus the "descending figure" also implies movement through time, through generations.

> Far away my sister is moving in her crib.
> The dead ones are like that,
> always the last to quiet.
>
> . . . . . . . . . . . . . . . .
> Now, if she had a voice,
> the cries of hunger would be beginning.
> I should go to her;
> perhaps if I sang very softly,
> her skin so white,
> her head covered with black feathers. . . . [ellipsis Glück's]
> (*Descending Figure*, 13)

The poem's final image—white skin and head covered with black feathers—visually links back to the last lines in the preceding section, "scraping the dark / paint from their faces," and to the earlier image of the gods "in their cloaks of feathers." This reappearance of imagery surely is an example of what Glück perceives as a "figure" descending through her poetry. Glück creates this densely interwoven texture of imagery throughout the book, as one image recalls and prepares for another. Thus, for this personal classicist, even imagery is a method of understatement.

She interweaves her themes and subject matter just as densely and quietly as she does her imagery. In "For My Sister," Glück imagines that if the dead sister could speak, "the cries of hunger would be beginning." Hunger asserts itself repeatedly in different settings in the later poems, and becomes a figure for artistic shaping. In a poem titled "Epithalamium," she writes of "the terrible charity of marriage," and in this context she sees "So much pain in the world—the formless / grief of the body, whose language / is hunger—."

Throughout *Descending Figure*, Glück presents a theme similar to that of *Firstborn*, while she continues to explore different sorts of articulation. Marriage is a union of only bodies and sex is an irresist-

---

41. "Recent Poetry," 99.

ible urge that is not celebratory, but wounding, humiliating, and inexorable. To a certain extent, all human relations except that between mother and child are depicted in these terms. In "Tango," the speaker describes the relationship between sisters as a state of inseparability that is nonetheless wounding: she writes of a moon that is "brutal and sisterly." The sisters are "actively starving," says the speaker; their hunger is the hunger not of sexual desire, but nonetheless of a desire to join, to either absorb or be absorbed. This section's final image is of the trees "disfigured" in the moonlight, emphasizing through imagery the fact that one thing—or person—can so easily disfigure another.

Whatever is inseparable is beyond control, and although Glück does not say it in so many words, she shows control to be the language of the spirit or soul. Hunger, she says explicitly, is "the language of the body": willed hunger is a kind of desperate articulation then, and anorexia becomes one of the important themes and metaphors of the book, exploring that strange middle ground where the bodily and the spiritual grapple. Whereas the corporeal speaks through desires and hungers, the spirit continually attempts to overcome the body's needs through mastery and denial. Such an approach to life is the only one that appears possible to the anorexic woman, and throughout much of the book we see the anorexic's own peculiar brand of existentialism informing the poetry's aesthetic.

As I have shown in the work of all the writers treated in this study, personal classicism is a mode dedicated to creating a shielding or controlling context—formal and thematic—for what is essentially quite personal poetry. Behind this dedication lies a supposition that personal poetry is somehow too vulnerable, too revealing, too seemingly unprofessional—in some way in need of a complementary dose of the impersonal. In Glück's adoption of anorexia as both subject matter and aesthetic approach, we see a brilliant use of the social forces that impel women—and women writers—to seek to efface the personal, even their very persons. Susie Orbach has written on the metaphoric implications of anorexia in contemporary culture.

A girl grows up learning to turn her own needs into the servicing of needs in others. She becomes accustomed to restricting her initiatives to those areas that are a response to others' declared needs. As a result she loses touch with her own needs so that they become not only repressed but unrecognized and undeveloped. More damaging, perhaps, she takes on the idea that needs that do arise from within her are somehow wrong, and that she herself is all wrong for having them.

The food refusal can be seen to be a graphic gagging of desire, a block on having what is so wanted. It becomes a model for deprivation in all areas. "If I can successfully deny myself food, I will be able to crush the other desires that arise in me." The determination associated with the refusal of food is much more than the expression of will, it is an example of the brake on desire in general that exists in the woman. It is a measure of perceived restriction in other areas of self-expression.[42]

As Orbach makes clear, anorexia is a struggle for control, not a matter of appetite loss. The body, in its physicality, is a seat of desire that must not go unchecked: the anorexic woman has internalized society's notions that women must be physically diminutive and pleasing to the extent that she sees her flesh as a monstrous enemy, an impediment to legitimate selfhood and happiness. "The body is experienced as an object that must be controlled or it will control," explains Orbach.[43] In other words, the physical desires of the body, especially for food, must be thwarted and denied or else they will retain too much power over an individual. The anorexic's struggle is a power struggle.

Throughout *Descending Figure*, Glück combines the writer's aesthetic search for a poetry reflecting postconfessional willed understatement with the anorexic's drive for control of physical desires. Helen Vendler has called Glück's technique indicative of a "renunciatory aesthetic" which is involved in "the acquiring, by renunciation, of a self."[44] In defining the language of the body as hunger, Glück fuses interest in linguistic/artistic mastery with that of physical restraint. In doing so, she explores the artistic extension of the anorexic's drive to refuse and reject.

Glück herself uses language very like Vendler's. "The tragedy of anorexia seems to me that its intent is not self-destructive, though its outcome so often is. Its intent is to construct, in the only way possible when means are so limited, a plausible self."[45] Glück identifies

42. *Hunger Strike: The Anorectic's Struggle as a Metaphor for Our Age*, 142.
43. Ibid., 100, 149.
44. *New York Review of Books*, 28 (July 16, 1981): 26
45. "Education," 4.

the anorexic's method of self-determination as a force of negation, of denial, of destroying the physical, public self in order to affirm a private, inner one. The act of will required to achieve such a goal can only be maintained through rigid ritual and self-discipline; the artist's method, similarly, is dedicated to the pursuit of perfection. As Glück says in "The Deviation," section four of "Dedication to Hunger," what the artist feels in "aligning these words" on a page—in constructing a coherent vision through poetry—is the pull of self-discipline an anorexic feels in trying to construct a "plausible self."

The first section of "Dedication to Hunger" is titled "From the Suburbs": it serves to locate the poem solidly in the landscape of post-war American culture.

> The little girl purposefully
> swinging her arms, laughing
> her stark laugh:
>
> It should be kept secret, that sound.
> It means she's realized
> that he never touches her.
> She is a child; he could touch her
> if he wanted to.
> (*Descending Figure*, 29)

In this opening section we see a little of what is important about the suburbs in forming a woman's dedication to hunger—the family structure: mother, whose pleasure comes out of the family, not out of herself, who is glad the child is "like" the head of the household, the father; daughter, who has already begun to internalize the power structure, knowing that she is, as a child, to some degree defenseless and passive; that powerful presence, the father. The touching the little girl does not receive from her father may simply be parental affection—like the speaker in "Tango," she may be "actively starving" for emotional warmth—but the language focuses simply upon "touch," the communication of the body, not the spirit. Even here, Glück concentrates on the demands and desires of the body, and of differences in power. Since "she is [only] a child," she remains passive while the father has the capability to be active. There is the beginning awareness of power as it manifests in familiar and societal roles, and the way roles are tied up with gender definition.

"From the Suburbs" certainly does not indulge in an expansive exploration of its subject, but it gains intensity as the sequence progresses. "Grandmother," the second section, again examines the role of a female in the family. The poem opens in the grandmother's own words, as memory takes her back to her youth—before children, before grandchildren. The speaker takes up the thread and is able to "watch" the figures of her grandparents; she reserves condemnation enough to claim, "I do not question their happiness." Yet she sees the passionate lives of her grandparents, in spite of the couple's happiness, as yet another example of sexuality as struggle.

This time the hunger is the man's; he is the instigator, the teacher—the assertive partner, not unlike the father in the preceding section. Yet any feminist criticism of marriage is once again muted: in its focus on miniature detail—light in the man's hair, the way he becomes recognizable only as he draws nearer—the poem avoids reliance on rhetoric or propaganda. Still, the final lines focus on the husband "rush(ing) in / with his young man's hunger" while the speaker pulls back from the scene to comment: "Of course, of course. Except / it might as well have been / his hand over her mouth." As this section immediately follows "From the Suburbs," Glück implies that the two situations are analogous, part of the same larger pattern. In both, the action implies a question: who controls a female's body—both when she is a child and when she is a wife?

"Eros," the third section, takes modern middle-class life in the suburbs into the mythic realm. This section follows essentially the same structure as that in "Grandmother." In both sections, four lines introduce the poem's subject. Although here the language is more arch and formal, these lines likewise set up a proposition of sorts: that male heterosexuality can be traced to a search for the mother. The lines following explore the plausibility of that proposition: while in "Grandmother" the speaker enters the world her grandmother has spoken of, in "Eros" the speaker explores further the Freudian implications already introduced. The girl child, an important figure in this section, follows the typical movement from love for the mother to love for the father; the way she "wills herself" toward the father, seems in this poem to be yet another instance of the terrible, inexorable drive to be merged. The final two lines correspond to the final three in "Grandmother," since the swift endings in both sections sum up knowledge wryly and emphatically. One cannot know one's paternal parentage—"the bond"—with the same knowledge one holds for the mother; it is this uncertainty that wills one into an Electra complex, the poem hints.

Out of this "desperate" urge for the father we see the penultimate section emerge.

### The Deviation

It begins quietly
in certain female children:
the fear of death, taking as its form
dedication to hunger,
because a woman's body
*is* a grave; it will accept
anything. I remember
lying in bed at night
touching the soft, digressive breasts,
touching, at fifteen,
the interfering flesh
that I would sacrifice
until the limbs were free
of blossom and subterfuge: I felt
what I feel now, aligning these words—
it is the same need to perfect,
of which death is the mere byproduct.

(Descending Figure, 32)

The deviation is anorexia, a *dedication* to hunger, and it grows out of the familial norm in a male-dominated society. What we have seen in the preceding sections has been disturbing, but not because of unusual violence or deviant behavior: each character has been "normal"; some have specifically known pleasure and happiness. They epitomize the superficially safe, apparently stable life of the suburbs, yet from them comes that haunting fear of non-being, of non-personhood in which the speaker can say a woman's body is a "grave" in its sexual capacity "to accept anything." Glück links the anorexic's need to control and perfect with that of the writer, so that in this section she declares her aesthetic and the forces that impel her to adopt it.

"Sacred Objects," the last section of the sequence, combines the mythic and the quotidian more fully than do the preceding four sections. Yet its power of conclusion, of combining and summing up, still is achieved through the spareness of language. The section begins:

Today in the field I saw
the hard, active buds of the dogwood

and wanted, as we say, to capture them,
to make them eternal. That is the premise
of renunciation: the child
having no self to speak of,
comes to life in denial—

                                    (*Descending Figure*, 33)

The section opens as if it will unfold a narrative event, but by the fourth line we see that the narrative serves as something of a parable, articulating the way an urge toward immutability might find its only expression in "denial" or "renunciation." Glück's "craving" for the "immutable" is part of the human condition and appears throughout literature of all ages. Yeats treated the subject repeatedly in the poems that are still among his best-remembered: "Sailing to Byzantium," "Lapis Lazuli," "The Circus Animals' Desertion." He sees his body as a "dying animal" to which he is chained; we are familiar with his metaphors and those of other great male poets. With "Dedication to Hunger" Glück has created a new metaphor—primarily based on female experience—to speak about the old craving to transcend the mortal and bodily confines. She hints as well that a woman's mortal restrictions are rather different from a man's. Her poems repeatedly emphasize the woman's body as an object, but it is an object that constantly threatens, through its own desires, to destroy its value or utility. Yet even though a political indictment lies deep within "Dedication to Hunger" and her other intimations of anorexia, that indictment and its accompanying anger are muted and not allowed to surface in the texture of her language in each individual section.

Through careful progression of sections, we see again how Glück is able to depend on the silence between statements—the renunciation of explicit narrative or transitional explanation—to imply the connections embodied in the poem. Glück's placement of "Dedication to Hunger" within the collection also helps to enhance the individual themes contained in the sequence. "Porcelain Bowl" precedes the "Hunger" sequence, and this brief poem introduces the notion of a woman's body relegated to the categories of use and ornamentation—societal attitudes that are directly responsible for anorexia.

The book's closing pages are another poem sequence, "Lamentations." This sequence is also subdivided into titled sections ("The Logos," "Nocturne," "The Covenant," "The Clearing,"), all of which return to the creation mythology of "Descending Figure." They focus on the loneliness that belongs to humankind, and trace the way God, too, "wanted to be understood"; he combats his loneliness by turning away from humans. First, he "turned to his angels"; the angels watch "how He divided them: / the man, the woman, and the woman's body." Finally "God arose, His great shadow / darkening the sleeping bodies of His children, / and leapt into heaven."[46] The man and woman are left alone on the earth, strange to one another, with a child to care for.

Thus, the book's end is loaded with the mournful loneliness of humans for the comfort of their immortal god; with "their human warmth, / their panic"; with the terrible divisions that set men apart from women and women apart from their own bodies; with the responsibility of a family. All the ingredients which have led to the clearly contemporary situations depicted in the book are manifest in "Lamentations." The sequence thus implies how time has changed little in the way humans connect with one another.

*Descending Figure* demonstrates eloquently how order and sequence can articulate a wider, more encompassing treatment of themes than that found in any single poem; indeed, I find that any single poem is slightly diminished in scope when removed from the entirety of the book. But "The Garden" appears to be the only poem sequence that Glück initially perceived *as a sequence.* Some of the others appear to have been conceived originally as separate pieces— and even published that way—and only later put together into the kind of development that distinguishes the collection.[47] Thus, from 1975, the year of publication for *Marshland*, until 1979, the year before publication of *Descending Figure*, the sequence apparently was not yet a major formal concern in Glück's poetry. Although the form had worked for "The Garden" as early as 1975, it did not seem to hold Glück's interest until shortly before the publication of her third book, nearly five years later. I suspect that the work of careful editing

46. Glück does not capitalize the deity in the first section, "The Logos," but she does in all the following sections, "Nocturne," "The Covenant," and "The Clearing."

47. From the title sequence, "For My Sister" was published in *American Poetry Review* in 1975; "The Sick Child" in *The New Yorker* in 1978; and a poem titled "Descending Figure" in *Antaeus* in 1976 which is precisely the same text as that which appears in the book as the first section titled "The Wanderer." "Grandmother," from "Dedication to Hunger" appeared in *Salmagundi* in the fall of 1979, several months before the entire sequence appeared in *Antaeus*. "The Logos" and "The Clearing" from "Lamentations" appeared in *Antaeus* in the winter of 1978 as distinct poems, months before the entire sequence would appear along with several other poems in the *New Republic*.

that must have been necessary to see *Descending Figure* as a whole may also have led to Glück's recognition of the sequence as a perfect form with which to extend her power for lyric concision into somewhat more expansive meditations.

None of the poems in the collection appears incidental, although they vary in quality. Indeed, some that were published in periodicals during these years have been omitted from the collection. One in particular, "In the Empty House," appeared in the *Iowa Review* in 1976 along with two other poems chosen for *Descending Figure*. "In the Empty House" shares much with the style of the poems chosen, but it emphasizes the act of writing distinct from the other hungers Glück chooses to combine in her collection; its surreal focus on the implements of writing seems caricatured. The house itself, with its furnishings, is said at the poem's end to be "counseling stillness," while, strangely, the speaker has a vision of a pencil appearing in a room, full of dreams and memory that will then dissolve into the act of writing. In spite of the way it voices an urge to silence, stillness, that is vital to Glück's aesthetic, "In the Empty House" is self-indulgent, more heavily romantic in its focus on the "I" without the emphasis on mythic implications we see in Glück's more successful poems. It does not belong in the collection: it is not in balance.

With *The Triumph of Achilles* (1985), Glück continues to emphasize the long poem, although the title poem itself consists of only twenty lines. Of the twenty-six poems that make up this collection, eight extend into several sections, many of them subtitled. Additionally, many of these long poems are longer than those in *Descending Figure*: "Marathon," for example, has nine titled sections, filling eleven pages, and "From the Japanese" likewise has nine sections, though these are not titled, and some are very brief. Yet an important distinction separates this book's approach from that of her previous collection. In a review, Edward Hirsch speaks of

> Glück's more open and intimate style and manner. Her most humane book thus far, *The Triumph of Achilles* is empowered by a complex struggle to live in the world as it is, to accept what the poet has learned to believe is the only world there is, to come to terms with the hard Stevensian proposition that "Death is the mother of beauty."[48]

48. "The Watcher," 33.

Similarly, Don Bogen notes, "The range of the work has expanded. . . . Language is looser, embracing the casual as well as the concise."[49] To return to Wayne Booth's terminology, whereas the implied author of *Descending Figure* recognized stasis, stillness, and death as important elements of existence, *Triumph* recognizes other elements as well, including humor. Poems like "The Mountain," a modern parody of the artist-teacher as Sisyphus, are more drily funny, self-mocking, and free of malice than any of the poems in Glück's three earlier books.

Yet Glück's new humor is never bawdy or slapstick. Glück's spareness and reliance on juxtaposition remain primary elements of her style; once again she has widened her subject matter. Although Glück has often relied on juxtaposition for effect, that juxtaposition has rarely included an almost Laforguian use of differing tones placed beside one another, as in "From the Japanese," where she combines serious statements like "Why love what you will lose? / There is nothing else to love" with amusing anecdotes about Gwen, a bilingual child of three, and the child's cat, Trixie. *Triumph* marks a new development in Glück's work for the formal use of tone.

The appearance of a new degree of tonal inclusiveness does not, however, replace Glück's dedication to narrative concision. The inclusiveness grows out of her earlier interests; moreover, this book contains poems that do not diverge from the postconfessional classicism we have seen in her two previous books. The second poem in the collection, a three-part sequence titled "Metamorphosis," continues Glück's work of imbedding the personal in the mythic: it is primarily an elegy for her father. The title sets the mythic context, with its reference to Ovid, and the elegy proceeds with the slow rhythmic dignity familiar in Glück. Many of the line breaks are dictated by syntax; predicate and complement are often set apart from each other, with the natural pause of a breath in between, while modifying phrases are likewise given lines by themselves. These lines are from the second section.

> Once, for the smallest
> fraction of an instant, I thought
> he was alive in the present again;
> then he looked at me
> as a blind man stares
> straight into the sun, since

49. "The Fundamental Skeptic," 53.

whatever it could do to him
is done already.

Then his flushed face
turned away from the contract.
      (*Triumph of Achilles*, 5)

To emphasize the emotional and linguistic control evident in this poem's craft, we might compare it with any of the poems by Sharon Olds concerning her father's illness and death, where the line breaks are as surprising and jolting as the imagery.[50] Glück's poem does not attempt to shock, but rather to see and to live with the responsibility of that sight. The poem is "about" maturity, gained at one of the defining moments of adulthood, the death of a parent.

Glück's interest in fusing contemporary experience with ancient myth continues throughout *Triumph*, and as the title might reflect, the mythology is largely from the classical Greek legends, rather than from the Judeo-Christian tradition. However, one poem, "Winter Morning," begins with a meditation on the death of Christ and moves into an enactment of the birth, fusing old fertility rites' yearning for spring with the promise of the nativity. Another, "Day without Night," carries a Biblical epigraph: "The angel of god pushed the child's hand / away from the jewels, toward the burning coal." After retelling how Pharaoh's daughter discovered Moses amid the rushes, the poem moves, in its eighth and final section, to a difficult, nearly existential appraisal of faith (and death):

Here is your path to god,
who has no name, whose hand
is invisible: a trick
of moonlight on the dark water.
      (*Triumph*, 49)

The stoical courage, the determination to endure, that ends this poem is an attitude familiar from earlier personal classicists, especially Bogan and Bishop. Glück wills herself to see the comfortless condition of humanity bereft of naive faith but with a tenacity reminiscent of that in the earlier "Dedication to Hunger," in which the speaker recalls her adolescent resolution to "free" herself of the flesh's "blossom and subterfuge."

---

50. I am indebted to Roger Mitchell's discussion of Sharon Olds's line breaks in "Thoughts on the Line," *Ohio Review* 38 (1987). See especially pp. 75–77.

Yet aside from these poems, the unmistakable atmosphere of the book is Hellenic, and, in its way, again reminiscent of H. D. "Mythic Fragment" is clearly a persona poem, spoken by Daphne, daughter of the river god Peneus. In order to avoid Apollo's pursuit, she begged her father to protect her: his solution reveals that only through renunciation of her female form can she avoid marriage. The appeal of this myth, given Glück's repeated interests, should be obvious. Glück's poem emphasizes Daphne's wistful loneliness and her desire for her father's love, not the passion of Apollo. The speaker is a female victim: she sees the god's praise as what Western culture's idealization of women has always been—a condition in which the woman's self is lost, "captivity." Yet, terribly, the only refuge offered by her father is both obliteration and a form of captivity, as well. She calls for her father's aid and then: "I was nowhere, / I was in a tree forever." Only through losing her female identity can she escape being "encompassed" by Apollo.

Glück's poem has a strong feminist message, but, unlike her earliest persona poems, its tone is quiet, making no rhetorical proclamations. Even the bitterness in the direct address—"Reader, / pity Apollo"—is a controlled stab at the canon's sympathy with Apollo's gesture toward tribute, or "praise," in wearing a laurel wreath in memory of the woman he could not possess. The indictment remains implied, not explicit. In this respect, it is much like some of the early personal classicist persona poems of H. D., not because the mythic characters correspond to and mask particular people or events in Glück's own life, but because the poem's speaker is seen anew in feminist terms, the woman's emotions—not Apollo's—are the heart of the work. We might easily compare "Mythic Fragment" to H. D.'s "Eurydice," "Circe," or "Evadne," for example, or to Bogan's "Cassandra." This is essentially what Alicia Ostriker calls revisionist mythmaking, as described in chapter 1.

Glück has said, "I am puzzled, not emotionally but logically, by the contemporary determination of women to write as women," explaining that gender differences will arise without an author's studied attention, so that one need not make a specific task of writing out of one's gender. She further explains, "The dream of art is not to assert what is already known, but to illuminate the hidden, and the path to the hidden world is not inscribed by the will."[51] Clearly, she

51. "Education," 3.

does not feel a responsibility as a woman poet to reeducate, through poetic rhetoric, her readers. Her use of myth continues to reveal her preference for subtlety, reticence, and control.

Glück has explained that her interest in myth is not the result of adult study, a kind of academic interest. Instead, the telling of myth was a part of her childhood; her parents told her fairy tales and myths, frequently making their own improvisations. Her father, for example, loved to tell the tale of St. Joan, excluding the final burning which martyred the girl. Thus, Glück says, "Before I was three I was well-grounded in Greek myths."[52] While myth was a part of her early development, so too was the revisioning of myth. Her earliest experiences with story-telling and literature included changing the accepted mythology to fit the teller's needs or desires. As we've seen, this is the approach she takes in her poetry, where the personal and the mythic are fused in the most recent manifestation of personal classicism, that of a postconfessional classicism.

The long poem sequence "Marathon" exemplifies just how Glück's fusion of mythic and personal take shape in *The Triumph of Achilles*. The sequence follows a brief poem, "The Embrace," which recounts a woman teaching her lover of "the gods" and in return being led by him "back" into "the original need." "The Embrace," then, sets a scene for mythology and sexuality to act out their drama, and "Marathon" provides the cycles of action. The sequence is divided into nine titled sections, "Last Letter," "Song of the River," "The Encounter," "Song of Obstacles," "Night Song," "The Beginning," "First Goodbye," "Song of Invisible Boundaries," and "Marathon." Together they trace the progress of a romantic relationship.

Much of the poem is placed in a Mediterranean coastal village. Section six, "The Beginning," recounts a dream where the speaker is in the market, recalling "Baskets," from earlier in the book, also clearly set in a Mediterranean village. The title of "Marathon," then, carries a connotation of place, or destination, as well as that of the arduous race. Within the dream recounted in "The Beginning," the speaker describes the marketplace full of fruit stands selling a single fruit—blood oranges—each stand exhibiting one of the ripe fruits cut open. The language reveals elements of Glück's vision familiar from *Descending Figure*: desires are hungers, and all desires long for structure. Says the speaker: "Then what began as love for you / became a

52. Ibid.

hunger for structure." This passage recalls Glück's earlier insistence that the urge to write poetry was the same as that which leads to anorexia: to give structure, to "perfect" as she said in "The Deviation," whether through hunger or through "aligning these words" on the page.

Similarly, Glück continues to work with language in context, allowing an image or phrase to reappear throughout the work; the next sequence, "First Goodbye," addresses the you directly, telling him to leave, to "go back"

> to increment and limitation: near the centered rose,
> you watch her peel an orange
> so the dyed rind falls in petals on her plate. This
> is mastery, whose active
> mode is dissection . . .
>
> (*Triumph*, 31)

As the orange image recurs, bringing the world of dream into the world of the present, Glück employs the same principles that led her to identify a "descending figure" as the appropriate metaphor for her work.

Throughout this book, however, the structuring metaphor is not chosen from music, but from myth, constantly implying that mythology is an actual part of our daily lives. "Marathon" ends like "The Triumph of Achilles," recognizing the inescapable mutability that defines human existence; however, it is more chilling, abandoning the physical world and seemingly entering a mythical dream world where nothing definite and lasting is possible, not even the abiding love that bound Achilles and Patroclus. The section recounts a dreamlike sequence during which the speaker hears a former lover speaking to her new lover, describing her body and how best to arouse it. The poem, and the sequence, end on a note of frightening uncertainty:

> For all I know, this happens
> every night: somebody waking me, then
> the first teaching the second.
> What happens afterward
> occurs far from the world, at a depth
> where only the dream matters
> and the bond with any one soul
> is meaningless; you throw it away.
>
> (*Triumph*, 34)

Glück has said that she has always preferred work that directly addresses the reader, that seems to need the reader.[53] Her own work is often difficult in its complexity, its spareness, and its intraconnectedness, yet I find throughout the development of her mature work a careful tone that, while it eschews extreme prosiness or direct confession, does imply a listener. Her best work exhibits courage, fortitude, and control—qualities that are important in an age when confessional "sincerity" is often substituted for craft.

Moreover, her use of the poem sequence demonstrates an important technique for offering a more wide-ranging meditation without losing any tension. Indeed, tension is often gained over the course of a poem sequence. It is interesting to recall what Richard Hugo told young poets in *The Triggering Town* about the importance of "writing off the subject" with his dichotomy of "triggering subject" and "real subject."[54] According to Hugo's model, the triggering or initiating subject is what catches the poet's interest and offers her or him an occasion to discuss emotions or memories or other truths buried somewhere in the poet's psyche. Hugo's discussion centers on ways of getting off the triggering subject and onto the real subject with skill and grace, to allow for greater possibility within the poem. In Glück's work it becomes increasingly difficult to distinguish between triggering and real subjects: the longer forms seem, for Glück, to be ways of distilling a returning concern—the real subject—into more than one section, each with its own contextual subject. What triggers, what initiates? At times it seems the voice itself is the starting point, as experiments in syntax "open up kinds of subject matter." In Glück's poetry the compression results repeatedly in a tension between expression and silence, and the long poem sequences present a form in which this tension can work: a kind of long-distance reticence.

In *Ararat* (1990), Glück continues to use the poem sequence, but in a hardly recognizable fashion. The book contains thirty-two titled poems, only one of which is broken into numbered sections. Yet Glück has said that she perceives the book as being essentially one long poem, one entire work, much the same way I have argued *Descending Figure* should be read. At least one reviewer saw the book in this manner, suggesting that the book "works almost as a single poem."[55] The most remarkable change in *Ararat*, however, is that

---

53. Ibid., 4.
54. *The Triggering Town: Lectures and Essays on Poetry and Writing.*
55. Introductory remarks, poetry reading at Ohio University's Spring Literary Festival, Athens, Ohio, May 4, 1989; Stephen Dobyns, "Will You Listen for a Minute?" 5.

Glück is returning to a more fully personal poetry. She has not abandoned her interest in classical, biblical, or mythic allusion, as the
title alone makes clear. Glück makes the present darkly numinous
with the past: the personal past and the mythic past.

The opening poem is titled *"Parodos"* (italics Glück's); Glück
becomes a Greek chorus of sorts, witnessing life, death, and its resul-
tant effects on individual and collective lives. But throughout the
collection, the sense of contemporary life actually participating in
the mythic is softened; instead, the book focuses on the speaker's act
of autobiographic witnessing—witnessing the death of her father and
the way the family deals with death, and, further, the way the family's shared past has prepared it for this event. The anonymous jacket
blurb describes the poetry this way: "It is the singular, pervasive
myth of family that she examines with a scientist's precision" and
"she now breaks free of it [her previous style], in a voice no longer
oracular but wry, idiomatic, undeceived, unrelenting."

Another reviewer saw the book as introducing something that
"seems new in Glück's work—a thoroughly human scale, without
ornament."[56] While I believe *The Triumph of Achilles* began Glück's
process of shifting emphasis back to the human level from the mythic
or archetypal emphasized throughout *The House on Marshland* and
*Descending Figure*, *Ararat* does seem to move beyond the sense of the
immortal that asserted itself as a kind of desperate need in some of
the earlier work. For example, the book's penultimate poem, titled
"Celestial Music," opens with these lines, sounding absolutely spoken,
and renouncing the need for the gods that pervades *Descending Figure*:

> I have a friend who still believes in heaven.
> Not a stupid person, yet with all she knows, she literally
>     talks to god,
> she thinks someone listens in heaven.

> (*Ararat*, 66)

Philosophical and searching in their meditations, the poems are generous with the way they draw upon biography, the way they openly
sift through the speaker's life. With *Ararat*, I find Glück moving
beyond willed stoicism and its attendant shielding of the self into a
new form of more personal poetry. For this book at least, she seems to
have left much of personal classicism behind. She has not, however,

---

56. Marianne Boruch, "Comment: The Feel of a Century," 17.

returned to the abrupt rhythms and syntax that characterized her earlier work. The greater generosity and sharing of autobiography of *Ararat* is not a return to her earlier confessional mode. Perhaps this should come as no surprise, since Glück has made clear that she wants to move in a new direction with each book, never simply repeating her achieved strengths. Having set the standard for contemporary personal classicism, she moves into different territory once again. In her own words, "Each book I've written has culminated in a conscious diagnostic act, a swearing off."[57]

57. "Education," 6.

# 6

# Endnote

All the poets in this study have struggled to achieve a balance between self-expression and silence; we have seen that each has chosen a slightly different approach to enclose the personal within the impersonal, with varying degrees of success. Certain characteristics are common to all their work, but each remains an independent, individual poet. Although I see a common element—personal classicism—linking their works, none of the poets would have identified herself as part of a historical movement called personal classicism. Indeed, although defined by social stereotypes and strictures that existed historically (and, alas, persist today), personal classicism is a mode, not a movement. The conscious manifestos of imagism, and the sense of identity and influence in a deliberate community of writers that H. D. must have shared, are lacking from the development of personal classicism. The mode is born more out of isolation than community.

Precisely rendered imagery is vital to all these poets, as they tend to draw scenes or landscapes with specific detail in such a way as to render them both visually and emotionally "true"—both grounded in the exterior world and evocative of an emotional, or interior world. Yet there are differences, such as H. D.'s hermetic equivalencies among time periods through allusions and setting as compared to Bishop's emphasis on specific "accuracy."

The personal classicists are lyric poets, even as they seek to mute and quiet the actual presentation of emotion and veil the biographical aspects of their work. Each writer relies on tone as a vital element of lyricism, although Bishop and Glück have shown the greatest resourcefulness in adopting tone as a formal element, combining naturalness with artifice to give greater understatement and heighten the moral or emotional importance of imagery.

H. D., Louise Bogan, and Elizabeth Bishop came to poetic maturity before the rise of confessional poetry as a major poetic mode. They therefore saw themselves participating in serious poetry, along with their more numerous male colleagues, largely by virtue of their interest in poetry as more than simply expression of personal emotion—unlike the more widely popular women poets of the late nineteenth and early twentieth centuries. Louise Glück, however, made a deliberate change in her work, choosing reticence over confession in a time when confessional poetry was an increasingly popular fashion for women writers.

While we should hope that what Gilbert and Gubar call the "anxiety of authorship," caused by the traditional conflict of society's perceived role of a woman with that of a writer, has begun to fade as a shaping force in contemporary literature, clearly the struggle exists for women to define their identities as poets within their identities as women. The fact that Glück could say she is "puzzled by the determination of women to write as women," reveals her own awareness that contemporary literature is marked by women writers who do feel that need—her postconfessional classicism is as much an answer to female poetic issues as to male ones.

The personal classicist mode continues to be of major importance for women writers like Chase Twichell, Jorie Graham, Linda Gregg, and perhaps most recently, Nina Bogin. Bogin's first book, *In the North* (1989), sounds so much like Glück that she may find herself in a position comparable to the one Glück describes herself facing after the publication of her own first book: needing to find a difference in style, in syntax, in language, that can somehow free her from her early influences. Bogin is an older poet than Glück was at the time *Firstborn* appeared and may be assumed to be less prone to undue influence, but *In the North* echoes Glück's mature work on every page. There are poem titles that themselves recall Glück's work: "All Souls"; "Through Marshland"; "The Garden"; and the tone of the poems is one of "infamous calm" as Bedient says of Glück. Bogin shares what I call Glück's ardent understatement. Here, for example, are lines from "Lost One," one of several poems in the collection treating the death of a child.

The days have done with you.
On a far hill the black
firs lose themselves in fog.

The morning is torn,
the sky flung out.
Rain drifts down

like something remembered
or once living—
how pure this absence is . . . [1]

The poem goes on for three more stanzas, continuing to imbed the speaker's loss and grief in the landscape. This quotation merely suggests the extent to which Bogin writes in the personal classicist mode; I do not intend to embark on a thorough study of her work here. My point is that the mode is becoming a popular one for talented women writers, a viable and visible alternative to the extremist statement gleaned from confessionalism that held such sway for younger writers throughout the 1970s.

Yet personal classicism may also become increasingly important among male writers who wish to write from their personal lives but wish to be recognized as much for their control and technique as for their themes. Jack Gilbert's book *Monolithos* seems to move in this direction, as does some—though certainly not all—of Michael Ryan's work. As the societal forces that have shaped both women's sense of self and their uses of language—in short, many of the gender-related forces that have in subtle or brutal ways shaped men and women differently—begin to drop away from our culture, however slowly, I suspect that the literary choices writers make will come increasingly to be made by aspects of their lives that are not necessarily gender-related.

Critics have traditionally talked about a writer's "vision" as a major element in his or her literary contribution, yet increasingly, the importance of "re-vision" has been recognized in women's writing. As Adrienne Rich has said, "Re-vision—the act of looking back, of seeing with fresh eyes, of entering an old text from a new critical direction—is for women more than a chapter in cultural history: it is an act of survival."[2] For the writer, the task is not merely to look back at an existing body of work and see it anew, but to look inward and envision a path for her own potential. The path that is personal

1. Nina Bogin, "Lost One," from *In the North*, 28.
2. "When We Dead Awaken," in *On Lies, Secrets, and Silence: Selected Prose 1966–1978*, 35.

classicism is not yet particularly long, and it is certainly not the only route women poets have chosen, but I believe it travels in a direction that will continue to interest contemporary and future writers: it travels at once into the known and the unknown, the spoken and the unspoken. It is a resonant quietude.

# Bibliography

Abrams, M. H. *The Mirror and the Lamp: Romantic Theory and the Critical Tradition.* New York: Oxford University Press, 1953.
———. "Structure and Style in the Greater Romantic Lyric." In *From Sensibility to Romanticism,* edited by Frederick W. Hilles and Harold Bloom, 527–60. New York: Oxford University Press, 1965.
Aleshire, Joan. "Staying News: A Defense of the Lyric." *The Kenyon Review* 10, no. 3 (Summer 1988): 47–64.
Alvarez, A. *Beyond All This Fiddle: Essays, 1955–67.* New York: Random House, 1968.
———. "Sylvia Plath." In *The Art of Sylvia Plath,* edited by Charles Newman, 56–68. Bloomington: Indiana University Press, 1970.
Ashbery, John. *"The Complete Poems."* in *Elizabeth Bishop and Her Art,* edited by Lloyd Schwartz and Sybil Estess, 201–5. Ann Arbor: University of Michigan Press, 1983.
Bedient, Calvin. "Birth, Not Death, Is the Hard Loss." Review of *Descending Figure,* by Louise Glück. *Parnassus* 9 (Spring/Summer 1981): 168–86.
Bishop, Elizabeth. *The Collected Prose.* Edited by Robert Giroux. New York: Farrar, Straus, Giroux, 1984.
———. *The Complete Poems, 1927–1979.* New York: Farrar, Straus, Giroux, 1983.
———. Postcard to Sandra McPherson. September 2, 1970.
Bly, Robert. "What the Image Can Do." In *Claims for Poetry,* edited by Donald Hall, 38–49. Ann Arbor: University of Michigan Press, 1982.
Bogan, Louise. *The Blue Estuaries: Poems, 1923–1968.* New York: Ecco Press, 1977.
———. *Body of This Death.* New York: Robert McBride & Co., 1923.

————. *Collected Poems, 1923–1953.* New York: Noonday Press, 1954.

————. *Dark Summer.* New York: Charles Scribner's Sons, 1929.

————. *Journey Around My Room: The Autobiography of Louise Bogan.* Edited by Ruth Limmer. New York: Penguin-Viking Press, 1980.

————. "Leave-taking." *Poetry* 20, 5 (August 1922): 250.

————. *Poems and New Poems.* New York: Charles Scribner's Sons, 1941.

————. *A Poet's Alphabet: Reflections on the Literary Art and Vocation.* Edited by Robert Phelps and Ruth Limmer. New York: McGraw-Hill Book Co., 1970.

————. *The Sleeping Fury.* New York: Charles Scribner's Sons, 1937.

————. "The Springs of Poetry," *New Republic* 37, sup. 9 (1923): 9.

————. *What the Woman Lived: Selected Letters of Louise Bogan 1920–1970.* Edited by Ruth Limmer. New York: Harcourt Brace Jovanovich, Inc., 1973.

————. "The Work! A Conversation with Elizabeth Bishop." Interview by George Starbook. In *Elizabeth Bishop and Her Art*, edited by Lloyd Schwartz and Sybil Estess, 312–30. Ann Arbor: University of Michigan Press, 1983.

Bogen, Don. "The Fundamental Skeptic." Review of *The Triumph of Achiles* by Louise Glück. *Nation* (January 18, 1986):53–54.

Bogin, Nina. *In the North.* St. Paul: Graywolf Press, 1989.

Boland, Eavan. "An Un-Romantic American." *Parnassus: Poetry in Review* 14, no. 2 (1988): 73–92.

Booth, Wayne C. *The Rhetoric of Fiction.* 2d ed. Chicago: University of Chicago Press, 1983.

Boruch, Marianne. "Comment: The Feel of a Century." *American Poetry Review* 19, no. 4 (July/August 1990): 17–18.

Bowles, Gloria. *Louise Bogan's Aesthetic of Limitation.* Bloomington: Indiana University Press, 1987.

Boyers, Robert. "Mixed Bag." Review of *Firstborn*, by Louise Glück. *Partisan Review* 36, no. 2 (1969): 306–15.

Brown, Ashley. "An Interview with Elizabeth Bishop." In *Elizabeth Bishop and Her Art*, edited by Lloyd Schwartz and Sybil Estess, 223–40. Ann Arbor: University of Michigan Press, 1983.

Bush, Douglas. *Mythology and the Romantic Tradition in English Poetry.* Cambridge: Harvard University Press, 1969.

Collins, Martha. *Critical Essays on Louise Bogan.* Boston: G. K. Hall & Co., 1984.

Cushman, Stephen. *William Carlos Williams and the Meaning of Measure.* New Haven: Yale University Press, 1985.

Dickinson, Emily. *The Complete Poems of Emily Dickinson.* Edited by Thomas H. Johnson. Boston: Little, Brown, and Co., 1960.

————. *The Letters of Emily Dickinson.* Vol. 2. Edited by Thomas H. Johnson. Cambridge: Belknap Press, 1955.

Diehl, Joanne Feit. *Women Poets and the American Sublime.* Bloomington: Indiana University Press, 1990.

Dobyns, Stephen. "Will You Listen for a Minute?" Review of *Ararat*, by Louise Glück. *New York Times Book Review,* September 12, 1990, 5.

Doreski, Carole Kiler. "Robert Lowell and Elizabeth Bishop: A Matter of Life Studies." *Prose Studies: History, Theory, Criticism* 10, no. 1 (May 1987): 85–101.

Doreski, William. "The Mind Afoot." Review of *Descending Figure*, by Louise Glück. *Ploughshares* 7, no. 1 (1981): 157–63.

DuPlessis, Rachel Blau. "Family, Sexes, Psyche: An Essay on H. D. and the Muse of the Woman Writer." In *H. D.: Woman and Poet,* edited by Michael King, 69–90. Orono, Maine: National Poetry Foundation, Inc., 1986.

————. *H. D.: The Career of That Struggle.* Bloomington: Indiana University Press, 1986.

Edelman, Lee. "The Geography of Gender: Elizabeth Bishop's 'In the Waiting Room.'" *Contemporary Literature* 26, no. 2 (Summer 1985): 179–96.

Eliot, T. S. *The Complete Poems and Plays, 1909–1950.* New York: Harcourt, Brace, Jovanovich, 1971.

————. *The Selected Prose of T. S. Eliot.* Edited by Frank Kermode. New York: Harcourt Brace Jovanovich; Farrar, Straus, Giroux, 1975.

Fishman, Pamela. "Interaction: The Work Women Do." In *Language, Gender, and Society,* edited by Barrie Thorne, Cheris Kramarae, and Nancy Henly, pp. 89–102. Rowley, Mass.: Newbury House Publisher, Inc., 1983.

Flint, F. S. "The Poetry of H. D." *The Egoist* (May 1, 1915): 72–73.

Frank, Elizabeth. *Louise Bogan: A Portrait.* New York: Alfred A. Knopf, 1985.

Friedman, Susan Stanford. *Psyche Reborn: The Emergence of H. D.* Bloomington: Indiana University Press, 1981.

Frye, Northrup. *Fables of Identity: Studies in Poetic Mythology.* New York: Harcourt, Brace, and World, Inc., 1963.

Fussell, Paul. *Poetic Meter and Poetic Form.* Revised edition. New York: Random House, 1979.

Gilbert, Sandra M., and Susan Gubar. *The Madwoman in the Attic: The*

*Woman Writer and the Nineteenth-Century Imagination*. New Haven: Yale University Press, 1979.

————. *No Man's Land: The Place of the Woman Writer in the Twentieth Century*. Vol. 1, *The War of the Words*. New Haven: Yale University Press, 1988.

————, eds. *Shakespeare's Sisters: Feminist Essays on Women Poets*. Bloomington: Indiana University Press, 1979.

Glück, Louise. *Ararat*. New York: Ecco Press, 1990.

————. *Descending Figure*. New York: Ecco Press, 1980.

————. "*Descending Figure*: An Interview." By Ann Douglas. *Columbia: A Magazine of Poetry and Prose* Spring/Summer 1981, no. 6: 116–25.

————. "Education of the Poet." *Envoy* 52 (1989): 1–6.

————. *Firstborn*. 1968. Reprint. New York: Ecco Press, 1983.

————. "The Garden." In *Fifty Contemporary Poets: The Creative Process*, edited by Alberta Turner, 110–14. New York: David MacKay Co., Inc., 1977.

————. "Gretel in Darkness." *New American Review*, 7 (1969): 171.

————. *The House on Marshland*. New York: Ecco Press, 1975.

————. "Jukebox." *Antaeus* 17 (Spring 1975): 67.

————. *The Triumph of Achilles*. New York: Ecco Press, 1985.

Goldensohn, Lorrie. "Elizabeth Bishop: An Unpublished, Untitled Poem." *American Poetry Review* 17, no. 1 (January/February 1988): 35–46.

Griswold, Rufus. *The Female Poets of America*. Reprint. New York: Garret Press, 1969.

Guest, Barbara. *Herself Defined: The Poet H. D. and Her World*. Garden City, N. Y.: Doubleday & Co., Inc., 1984.

H. D. [Hilda Doolittle]. *Bid Me To Live*. Redding Ridge, Conn.: Black Swan Books, Ltd., 1983.

————. *End To Torment: A Memoir of Ezra Pound*. Edited by Norman Holmes Pearson and Michael King. New York: New Directions Books, 1979.

————. *The Gift*. New York: New Directions Books, 1982.

————. *H. D.: Collected Poems, 1912–1944*. Edited by Louis L. Martz. New York: New Directions Books, 1983.

————. *Helen in Egypt*. New York: Grove Press, Inc., 1961.

————. *Ion: A Play After Euripides*. Redding Ridge, Conn.: Black Swan Books, 1982.

————. *Notes on Thought and Vision*. San Francisco: City Lights Press, 1982.

————. *Palimpsest*. Carbondale: Southern Illinois University Press, 1968.

————. "Priapus, Keeper-of-Orchards." *Poetry* 1.4 (January 1913), 121.

————. *Tribute to Freud.* Boston: David R. Godine, 1974.

Hall, Donald, ed. *Claims for Poetry.* Ann Arbor: University of Michigan Press, 1982.

Hamilton, Ian. *Robert Lowell: A Biography.* New York: Random House, 1982.

Handa, Carolyn Patricia. "The Poetry of Elizabeth Bishop." Ph.D. diss., University of California, Los Angeles, 1983.

————. "Vision and Change: The Poetry of Elizabeth Bishop." *American Poetry* 3, no. 2 (Winter 1986): 18–34.

Hartman, Charles O. *Free Verse: An Essay on Prosody.* Princeton: Princeton University Press, 1980.

Hawkes, John E. Letter to the Editor. *American Book Review* 6, no. 1 (1983) 4+.

Hirsch, Edward. "The Watcher." Review of *The Triumph of Achilles*, by Louise Glück. *American Poetry Review* 15, no. 6 (November/December 1986): 33–36.

Hoffman, Steven K. "Impersonal Personalism: The Making of a Confessional Poetic." *ELH* 45, no. 4 (1978): 687–709.

Holbrook, David. *Sylvia Plath: Poetry and Existence.* London: Athlone Press, 1976.

Holden, Jonathan. *Style and Authenticity in Postmodern Poetry.* Columbia: University of Missouri Press, 1986.

Hollenberg, Donna Krolik. "Art and Ardor in World War One: Selected Letters from H. D. to John Cournos." *The Iowa Review* 16, no. 3 (Fall 1986): 126–55.

Hugo, Richard. *The Triggering Town: Lectures and Essays on Poetry and Writing.* New York: W. W. Norton & Co., 1979.

Hulme, T. E. "Romanticism and Classicism." In *Speculations: Essays on Humanism and the Philosophy of Art*, edited by Herbert Read, 113–40. New York: Harcourt, Brace, & Co., Inc., 1936.

Jarrell, Randall. "On *North & South.*" In *Elizabeth Bishop and Her Art*, edited by Lloyd Schwartz and Sybil Estess, 180–81. Ann Arbor: University of Michigan Press, 1983.

Jones, A. R. "Necessity and Freedom: The Poetry of Robert Lowell, Sylvia Plath, and Anne Sexton." *Critical Quarterly* 7, no. 1 (1965): 11–30.

Juhasz, Suzanne. *Naked and Fiery Forms, Modern American Poetry by Women: A New Tradition.* New York: Harper and Row Books, 1976.

Jung, C. G. *The Spirit in Man, Art, and Literature.* Translated by R. F. C.

Hull. Bollingen Series 20. New York: Bollingen Foundation, 1966; distributed by Pantheon Books.

Kalstone, David. *Becoming a Poet: Elizabeth Bishop with Marianne Moore and Robert Lowell,* edited by Robert Hemenway. New York: Farrar Straus Giroux, 1989.

――――. "Elizabeth Bishop: Questions of Memory, Questions of Travel." In *Elizabeth Bishop and Her Art,* edited by Lloyd Schwartz and Sybil Estess, 3–31. Ann Arbor: University of Michigan Press, 1983.

Kammer, Jeanne. "The Art of Silence and the Forms of Women's Poetry." In *Shakespeare's Sisters: Feminist Essays on Women Poets,* pp. 153–64, edited by Sandra M. Gilbert and Susan Gubar. Bloomington: Indiana University Press, 1979.

Keller, Lynn, and Cristanne Miller. "Emily Dickinson, Elizabeth Bishop, and the Rewards of Indirection." *The New England Quarterly* 57, no. 4 (December 1984): 533–53.

Kenner, Hugh. *The Pound Era.* Berkeley: University of California Press, 1971.

King, Michael, ed. *H. D.: Woman and Poet.* Orono, Maine: National Poetry Foundation, Inc., 1986.

Kroll, Judith. *Chapters in a Mythology: The Poetry of Sylvia Plath.* New York: Harper Colophon Books, 1976.

Kunitz, Stanley. "Land of Dust and Flame." In *Critical Essays on Louise Bogan,* edited by Martha Collins, 63–65. Boston: G. K. Hall & Co., 1984.

――――. *Next to Last Things: New Poems and Essays.* Boston: Atlantic Monthly Press, 1985.

Lerner, Lawrence. "What is Confessional Poetry?" *Critical Quarterly* 29, no. 2 (Summer 1987): 46–66.

Levenson, Michael H. *A Genealogy of Modernism.* Cambridge: Cambridge University Press, 1984.

Limmer, Ruth. "Circumscriptions." In *Critical Essays on Louise Bogan,* edited by Martha Collins, 166–74. Boston: G. K. Hall & Co., 1984.

Lowell, Robert. "From 'Thomas Bishop and Williams.'" In *Elizabeth Bishop and Her Art,* edited by Lloyd Schwartz and Sybil Estess, 186–89. Ann Arbor: University of Michigan Press, 1983.

Malkoff, Karl. *Escape from the Self: A Study in Contemporary American Poetry and Poetics.* New York: Columbia University Press, 1979.

Maraffino, Elizabeth. "Missed Books: *Descending Figure.*" Review of *Descending Figure,* by Louise Glück. *American Book Review* 5, no. 15 (1982): 12.

Merwin, W. S., and George E. Dimock, Jr., trans. *Iphigenia at Aulis,* by Euripides. New York: Oxford University Press, 1978.

Millay, Edna St. Vincent. *Collected Poems.* New York: Harper and Row, 1956.

Miller, James E., Jr. *T. S. Eliot's Personal Wasteland: Exorcism of the Demons.* University Park: Pennsylvania State University Press, 1977.

Millier, Brett Candlish. "Elusive Mastery: The Drafts of Elizabeth Bishop's 'One Art,'" *New England Review.* Middlebury Series, 13, no. 2 (Winter 1990): 121–29.

Mitchell, Roger. "The 15th Century Again," *American Poetry Review* November/December 1988, 23–25.

———. "Thoughts on the Line." *Ohio Review* 38 (1987): 69–80.

Mitgutsch, Waltraud. "Women in Transition: The Poetry of Anne Sexton and Louise Glück." *Arbeiten aus Anglistik und Amerikanistik* 9, no. 2 (1984): 131–45.

Mizener, Arthur. "New Verse: *North & South.*" In *Elizabeth Bishop and Her Art,* edited by Lloyd Schwartz and Sybil Estess, 190–93. Ann Arbor: University of Michigan Press, 1983.

Moore, Marianne. "A Modest Expert: *North & South.*" In *Elizabeth Bishop and Her Art,* edited by Lloyd Schwartz and Sybil Estess, 177–79. Ann Arbor: University of Michigan Press, 1983.

Mossberg, Barbara Antonina Clarke. *Emily Dickinson: When a Writer Is a Daughter.* Bloomington: Indiana University Press, 1982.

Mullen, Richard. "Elizabeth Bishop's Surrealist Inheritance." *American Literature* 54, no. 1 (March 1982): 63–80.

Muller, John. "Light and the Wisdom of the Dark: Aging and the Language of Desire in the Texts of Louise Bogan." In *Memory and Desire: Aging—Literature—Psychoanalysis,* edited by Kathleen Woodward and Murray M. Schwartz, 76–96. Bloomington: Indiana University Press, 1986.

Newman, Charles, ed. *The Art of Sylvia Plath.* Bloomington: Indiana University Press, 1970.

Nichols, Ashton. *The Poetics of Epiphany: Nineteenth-Century Origins of the Modern Literary Moment.* Tuscaloosa: University of Alabama Press, 1987.

Olds, Sharon. *The Dead and the Living.* New York: Alfred A. Knopf, 1985.

Olson, Charles. *Selected Writings of Charles Olson.* Edited by Robert Creeley. New York: New Directions, 1966.

Orbach, Susie. *Hunger Strike: The Anorectic's Struggle as a Metaphor for Our Age.* New York: W. W. Norton & Co., 1986.

Ostriker, Alicia Suskin. *Stealing the Language: The Emergence of Women's Poetry in America.* Boston: Beacon Press, 1986.

Parini, Jay. "After the Fall." Review of *Descending Figure*, by Louise Glück. *Times Literary Supplement*, April 24, 1981, 466.

Parker, Robert Dale. *The Unbeliever: The Poetry of Elizabeth Bishop.* Urbana: University of Illinois Press, 1988.

Pater, Walter. *Appreciations with an Essay on Style.* 1924. Reprint. Folcroft Library Editions, 1978.

Pearson, Norman Holmes. "An Interview." *Contemporary Literature* 10, no. 4 (Autumn 1969): 435–46.

Perlmutter, Elizabeth P. "A Doll's Heart: The Girl in the Poetry of Edna St. Vincent Millay and Louise Bogan." *Twentieth Century Literature* 23, no. 2 (May 1977): 157–79.

Phillips, Robert. *The Confessional Poets.* Carbondale: Southern Illinois University Press, 1973.

Pinksy, Robert. "The Idiom of a Self: Elizabeth Bishop and Wordsworth." In *Elizabeth Bishop and Her Art*, edited by Lloyd Schwartz and Sybil Estess, 49–60. Ann Arbor: University of Michigan Press, 1983.

Plath, Sylvia. *Collected Poems.* Edited by Ted Hughes. New York: Harper and Row, 1981.

"Poets: The Second Chance." *Time*, June 2, 1967, 67–74.

Pope, Deborah. *A Separate Vision.* Baton Rouge: Louisiana State University Press, 1984.

Pound, Ezra. *Literary Essays of Ezra Pound.* Edited by T. S. Eliot. New York: New Directions, 1968.

———. *Personae: The Collected Shorter Poems.* New York: New Directions, 1971.

———. *Selected Letters of Ezra Pound, 1907–1941.* Edited by D. D. Paige. 1950. Reprint. New York: New Directions, 1971.

———. "Vorticism." *Fortnightly Review* 102 (1913): 461–71.

Pratt, William. *The Imagist Poem.* New York: E. P. Dutton & Co., Inc., 1963.

Procopiow, Norma. "Survival Kit: The Poetry of Elizabeth Bishop." *The Centennial Review* 25, no. 1 (Winter 1981): 1–19.

Quinones, Ricardo J. *Mapping Literary Modernism: Time and Development.* Princeton: Princeton University Press, 1985.

Ransom, John Crowe. "The Poet as Woman." *Southern Review* 2 (1937): 783–806.

Reeves, James. *Georgian Poetry.* Harmondsworth, Middlesex: Penguin Books, 1962.

Rich, Adrienne. "The Eye of the Outsider: The Poetry of Elizabeth Bishop." *Boston Review* 8, no. 2 (1983): 15–17.

―――. "When We Dead Awaken: Writing as Re-Vision." In *On Lies, Secrets, and Silence: Selected Prose 1966–1978.* New York: W. W. Norton & Co., 1975.

Ridgeway, Jacqueline. *Louise Bogan.* Boston: Twayne Publishers, 1984.

Roberts, Michael. *T. E. Hulme.* Manchester, England: Carcanet New Press, 1982.

Roethke, Theodore. "The Poetry of Louise Bogan." In *Critical Essays on Louise Bogan,* edited by Martha Collins, 87–96. Boston: G. K. Hall & Co., 1984.

Rosenthal, M. L. *The New Poets: American and British Poetry since World War II.* New York: Oxford University Press, 1967.

Rumens, Carol. *Making for the Open: The Chatto Book of Post-Feminist Poetry, 1964–1984.* London: Chatto and Windus, Hogarth Press, 1985.

Ryan, Michael. "A Dark Gray Flame." *New England Review and Bread Loaf Quarterly* 6, no. 4 (Summer 1984): 518–29.

Schneidau, Herbert N. *Ezra Pound: The Image and the Real.* Baton Rouge: Louisiana State University Press, 1969.

Schwartz, Lloyd. "Annals of Poetry: Elizabeth Bishop and Brazil." *New Yorker,* Sept. 30, 1991, 85–97.

―――, and Sybil Estess, eds. *Elizabeth Bishop and Her Art.* Ann Arbor: University of Michigan Press, 1983.

―――. *That Sense of Constant Readjustment: Elizabeth Bishop's 'North & South.'* New York: Garland Pub., Inc., 1987.

Sewall, Richard, ed. *Emily Dickinson: A Collection of Critical Essays.* Englewood Cliffs, N. J.: Prentice-Hall, 1963.

Sexton, Anne. *The Complete Poems.* Boston: Houghton Mifflin Co., 1981.

Showalter, Elaine, ed. *The New Feminist Criticism: Essays on Women, Literature, and Theory.* New York: Pantheon, 1985.

Smith, Dave. "Some Recent American Poetry: Come All Ye Fair and Tender Ladies." *American Poetry Review* 11, no. 1 (January/February 1982): 36–46.

Snodgrass, W. D. *Selected Poems, 1957–1987.* New York: Soho Press, Inc., 1967.

Stevenson, Anne. *Elizabeth Bishop.* New York: Twayne Publishers, 1966.

Sultan, Stanley. *Eliot, Joyce and Company.* New York: Oxford University Press, 1987.

Swann, Thomas Burnett. *The Classical World of H. D.* Lincoln: University of Nebraska Press, 1962.

Thackrey, Donald E. "The Communication of the Word." In *Emily Dickinson: A Collection of Critical Essays*, edited by Richard B. Sewall, pp. 51–69. Englewood Cliffs, NJ: Prentice-Hall, 1963.

Thorne, Barrie, Cheris Kramarae, and Nancy Henley, eds. *Language, Gender, and Society*. Rowley, Mass.: Newbury House Publisher, Inc., 1983.

Tomlinson, Charles. *Poetry and Metamorphosis*. Cambridge: Cambridge University Press, 1983.

Tompkins, Jane P. "Sentimental Power: *Uncle Tom's Cabin* and the Politics of Literary History." In *The New Feminist Criticism: Essays on Women, Literature, and Theory*, edited by Elaine Showalter, pp. 81–104. New York: Pantheon Books, 1985.

Travisano, Thomas J. *Elizabeth Bishop: Her Artistic Development*. Charlottesville: University Press of Virginia, 1988.

Valentine, Jean. Untitled (discussion of "Sonnet"). *Field* 31 (Fall 1984): 45.

Vendler, Helen. *Part of Nature, Part of Us: Modern American Poets*. Cambridge: Harvard University Press, 1980.

————. "The Poetry of Louise Glück." *New Republic*, June 17, 1978, 31–37.

————. "A Quarter of Poetry." Review of *The House on Marshland*, by Louise Glück. *New York Times Book Review*, April 6, 1975, 4+.

————. Review of *Descending Figure*, by Louise Glück. *New York Review of Books*, 28 (July 16, 1981): 24–26.

Wagner, Linda W., ed. *Sylvia Plath: The Critical Heritage*. New York: Routledge, 1988.

Walker, Cheryl. *The Nightingale's Burden: Women Poets and American Culture before 1900*. Bloomington: Indiana University Press, 1983.

Wehr, Wesley. "Elizabeth Bishop: Conversations and Class Notes." *Antioch Review* 39, no. 3 (Summer 1981): 319–28.

Williams, William Carlos. *Selected Essays*. New York: Random House, 1954.

————. *Selected Poems of William Carlos Williams*. New York: New Directions, 1969.

Williamson, Alan. "*A Cold Spring*: Poet of Feeling." In *Elizabeth Bishop and Her Art*, edited by Lloyd Schwartz and Sybil Estess, 96–108. Ann Arbor: University of Michigan Press, 1983.

————. *Introspection and Contemporary Poetry*. Cambridge: Harvard University Press, 1984.

Woolf, Virginia. *A Room of One's Own.* New York: Harvest/HBJ-Harcourt Brace Jovanovich, 1929.

Wooten, Anna. "Louise Glück's *The House on Marshland.*" *American Poetry Review* 4, no. 4 (July/August 1975): 5–6.

Yenser, Steven. "Recent Poetry: Five Poets." *Yale Review* 71, no. 1 (Autumn 1981): 97–103.

# Index

Abrams, M. H., 2, 13

Aldington, Richard: affair with Flo Fallas, 51, 54; "Imagist Manifesto," 18; marriage to H. D., 51; translations of Sappho, 10, 24

Alvarez, A., 96. See also Confessional poetry, definitions of

Anorexia nervosa, 4, 150, 170, 181–86

Auden, W. H., 97

Beerbohm, Max, 42–43

Bishop, Elizabeth: and confessional poetry, 126–29; formalism, 6, 120, 142–44, 154; lesbian interpretations, 108–10, 115–18, 121, 125, 133–34; and literal "truth," 107–8, 118, 129; and natural tone, 104, 118–22, 149; personal reticence, 61; and Robert Lowell, 123–29; surrealism, 112–16, 118; use of description, 104–5
—works: "Argument," 135; "The Bight," 132; "Brazil, January 1, 1502," 112; "Casabianca," 113; "A Cold Spring," 129, 130–32, 138; A Cold Spring, 107, 110, 129, 139–40; The Complete Poems, 135; "Conversation," 135, 136, 138; "Cootchie," 147; "Exchanging Hats," 110; "Faustina, or Rock Roses," 112; "Five Flights Up," 119, 129, 144–45; "Four Poems," 129, 135–41, 147, 172; Geography 3, 129, 130; "Gwendolyn," 124, 129; "In the Village," 123–24, 125, 127–28, 129, 175; "In the Waiting Room," 109–10, 132; "Insomnia," 129, 133–34; "Invitation to Miss Marianne Moore," 107, 130; "It is marvellous to wake up together," 146–47; "Letter to New York," 130; "The Monument,"

112; "The Moose," 137; "O Breath," 135, 140; "One Art," 119, 120, 135, 142–44, 145, 167; "Over 2000 Illustrations and a Complete Concordance," 130; Questions of Travel, 123, 124, 142, 175; "Rain Towards Morning," 135, 136–38; "Rainy Season; Sub-Tropics," 145; "Roosters," 111; "The Shampoo," 129, 141–42; "Sonnet," 116–18, 138; "A Summer's Dream," 129, 132–33; "Varick Street," 129, 130, 134–35, 140; "The Weed," 114–16; "While Someone Telephones," 135, 138–40

Black Mountain Poets, 140

Bly, Robert, 161–62

Bogan, Louise, 25, 151; Bennington College lecture, 94; dislike of confession, 89, 96, 100–101, 106, 122; formalism, 6, 80; hospitalization, 85, 90, 97, 99; marriage to Curt Alexander, 75–76; marriage to Raymond Holden, 85; use of poetic personae, 78–79
—works: "Ad Castitatem," 82; "Beginning and End," 81; "Betrothed," 76–79, 81–82; The Blue Estuaries, 76, 79, 87; Body of this Death, 71, 75, 79, 81, 84, 88; "Cassandra," 191; Collected Poems, 79; Dark Summer, 79, 85–87; "Evening in the Sanitarium," 97; "Fifteenth Farewell," 81; "The Flume," 80, 85–87, 88, 89; "The Frightened Man," 77; "The Heart and the Lyre," 92–93; "Henceforth, from the Mind," 90; "Homunculus," 89; "Hypocrite Swift," 89–90; Journey Around My Room, 74, 88, 96, 98; "Knowledge," 81, 82; "Late," 79; Laura Daley's Story, 96, 98; "Leave-Taking," 81–82; "A Let-